Sociological analysis

International Library of Sociology

Founded by Karl Mannheim

Editor: John Rex, University of Warwick

Arbor Scientiae
Arbor Vitae

A catalogue of the books available in the **International Library of Sociology,** and new books in preparation for the Library, will be found at the end of this volume.

Sociological analysis

Arun Sahay

Department of Sociological Studies,
University of Sheffield

Routledge & Kegan Paul

London and Boston

First published 1972
by Routledge & Kegan Paul Ltd
Broadway House, 68–74 Carter Lane,
London EC4V 5EL and
9 Park Street,
Boston Mass. 02108, U.S.A.
Printed in Great Britain by
Ebenezer Baylis and Son Ltd,
The Trinity Press, Worcester, and London
© Arun Sahay 1972

Library of Congress Catalog Card Number 72-85958
ISBN 0 7100 7363 1

FOR INDIRA

Contents

		page
	Preface	viii
1	Problems of sociological analysis	1
2	Weber's ideas on the analysis of rationality and its effects on modern society	17
3	Pareto's analysis of sentiments and tradition in society	49
4	Comparative analysis of Weber and Pareto	98
5	Mannheim and social conditioning of knowledge	112
6	Parsons's 'theoretical' sociology and the solution of the problem of order in society	132
7	Merton and Bendix: generalizations of limited range and comparative study of societies	153
8	Dahrendorf: conflict as a reorientation of sociological analysis or a substitute 'grand' theory	165
9	Conclusion	173
	Notes	187
	Bibliography	203
	Index	207

Preface

This book is written mainly as an attempt to provide an introduction to the analytical aspects of sociological theory, because there is none. It has become necessary now because the explicit awareness of the range of sociological thought and analysis is much greater now than it has ever been. But it also makes it difficult to organize one's study of the subject or to judge its fundamental premises. It is an essay in criticism, therefore, in the sense that the function of criticism is to clarify, define and consolidate the essential point.

Many of the points raised in the following pages—which I have attempted to deal with—came from my students in these last few years. I should like to acknowledge my debt to them collectively for clarifying many things for me through their questions.

I also wish to thank the secretarial staff of the department who typed the manuscript in an exceedingly short time.

1 Problems of sociological analysis

It soon becomes apparent to anyone dealing with sociology that the questions of validity and objectivity cannot be decided by pure reasoning alone. The solutions offered by writers who have never done any systematic analysis of a sociological problem, i.e. right through to the question of the validity of their conclusions and the justification of their assumptions, seem quite reasonable superficially, but as soon as one begins to use or apply them they fall apart at the seams.

The first task, of course, is to identify the real problems; and the second is to decide why these problems must be solved before one can separate speculations on the nature of society, or correlations of beliefs, values and conduct, on the patterns of change, movement and calm in various periods of history, either in a specific society or the whole world, and other such phenomena, from sociological analysis, which is entirely an intellectual search for knowledge of the realities of social aspects of human life, in both historical and contemporary times, as the historical and the contemporary are only extensions of one another, and, in any actual sense, indistinguishable. However, in philosophizing it is the *belief** that a solution is correct that counts, but in sociological analysis it must inevitably be that one should examine the bases of explanations, solutions, assumptions, hypotheses, etc., on the evidence of the reality itself that one is

* This is the reason why attempts to develop a sociology of knowledge are necessary but which has also contributed to the failure of many such endeavours to answer the fundamental question of the social conditioning of knowledge: what is knowledge in sociological terms? In so far as this is answered, we have a valid theory of society: cf. chapters on Weber and Pareto.

attempting to explain, i.e. the *results of social processes* one observes in society.

The first obstacle that one has to face in this examination is the nature of social reality. This problem is indeed a philosophical one: there is no tangibility about the nature of such a reality, yet one cannot deny that social norms, institutions and organizations, and their effects on the individual, are real. The determination of this problem is entirely conceptual. It has to be defined; which creates what seems to be another complex problem: the use of logic. Definitions of social reality have been made, more often than not, tautologically. The most esteemed at the present time seems to be the one through the use of language, derived in one way or another from the notions of Ludwig Wittgenstein, who set out to delimit philosophically 'sense' and 'nonsense'* in language, by investigating its structure and function. He assumed that the structure of language was logic and its function was to describe or picture the world. He also assumed that 'Thought is surrounded by a halo—its essence, logic, presents an order, in fact the *a priori* order of the world: that is, the order of *possibilities*, which must be common to both world and thought.'[1] The great problem, round which everything he said turned—'Is there an order in the world *a priori* and if so what does it consist in'?[2]—should have been no problem at all, as he had already assumed that the order of logic presents an *a priori* order of the world, and that logical possibilities, i.e. pure logical or linguistic inferences, are inferences on the nature of the world. Nevertheless, even if we regard this extension of the linguistic structure as a hypothetical assumption rather than a doctrine, Wittgenstein's theory of language only produces the notions of 'picture' and 'truth-function', which is just a different way of saying that language is the mirror of the world. It follows, therefore, quite simply, that the structure and function of language is the source of his notion: 'How are propositions related to one another?' Wittgenstein, to mitigate the circularity of this proposition, would refer at this point to his sentence: 'The world is all that is the case';[3] thus, making the truth or falsity of propositions dependent on 'the world' rather than on other

---

* Mainly in his *Tractatus Logico-Philosophicus*, but also in his *Philosophical Investigations*. The solemnity of his followers, in making his earlier and later notions on language and the world seem profoundly different, is understandable only as part of the ritual tribute due to a *guru* in which his most trite and unoriginal ideas must be received with the utmost respect.

propositions. But, one has to point out, the world is *either* determined by propositions, if we accept his original set of assumptions; *or*, if not, it is unknown. The tautology, therefore, is not broken: the assertion is true by definition or by reference to an unknown object, the world.

However, if we accept the notion, for the moment, that certain propositions can picture the elements of the world, then, his 'truth-function' theory begs the question: how can complex propositions be truth-functions of the elementary ones, unless *all* purely logical propositions are separate but consistent reflectors of the world? The world, one must remember, can be in Wittgenstein's philosophy either a logical composition or an unknown object. If it is a logical composition, then logic needs no reference to an object called the world; but, if one insists that the world 'is all that is the case', then it can never be *known* by pure logic.

The inevitable conclusion from Wittgenstein's philosophical endeavours is simply that one can either investigate the logic of language, i.e. make a linguistic analysis of concepts, propositions, etc., without referring to anything else but grammar and meaning; or investigate the structure of the world, i.e. the conceptual reality contained in evaluations, beliefs, institutions, norms, descriptions, etc., and their consequences. These are both inevitably empirical investigations: there can be no knowledge, *a priori*, of either language, which can only be an abstract concept referring to the common characteristics of the known languages, or the conceptual reality of the world, which is a generalized description of all notions, beliefs on the form and nature of reality. It is inconceivable that language or the world, even as philosophical notions, can be *a priori*. Philosophical notions are simply one of many conceptual forms or ideas believed in by human beings. Thus, there seems to be no ground for assuming, even hypothetically, their synonymity, even at the level of pure form, as the 'philosophers' of science and social science have done. Such an assumption will lead either to a simple-minded theory of language as sociology or as an unending whirl of agonized assertions. The freedom which has been allowed in such cases to hypotheses is only possible in *pure speculation*, not if they are made to explain *knowable* phenomena like language or conceptual beliefs, for both language and conceptual beliefs refer to an objectivity, for their truth or falsehood, and not to the aesthetics of reasoning.

3

This point becomes incontrovertible when one realizes that Wittgenstein was concerned with delimiting the language of natural science, in order to clarify 'what can be spoken of' and 'what cannot be spoken of'[4] and especially when it may be added that 'scientific' propositions are descriptions, and Wittgenstein was referring to the truth of these descriptions. But any description, scientific or otherwise, cannot be a total representation of the object described. It is only possible to make a total representation of the point of view, or the premise, and not of the object in a description: such is the nature of logical reasoning, until the object has been identified or defined, completely, through these descriptions. A description may be presented as a total representation of an object in situations where only one view is possible, and the natural-scientific knowledge is one such situation. Even within it, if one takes the specific sciences and how they illuminate, and co-ordinate with, other descriptions, it illustrates, first, the point that a description is governed by a point of view and, second, that a synthetic representation is all that is possible through descriptions.

The shift, therefore, from the *a priori* structure of language to 'the way in which language signifies is mirrored in its use'[5] is only a shift in phraseology. This may seem a distinct change in Wittgenstein's thinking from *a priori* analysis to the *a posteriori*; but the simile of the tool box in *Philosophical Investigations*[6] is only a change of imagery, not of method. For, even if we can recognize the tool box, do we know the variety of uses a set of tools can be put to, without the skills of which they are instruments? We can speculate, as philosophers will, how the tools could 'logically' be used: but what the speculator can make of the tools will depend on his knowledge of the skills involved, not on the logic of his speculation. This shift from the *a priori* to the *a posteriori* in Wittgenstein's analytic thought was inevitable because without a knowledge of the use of language no statements on its nature can even begin to be made. But his solution certainly is not logical. For the logical conclusion is the inevitability of sociological analysis in determining the use of language as a set of concepts on reality, for linguistic *or* logical analysis will not suffice in illustrating the relationship between concept and reality even in philosophical assertions.

Wittgenstein had assumed that every proposition should have a definite sense, as a philosopher is free to do, but he found that the facts of language did not conform to his *a priori* assumption. Therefore, the simple and the complex propositions could not be seen as extensions of one another, but were dependent on the context of meaning and use.

Again, his conclusion is simply one of recognition of the fact that there are no definite senses to propositions and that the simple is not the source of the complex. But what comes after this acknowledgment of a barrier against philosophical analysis of language? Not, as Wittgenstein suggests,[7] 'Ask yourself: on what occasions, for what purpose, do *we* say this? What kinds of actions accompany these words? In what scenes will they be used; and for what?'

These are empirical questions, which the philosophical or any other individual cannot answer from his *own* experience, because the experiences of one individual in the use of language will never be identical with that of another individual. Their experiences will, on the other hand, be understandable to each other, if they agree on the meaning of words, sentences and propositions, and use the language according to the grammatical form. This is not to say that the contents of their statements will also be determined in the same way as their formal use of language. This difference in the form and content of language is not made by Wittgenstein: one is not interchangeable with the other, and use explicitly refers to the content and implicitly to the form. It seems that in spite of the change of phraseology and imagery, Wittgenstein is still looking for *a priori* or formal answers to empirical or substantive questions. The shift, however agonizing to him personally, has not happened.

This discussion of Wittgenstein's confusion, in fact, highlights one of the basic intractable struggles between *a priori* thinkers and empirical theorists; especially in sociology, which is the primary discipline concerned with the subject-matter of this duality of thought and knowledge. On the social world, the theoretician can only justify his assertions on the nature of its reality by claiming the precedence of thought over knowledge; on the natural world, he can claim with more justification that all knowledge is necessarily of thought and logic. In the knowledge of social reality, thought may preface empirical analysis but it can neither supplant nor anticipate it. As we can find in Wittgenstein's preoccupations, the subject-matter of sociology is the same in its constituents as linguistic philosophy's:

concepts, contexts and meanings with their descriptive and explanaory qualities. And the aim of both is the knowledge of the conceptual reality of the world. However, the belief, of Wittgenstein and others, that this conceptual reality is the same as the scientific description of the world is, to say the least, naïve. In natural sciences the description of the world has been pursued through observation and perception, and through experiments in validation of hypothetical concepts. But neither observation nor perception is possible without a point of view, and the logic of experiment is governed by the logic of thought and understanding. There is, thus, no *a priori* knowledge, only *a priori* thought, in science. In the so-called *a priori* theoretical explanation, the presupposition of rational determinism is the invariable premise of inferences—as it is of empirical explanation. The correctness of theoretical explanations, even if judged by purely logical tests, lies in this common doctrine of rationality, and not in their logical structure. In other words, the logic of explanation will remain intact even when the premise is not rational in any absolute, metaphysical or philosophical sense. Therefore, the point which should be distinguished in all scientific analysis, whether natural or social, is that the premise of rationality is legitimate and applicable only in the case of explanation: it is neither transferable nor applicable to any form of reality, natural or social. If applied to reality, it must be seen for what it is: a *metaphysical* principle. Metaphysical principles, it must further be noted, are governed by presuppositions of thought, and, therefore, are not even hypothetically empirical generalizations. They can only be considered *a priori* empirically if no explanation is possible except by deduction from them, i.e. when there is no other source of logical reference available. It is only in this way that natural phenomena seem amenable to rational explanation, which may seem inductive if judged from a specific point of view, that of a particular investigation. Again, it has to be realized that hypotheses made in particular studies are based invariably on intuitive or studious *deductions* from the metaphysical principle of rational determinism. If they were not, it would be impossible to recognize, let alone analyse, the minutiae of the natural world. The validity of such *deductive* explanations, therefore, is only demonstrable by replicating hypothesized results—and by eliminating false hypotheses if the result is not replicable—as, in effect, justifications of the principle of rational determinism, the original

6

assumption of science.* However, this shows that the truth of a scientific proposition is not inherent in the presuppositions but in the correctness of its empirical reference. It is through demonstrations of such a correctness that the assumption of rationality, still, both logically and empirically, holds in natural scientific knowledge.

As long as rationality is seen clearly as only the determinant of explanation, and not of reality to which it refers, the *principles* of scientific knowledge are as accurately applicable in natural as in social scientific analysis. But, if rational determinism is understood, or misunderstood, as *realized* metaphysics, scientific analysis becomes an imitation of various natural scientific techniques; and when results appear inaccurate, meaningless or trivial, one claims to be exonerated by 'a lack of sophistication' in social scientific methodology, or the inseparability of one's creative intervention (which in other circles may have been seen as fraudulent experiment) from the origins of social data, or by one's ignorant acceptance of the myth that social scientific activity is a recent invention.

All these self-justifications would have been unnecessary if one had realized that rational principles, in any case, work only when applied to the methods of explanation, and a rational explanation is not a representation of the subject-matter—or that the subject-matter is not a reification of the explanation—but an *independent* conceptualization of reality.

This lack of realization has led to a fundamental confusion between description and explanation. Since it should be fairly clear by this stage of the discussion why natural scientists can only describe and therefore need make no distinction between description and explanation, the problem which arises in the examination of social reality is fundamentally that of the relationship between description and explanation.

What one deals with in social scientific, primarily sociological, analysis is not social behaviour, conduct or phenomena or events, but their descriptions. The raw data of analysis is the description itself: it contains both an account and a justification of behaviour, conduct or events: a description or justification which may or may

* Popper's analytic description of the process of scientific knowledge, if interpreted in this way, is undoubtedly correct; but when it is related to the notion of progress in scientific knowledge, then, of course, it becomes problematic and, thus, a philosophical issue and it must be judged as such.

not be rational in the sense of being fully understandable to others. In the structure of any given description or justification of social behaviour, conduct or event we can discover the logic of social scientific explanations. But although we can recognize a similarity of structure in all descriptions and justifications, social, linguistic, motivational or objective, it does not mean that all these accounts are either variants of the same explanation, or reflect the same reality, or that *a priori* analysis is all that is needed to deduce them.

All these descriptions, whether given by a participant, actor or observer, are subjectively valid, because they reflect the individual's point of view, i.e. they have a valid meaning. But their validity as explanation of the behaviour or event concerned will depend on the *correctness* of the perception underlying the meaning or significance which the conduct or event has for the participant, actor or observer. Two points emerge clearly from this formulation of the distinction of explanation from description. First, the recognition of an intrinsic context of meaning which every perception of reality has; and second, the context of meaning in itself does not provide a rational, objective or scientific explanation of a behaviour, conduct or event.

Why, however, should this distinction have to be made? Because, this is the fundamental distinction in the perceptibility of natural and social reality, a difference which has turned to a chasm of failure for many a philosopher of science, epistemologist and sociologist of knowledge, who has in exploring its depths fallen into it and been lost. Without this distinction, social scientific thought is blocked. It cannot do more than present a behavioural chart in the velvet covers of the latest banality on the nature of logic, language and society.

Because a description, whether made from a rational, ideological or emotional point of view, always has an objectively recognizable meaning which cannot be logically subordinated to any other meaning, even the scientific: the problem is neither of rationalization nor dogmatic censorship, but of translation. How can one translate what are logically truths of existence into objective statements? This is another question on which many answers continue to be given, but there could be no solution without the fundamental distinction between natural and social reality.

The translation from the subjective meaning of a description to its objective validity as an explanation is a direct one if the relation between its point of view and its perception of reality is logical, i.e. the description is an account of the conduct or event which is consistent with experience. Experience cannot be confined to any individual at any place or time: it is the knowledge of the whole of human life and possibilities. Possibilities are precisely what logic allows us to judge, by separating, in a conjectured possibility of experience, the elements which are consistent with past experience from those which are not. But it does not itself create experience, a point which has been ignored; and the process has been reified to make logic the source of experience, or vice versa. Although these questions of origin are impossible to answer because they are enigmas of existence, they are in fact irrelevant to the decision of *how* they are related to each other and how they must be used. It is the relationship and use which concern us, both in subjective and objective description and explanation. The relationship allows us to understand experience, and the use allows us to analyse its content. Any attempt to analyse relative descriptions of experience scientifically is only an attempt to translate them from ambiguity and autonomy of individual perceptions to certainty.

This certainty, which rational knowledge enables one to have, could be said to be the primary defining quality of science. This certainty does not depend on the unshakeability of belief, emotional attachment or assertion of truth but on the demonstrable qualities of scientific analysis, which are not available, to the same degree of explicitness, even in other forms of rational knowledge. Scientific analysis is primarily recognizable as such because it makes itself *independent* of the individual psyche at all stages. All other branches of rational knowledge eventually refer to the source, the giver of knowledge, the individual, even though they are judged for their details on the principle of rational knowledge. All knowledge in this way is subjective, but the decisive point is not its subjective origin or reception, but its criteria of certainty. All forms of knowledge refer to a subjective conviction of truth, but rational knowledge subordinates such subjective conviction to experience; and science, to an objective analysis of experience itself. In sociological terms, this means that all knowledge is in fact belief. Rational knowledge is belief on rational grounds; and science is such a rational belief on the certainty of the evidence itself. The progress of knowledge in a society or in world history is a sociological phenomenon, a problem of social conditioning, but the knowledge itself is not determined by any existential context of its discovery. It is determined by this quality of certainty, inherent in the faculty of reason, which all human beings possess, but may not use at all times for the growth of knowledge. It does seem rather absurd from this point of view that the idea of 'civilized' and 'primitive' mentalities should have such a fascination for social anthropologists and sociologists as it has—but as a sociological problem, their own descriptive endeavours are, of course, another matter . . .

This quality of certainty, which distinguishes science more than other forms of knowledge, is realizable only by analysis. The intuitive aspects of certainty are not insignificant for an individual, but they are simply irrelevant to any proof of certainty that he may provide, except in axiomatic stages of his analysis. It may be said that all proof, since it is subjective conviction, is intuitive and science may thus be designated systematic intuition. But intuition by its very nature precludes systematic arrangement, which is only possible by deliberate experimental analysis.

In sociology the analysis proceeds with the logic of experiment and not with intuitive organization, however apt it may seem to the observers of sociological activity—because the relationship between thought and knowledge is exactly the same as in all science, except that certain formal distinctions of the elements of analysis have to be maintained more sharply and constantly than in the natural scientific analysis.

First, the distinction of the reality from its description; second, the specific context of meaning of the description from its general contexts; third, its specificity from that of analogous descriptions. These distinctions are formal because they are the *basis* of the explanation of social reality. The context of meaning gives the description—and through it the conduct or event—a specificity which enables one to understand the relationship between an individual perception of reality and the kind of belief (not simply the ideas or the category) it reflects; and through the common links between perception and belief, the relationship between thought and experience. Although meaning defines in this way the whole of social reality, obviously the problem is not that it does, but *how* the definition is made. In this definition, moreover, we find the principles of sociological knowledge, the relations of theory and empirical analysis, realized in a way which makes the task of the *a priori* thinker far from simple.

Any theory of sociological knowledge, whether philosophical or empirical, is impossible to formulate without an understanding of the actual *processes* of definition by meaning and significance, i.e. between belief and action. The categories of belief, like religious, political, ritual, civilized or primitive, are superfluous to this definition, because the categories are not based on the form or the relationships of these notions and perceptions of reality but on their substance—judged from points of view in which a particular relationship is assumed to be ubiquitous.

The substantive categories which form so much of what is considered theory in the social sciences are in fact a direct contradiction of both the characteristics of social reality and the principles of its explanation. First, because substantive categories in social sciences are also empirical generalizations. A belief, for example, which is categorized as religious necessarily implies a definition of religion. This definition can, of course, be *a priori* or subjective, or, hypothetical. Hypothetical definitions therefore only suggest empirical generalizations; they do not necessarily imply them. In so far as a category remains hypothetical, it has to be justified by empirical analysis.

A justification of substantive categories, therefore, can only be specific. It can appear, on the other hand, to be general when a universal explanation has already been assumed. Then the categories follow automatically: they do not need any empirical justification. But this makes the whole process entirely arbitrary, given the nature of social reality.

Therefore, theory in sociological, and by implication in other social scientific, analysis cannot be a series of categories, but analytical explanations. This is not to say that sociological analysis has no categories of conduct or events, but that these categories are hypothetical. Their validity depends not on their usefulness to the individual sociologist, but on the validity of specific investigations. This may suggest that sociology has or should have only unrelated, ungeneralizable investigations and that the general principles of sociological analysis are superfluous. But the validity of the categories is dependent on the correctness of specific investigations, because they are not inferences from any principle of determinism. Further,

11

their usefulness or significance cannot be made a methodological principle, because the use of a category is simply a practical decision and refers only to the preliminary arrangement of the material, and does not determine either the form, or the results, of analysis. In fact, the analysis is a test of the empirical correctness of the definition of the categories. A category does not provide any clue of its relationship to another category: the relationship of one class of conduct or events to another, in social reality, is always to be discovered. It cannot be assumed to be rational, as in natural reality, and therefore deducible from the categories themselves.

This shows fairly clearly that several of the techniques of validation borrowed from natural scientific practice are quite irrelevant for social scientific analysis, mainly because there cannot be any valid general categories to which individual facts could be attributed and explained as examples. All *a priori* attempts to systematize sociological theory, then, become an exercise in subjective rationalization, because invariably the principle to which such systematics can be made dependent on is that of rational determinism. All attempts therefore to validate empirically such theories fail, first, because the categories of sociological objects based on a rational relationship of objects is simply *one* meaningful definition of reality among several possible. For the rationality of systematic sociology is only that of ends which govern men's action. To determine whether the systematized ends do govern men's action is not the same thing as to assume the ends to be rational in themselves. The significance of *a priori* systematic theory depends completely on this assumption, otherwise it becomes hypothetical, unproven and tentative and to be judged on the subjective belief—that it is comprehensive and true—of the individual sociologist. He cannot in application prove or disprove the theory, because he must first of all *prove* the correctness of the assumption that social conduct is invariably rational in relation to the ends which, according to the theory, govern it. This proof is only possible if the natural scientific assumption of rational determinism is shown to be applicable without any modification to all aspects of social reality. The tautological demonstration of applicability is too familiar to need examination in any detail, but the process is of a formation of general categories—as concepts of sociology—from axioms of experience like 'man has needs': biological, psychological, social, political, economic, etc. How needs—or intentions, if psycho-

12

logical freedom is favoured—are to be satisfied rationally, then, simply becomes a matter of subjective inference, and all social reality, past, present and future, becomes reducible to biological or psychological factors. A theoretical edifice on this basic assumption is thus created in the name of systematic sociology, which may become an expression of genius or a tissue of platitudinous jargon; how is one to judge? On the other hand, the misunderstanding of natural scientific knowledge may lead to an 'inductive' study in which a hypothesis is formed and subjected to an empirical test in which the ultimate precision is 'measurement'. The hypothesis is considered an empirical generalization and in a further abstract form becomes a sociological concept. This process is, as one can easily notice, no more inductive than the 'theoretical' process. First, because the hypothesis is obviously an *a priori* notion, depending for its relationship of categories of objects on the principle of rational determinism and for its immediate, substantive relationship on the perception of the hypothesizing individual which may be, again, an intuition of genius or an arbitrary assertion of limited imagination. Since the hypothesis is the framework of both recognition and selection, i.e. relevance, of facts, the process of induction is still unused. Induction may make some contribution when the facts gathered in research show a different pattern, which cannot be easily assimilated to the one hypothesized. Analysis, in this case, is simply a process of exemplification and not of exploration or experimentation. The use of experiment in such an analysis refers to the rituals of natural scientific experimentation, and not to its fundamental principle, i.e. analytical validation. Thus, an adaptation of a technique of measurement, however logically rigorous, remains a ritual exercise, because the question 'When is measurement empirically relevant and possible?' remains unanswered. Measurement, including rank ordering, is only possible and relevant when an indication of the degree of a *determined* variation is necessary. The determination of the variation is already postulated in the hypothesis, which has remained an *a priori* inference throughout the process of exemplification. Thus, the measurement of the variation is a measurement of an arbitrarily determined relationship which has at no stage been empirically justified. It does seem that in these circumstances measurement is a magical rather than a scientific concept.

There is another way of analysis which, although directly intuitive

13

in its affirmation, seems, on first acquaintance, to relate theory and research more fruitfully, by rejecting all presuppositions on the validity of generalized descriptions of observable behaviour in terms of *a priori* hypotheses, and proposing, instead, an 'intentional' exploration of hypothetical situations to reveal the totality of an experience. The approach seems to relate thought to reality by, first, referring to the philosophical implications of intentionality, then, constructing 'ideal types'—as opposed to any quantified construct— of 'sympathetic' understanding. The actor is not simply 'one who acts' but becomes one who plays a role: the analyst, to understand, explores or dramatizes the situations in which the individual role is, or has been, or may be, played. His conclusions are then generaliz- able on both the possibilities and limits of experience. One may see in this a marriage of *a priori* thought and empirical exploration. But the most important question, which remains unanswered in this approach, is: 'how are the conclusions of an essentially artistic reconstruction generalizable?' They, i.e. the phenomenologists, would say: by inferences from the consistency of one reconstruction with another and by the use of logic and, finally, by referring to one's sympathies; but, if the fundamental point of view of this approach is taken, that of the understanding of social reality, then all these processes cannot be proved as anything but the subjective under- standing of individuals, which is not generalizable as the objective understanding, in terms of meaning and significance, of the *actual* situation. But these reconstructions are supposedly made, not for private individual understanding, but as indications of the general characteristics of social experience. These general characteristics are not inter-personally, but universally, understandable; further, experience is not inter-personal but personal. So the introduction of an extra personality as a 'role-playing' actor in reconstructed or hypothetical situations is not to objectify it. The objectivity of experience (which is invariably personal) lies not in the experience itself, but in its expression and interpretation. If, however, one takes the extra personality (who may, in some cases, be the second per- sonality in an interaction) as the catalyst of expression, or the inter- preter of the experience, then, the objectivity is not referable to the experience itself but to *his* interpretation. But his interpretation may or may not derive from the meaning or significance the experience has for the first individual. In judging this ambiguity, the other forms

14

of understanding[8] inevitably become more important, in the objectivity of interpretation of experience, than sympathy. Therefore, the arbitrariness of attributing objective validity to one's reconstruction of another's experience is similar to the 'empiricism' of explanation by hypothesis-testing.

How, one may ask at this point, is theory in sense of *a priori* definitions to be related to empirical analysis, if neither the assumption of rational determinism of experience in general nor the sympathetic understanding of other individuals' experience is objectively possible? First, through a clarification of the form of understanding involved in the knowledge of both the general characteristics of experience and of the individual's perception of his own experience. And, second, through the process of analytical translation of individual's perception of his experience into a generalizable form of such perceptions. It is only through these means that sociological theory, i.e. a body of general statements on the determinants of social action, is possible. The formulation of these means in actual analysis is what Weber's and Pareto's contributions to sociological knowledge achieve in a complete form.

Their demarcation of definitional concepts, methodology and empirical generalizations is validated by them in their very different ways through experimentation and exploration of varieties of meanings, values and sentiments found in the actual descriptions, interpretations and rationalizations of the basic impulses of social experience; and, more significantly, the formal principles of analysis which they postulated and developed in their empirical analyses answer all the fundamental questions of sociological analysis. Further, on the original question of validity in scientific knowledge, that of generalization—on which many attempts to make sociological descriptions objective have foundered—their answer is definitive, and extends the exact applicability of scientific principles into regions of human experience which had, before them, seemed impossible to explore in such a way.

Generalization in science has been traditionally regarded a matter of discovering general categories of objects on the basis of observation and experiment. What has not perhaps been noticed is the role of inferential generalization, which relates *a priori* thought with observation, in experimental analysis. It is the inferential generalization which is the most important form in sociological analysis. The

15

subject-matter of sociology has always presented the difficulties which have become significant in natural sciences only recently, when the role of *a priori* thought has become crucial in empirical analysis and generalization. The fundamental difference between the inferential generalization of sociology and the *a priori* generalization of modern natural sciences is that sociological thought must make simultaneous inferences at all levels, while *a priori* thought in natural sciences is necessarily progressive.

The simultaneity of inferential generalizations in sociology is necessary because the simple is not always the source of the complex: they are relative categories, and explanations must, therefore, always be individual. But individual analyses do not preclude generalizability of explanations: a point which only Weber and Pareto grasped and made fully realizable. Although their substantive analyses can be seen as refinements of the original Marxian analytical ideas on the role of human consciousness in the formation of social reality, their methodological principles give their analyses the characteristics of scientific prediction—which Marx's empirical analysis wholly lacks. It is only from a knowledge of their analyses that we can differentiate in sociology scientific prediction, as an objective judgment of future developments on the basis of our causal understanding of past developments; from prophecy, as an intuitive projection of thought; and revolution, as a philosophical prediction. These three kinds of prediction are, however, still confused with one another; but to understand historical and contemporary social processes one must separate them. It is only from Weber and Pareto that we learn exactly how the separation can be made.

2 Weber's ideas on the analysis of rationality and its effects on modern society

The theme of Max Weber's sociology as a whole is rationalization of life: in the methodology, he is concerned with the translation of sub-jective rationality into objective knowledge; and in the analysis of world civilizations, with the social conditions of the varieties of rationalization. While the centre of his methodology is the logical structure of individual causal explanations, his study of capitalism provides a general analysis of the conditions of rationalization in the modern civilization, which, although historically rooted in Western Europe, has become a force of world-wide significance. These seemingly paradoxical analyses—of rationality and individual explanation, of civilizations and the uniqueness of industrial capitalism—provide us with a complete investigation into the form and substance of social reality and a definition of sociological knowledge, both of which, in comparison with other similar attempts, remain unsurpassed and, in application, irrefutable.

The basis of his methodology, the structure of individual causal explanation, does not lead in Weber's work to a preoccupation either with the form of historical description or a causal, compara-tive study of the implications of a particular institution, or with the means of perceiving the 'meaningful' unity of a phenomenon, as it does in the numerous derivations from his ideas. The methodology is a framework for relating historical causes and the meaningfulness of ideas and interests with the sociological significance of particular historical-social movements and institutions in which they are realized. Weber was not concerned with inventing new methods of analysis, but with a clarification of the form of sociological

17

knowledge through its contents. If his clarification developed into an original methodology, it is because he did not assume logic to be the source of knowledge, nor rationality the source of reality.* For him, logic only provides the form of knowledge and rationality the means to translate the contents of reality into scientific knowledge. These assumptions lead in Weber's work to some very original conclusions, not because these assumptions are new, but because he analyses the material, both formal and substantive, precisely.

The first concern of knowledge is obviously the question of its validity, to which historical or social-scientific knowledge can be no exception. There are four ways in which the patterns of thought which may designate the past can be distinguished: first, as defying all criteria of validity; then, as valid if judged by present ideals; or if one could imagine oneself in the actual situation; and, finally, as being considered completely valid because we cannot even gradually surpass them.†

These are theoretical values of the thought-patterns, which are taken as various premises in a valid analysis. The validity of the analysis will not be affected, whether these values, or interests, in reality lead to errors, retrogressive steps or deviations, because they are its facts. The presupposition of every attempt at historical or sociological knowledge is that the theoretical value is related to the theoretical premise of the object in such a way that the formal premises of knowledge can measure the validity of the knowledge thus gained.

The formal bases of knowledge themselves, which are derived from the constitution of human reason, cannot, conceivably, change. Methodology is, thus, not concerned either with the question of how raw experience can be changed into an object of analysis or with the *a priori*, subjective assumption on which the possibility of experience itself depends. The metaphysical meaning of an experience,

* Cf. comments on Wittgenstein's assumptions above, chapter 1.

† Cf. A. von Schelting, *Max Webers Wissenschaftslehre*, p. 83. Von Schelting's work is a definitive study of Weber's methodology in the context of the logical problem of historical cultural knowledge, which, through its analyses of Weber and Mannheim, makes an independent contribution both to the understanding of the implications of Weber's ideas and the clarification of the principles of sociological knowledge. Without this study it would be difficult to judge Weber's ideas, and it is a pity that it has never been translated into English.

which these questions imply, is simply a constituent of its objective knowledge: the problem that has to be solved, for Weber, is that of the logical structure of all those social and cultural sciences which are not amenable to the natural scientific method. How does, in other words, this structure work? What is, further, the specific characteristic of social scientific concepts, and the connection between these concepts—in contrast to the natural scientific ones—and the diversity of reality? In the analysis of these questions Weber refutes both the objectivist and the intuitionist theories on the logical difference between the social and natural sciences.

The objectivist theories on the 'irrationality' of historical events, deriving from human action and personality, base it on the irrationality and freedom of the human will, physical causality of human action, qualitative differences among individuals; which make it impossible to predetermine events or give explanations of them and, consequently, to formulate either general concepts or historical laws. The basic theme of intuitionist theories, on the other hand, is that an historical experience is understandable without concepts, and, therefore, explanations are to be based on the certainty of this inner, sympathetic understanding.

These theories continue to form the assumptions of contemporary sociological thought—leading either to the formation of apparently new or irreconcilable schools of sociology or to the recurrence of various arguments on the generalizing and individualizing methods in behaviourism and phenomenologism, or in philosophical distinctions between objectivity and meaningfulness, facts and values— mainly as the result of either a complete incomprehension of the implications of Weber's refutation or through ignorance of them.

Weber's refutation includes two fundamental discussions: (a) on an objectively workable theory on the historical knowledge of a particular phenomenon, and (b) on the concept of individuality as its essential constituent. In these discussions the questions which he considers are: (i) whether the 'irrational' qualities of history, attributed both by the objectivist and the intuitionist, exist at all; and if they do (ii) whether they have any logical relevance for differentiating between natural and social sciences. First, Weber finds no logical relevance in them for the differentiation, because the factors underlying a subject of knowledge are decisive for its logical structure, not the qualities of its content. But it is not to be inferred from this irrelevance of the material qualities of a science, that there are no differences in the logical character of the various sciences. There are specific points of view in the social sciences, which do not permit certain forms of thinking—or at least the meaning which they have for them—available to the natural sciences and create the 'deepest difference' between them,[1] in spite of a possible similarity in the formation and the logical structure of concepts.

Weber's development of this particular notion is, again, to be found in his refutation of the objectivist view, and in his inferences, from his position, of the differences within the range of empirical scientific knowledge. The logical importance of the 'understandability' of historical objects in his methodology is, on the other hand, to be found in his refutation of intuitionism.

His discussion of the objectivist methodology is centred on the concept of irrationality. The questions, on the existence of the specific irrationality of an historical event and on the possibility of constructing a logical structure of explanation on such a notion, imply three different meanings of irrationality. Weber discusses them all with a surprising originality and conviction, and concludes that in all the three meanings it is impossible to make irrationality the logical basis of explanation. In the meaning derived from the point of view of the present, irrationality is the impossibility of putting historical events together in terms of causal laws or general concepts, because of a lack of predetermination of events; but neither is the course of nature predetermined in any empirical sense. As the principle of rational determinism is only a principle of explanation, governing the formation of causal laws or general concepts, Weber finds nature as irrational as history in this logical sense.[2] Irrationality in this sense is ascribable to history only if the principle of explanation is reified and considered an inherent characteristic of natural processes. The irrationality of history is exaggerated by this reification, which, however, also makes the complete individuality of an historical phenomenon much more obvious than that of a natural phenomenon. For Weber, this more obvious individuality of history in itself as an object is no more comprehensible than that of nature, but the distinctive characteristic of this historical individuality lies in the subjective interest of the individual in the qualitative diversity of historical reality. This characterization of the recognition of the individuality of historical

20

facts is probably the most misunderstood notion of Weber's sociology. The logical separation between the theoretical and the subjective points of view of the historian or social scientist is not made by the commentators, in the same way as it is not made in the various schools of generalizing and individualizing methodology, either because the analyst or the observer is considered objective *per se* or merged in the general, metaphysical subjectivity of historical and social reality. The four ways mentioned above, in which the theoretical value of an historical process or event can be determined, are obvious enough in themselves, but not so obvious to historians and sociologists in their implications for a valid theory of social scientific knowledge.

The second meaning of irrationality, that of a lack of any attributable individual motivation or impulse—which is an essential ground for any sympathetic reconstruction in historical events—makes it impossible to develop historical explanations from it. Irrationality in this sense is, in Weber's phrase, 'the privilege of the mad'.[3]

The lack of motivation which one finds in history is due to the impossibility of directly applying the rational means-end relationship of an individual's action to it; on which, nevertheless, the 'irrationality' of history is judged by the intuitionist theorists. Thus, the situation in which a person would be declared 'mad' (because no recognizable motives can be attributed to his actions), when applied to a historical sequence of events without regard to the absurdity—which Weber points out—of the transference, becomes more confusing when the freedom of the will seems to be equated, in reality, with the irrationality, i.e. of apparent motivelessness, of insane behaviour.

Weber further distinguishes the freedom of the will clearly from its vague and distorting accretions of irrationality by discussing how it is associated with rational action rather than with wilfulness or insanity—a point which emerges as extremely important in relation to the more recent sociological theories based on rationality as a composite norm of action and analysis.

Free action is, in Weber's view, specifically rational, calculable and understandable. Every actual human action is rational only within given circumstances, but a pure rational action—taken as an extreme case—is not influenced by transcendental motives and circumstances and its end is determined by the adequacy and objectivity of the means available. The calculability and under-standability of such a rational action, therefore, depends on the empirical objectivity of both the end and the means; thus, making it clear how it is the only basis of the theory of general concepts and rules governing general empirical connections between means and end as valid determinants of knowledge. Human behaviour, similarly, shows coherence and regularity,[4] and the formulation of rules governing these empirical connections between means and end in it is as justified as in the case of natural objects. For, the indispensable premise of rationality, the causal relationship, is related to the explanation, both for the actors, subjectively, and for the analysers or observers or actor-observers, objectively, as it is in natural sciences. These empirical formulations of means-end relationship are thus general concepts as well as empirical laws, in the same way as the general concepts and laws on natural objects.

The third meaning of irrationality, that of the physical causality of human action, cannot be made a logical element of historical knowledge as opposed to natural scientific knowledge, because its explanation can only be in terms of natural scientific knowledge.

The answer to the question about the basis of social scientific as opposed to natural scientific knowledge (it should be obvious by now) is given by Weber implicitly in the concepts of individuality, values and understanding. But the difficulties of individualism as a methodological principle, implicit in the notion of reconstruction of reality in its endless variety, are not resolved for Weber by intuitive sympathy because of another methodological principle, that of concept-formation and generalization, which Weber's discussion of irrationality affirms as a fundamental principle of knowledge. In concept formation the endless variety is only bridged over,[5] never reconstructed or reproduced, necessarily, because if it were possible to reconstruct or reproduce the individuality of reality in its endless variety, it would preclude any form of generalizability of such descriptions. Further, the subjective, qualitative interest which characterizes the formal individuality of a perception of reality is in the existence and combination of different 'new' and 'old' historical times in one social situation or period, which can be represented by contemporary as well as anachronistic forms or heterogeneous ideals of individual groups. This quality of individual perception of, and interest in, social reality, past and present, is the basis of Weber's famous principle of value-relevance, because it is not simply the new elements of reality which have logically to be explained, but meaningful new elements. Without the concept of value-relevance, i.e. description of reality from varying individual points of view or perceptions—which make up, as a whole, the conceptual reality of the world—as a principle of selection of facts and perspective, it would be impossible to have empirically valid historical, or social scientific, knowledge. Another concept which defines this principle of selection, in combination with value-relevance, is effectiveness (*Wirksamkeit*). First, however, the changeability of values, points of view and perspectives must not affect the validity of the formal structure of historical knowledge. This is possible, as a claim to objectivity, by supposing —as Rickert and Weber do—that values are unconditionally valid *on the basis of* the connections that exist between value-ideas as facts and evaluations. Evaluations are, in any case, unconditionally valid, but without this basis value-ideas cannot be considered as facts. Therefore, these objects, in themselves, become important from all points of view and are generally accepted as the content of valid historical concepts. In other words, values, both as points of view and ideas, are to be taken as facts, because historically either evaluations of human beings become facts themselves or give meaning to facts.

This, however, is not enough. It does not resolve the problems of valid selection, because the subjectivity of values cannot yet be delimited in methodological terms. How, for example, is one to decide when a value-position becomes completely a theoretical premise, to be judged by the formal principles of valid knowledge, and does not remain a subjective premise of either the participant or the historian/social-scientist? Value-relevance on its own cannot resolve this dilemma. Rickert, in spite of his precise formulation of value-relevance *and historical effectiveness*, was unable to suggest an unconditionally objective principle. Historical effectiveness delimits the relationship between values and facts, by showing when values become facts and how values influence the becoming of facts *in reality*. But he fell back on the traditional notion of 'supra-historical values' which all 'civilized' men accept. Weber, following his discussion of the complementary nature of value-relevance and effectiveness, agrees with Rickert that mere effectiveness—i.e. whatever happens or has an effect—is not a sufficient criterion of

23

what is historically essential.[6] It is not 'obvious' to Weber that the point of beginning of a causal explanation of history is the result itself, i.e. the present; or that the effective and the historical are inherent in the process that has resulted in the present. If it were so, then we would have to include in history all those events of the human past which have no *causal* relevance for the present and make them the beginning of their own causal explanation.

The understanding of history in this narrow sense of causal explanation is the basis for understanding other ways of analysis of historical phenomena. Thus, effectiveness gives no support, in Weber's view, to the principle of value-relevance as Rickert formulated it.

A past event is valuable to us not just because it is a stage in the development towards the present, but also because it is an individual and self-sufficient form of human destiny.* Effectiveness as such cannot be the only criterion of the value or truth of ideas or thoughts: what is effective in history or social reality is recognizable only in terms of its perception and meaning, which presupposes a relevance to value-ideas. Then, the question arises, whether the truth of value-ideas is based on the present or effective reality or is independent of it?

This question can only be answered if the value-ideas which are relevant to a perception of reality are analysed to determine and delimit it as an object of study from the world of values, the historical or conceptual reality. A perception of reality is a value-judgment, and without this analysis the subjectivity of value-relevant descriptions cannot be objectified as conscious or articulate presentation of a point of departure from a possible value position. This step gives an historical—or, in a general sense, sociological—description an objective identity in terms of a theoretical premise, to govern the logical selection of facts. This resolution of 'subjectivity' begins in practice when the historian or social scientist does not rely on his subjective judgment of what is value-relevant, but considers all those elements which are relevant or should be relevant, logically, to the value object, the theoretical premise. Weber does not characteristi-

* A point which clearly indicates the distinction between historical and sociological analysis, because historically one is unable to envisage an event without its chronological and real antecedents and concomitants, thus diminishing the generalizability of its significance which, sociologically, is its most valuable aspect.

cally—and justifiably*—enumerate or formally delimit the particular values which the historian or sociologist should make his theoretical premise. Objectivity in this context is neither related to the value of 'truth' nor to the subjective value of the historian, but to the theoretical value-premise; and objective validity, then, concerns the specific scientific result of the analysis. It will be true in this logical sense, even when its ultimate truth remains problematical.

The logical distinction between value as meaningfulness and as theoretical premise in Weber's work is of fundamental importance, because without this distinction any recognition of the meaning of value as a subjective perception of reality and its *objective* implications becomes impossible. The concept of meaningful explanation includes the whole variety of interpretations which form the conceptual reality of the world; they are individually and subjectively valid and include the ideal typical descriptions of reality as such, i.e. if they are not part of a causal explanation. If they are part of a causal explanation, as they are in Weber's methodology, they are descriptions with values as theoretical premises.† In this formulation there is no contradiction when the meaningful explanation is also a causal explanation, i.e. both subjectively and objectively valid—it is simply not problematic. Neither is there any actual dichotomy between value as meaningful subjective validity and as theoretical premise of a causal analysis; nor is the distinction between them confused.

This notion of meaning, which is what one 'understands' in Weber's sociological analysis, is the basis of his concept of action. If the distinction between meaningful explanation and causal explanation were not made, then action would have been synonymous with some form of substantive rationality, which would have been made the norm of actual conduct. Action is definable only on the basis of the means-end relationship of motive and behaviour. Meaning is

* Cf. A. von Schelting, *Max Webers Wissenschaftslehre*, p. 249. Von Schelting's comment on this point, that the presupposition of fruitful historical research must be a knowledge of possible value-relevances implying the ability to change standpoints according to the object, can only be interpreted as a prior knowledge of 'value-relevances'. This would be a form of value judgment; but if one takes Weber's lack of enumeration of relevant values as a positive step—it is consistent with his methodological discussion as a whole—it is completely unnecessary.

† A point which does not seem to have been realized by many commentators on Weber.

the defining quality of motive and behaviour together. They are inseparable for analytical purposes because one without the other is not understandable, and certainly cannot be ascribed any *intrinsic* meaning.

Causal imputation is possible only when the inexhaustible reality of phenomena is thus analysed and reduced to its value-relevant descriptions or meaningful constituents. Only when these descriptions, or ideal types, are made points of departure and the subject-matter of the causal analysis or regression, is it possible to give causes of historical phenomena. The construction of an ideal type, i.e. the formation of reality, through abstraction and synthesis, as a recognizable entity—which Weber designates 'the construction of an historical individual'—is the first assumption in the possibility of individual historical knowledge. For, through this assumption it becomes possible to separate, within the multitude of facts which cause the full variety of reality, those which modify the actual course of events under consideration from those which do not. This is the way the first question on the possibility of causal imputation—i.e. how can a concrete result be imputed to one particular cause when there are innumerable causal factors which have conditioned a particular development?'—is answered by Weber.

Now the question to be answered is: 'in what logical form is the causal explanation of value-relevant individuality of an historical phenomenon to be validly realized?'[7] The first step, obviously, would be simply to show how the logical structure of this explanation is constructed by analysing a concrete example on the basis of a number of hypothesized factors; but the structure must apply to every concrete example, to be valid. It should not matter at all whether the example is a significant historical event or a domestic incident, whether it is a 'meaningless' natural event or a meaningful human behaviour, whether it is one's own subjective experience or another's (p. 258). The logical structure becomes clear only by 'control' or contrast of hypothetical contents, it does not change the circumstances. It is implicit in every causal analysis that we must presume the substance of the hypothesis to be realized, or that it has the possibility of realization. Weber again, characteristically, would not generalize a practical analysis, but show the necessary logical form of all causal analysis, both as commonly used and as implicit in historical knowledge.

26

The proof of this statement is to be found in the main part of Weber's essay on the Protestant ethic and the spirit of capitalism, in which, however, the material enumerative question—which particular qualities, and in what measure compared to other causally relevant factors, can be specially attributed to the economic ethic of ascetic Protestantism—remains unanswered in an absolutely precise sense (pp. 281–2); mainly because it cannot be answered until the primary relationship between the particular ethical orientation of Protestantism and its result, the spirit of capitalism, has been established and its generalizability to the relationship of ethic and action has been determined. The enumeration is a matter of detailed research which cannot be undertaken before the general relationship is proved.* It is not a fundamental problem, because it is the general theoretical analysis that would establish the limits of factual correlations, not the facts themselves. The general theoretical analysis of ethic and action is not exhausted—as it has gradually become recognized—by the Protestant ethic essay, but includes the studies in religion and society as well as in economic history.†

In the Protestant ethic essay, Weber emphasizes the importance of the economic ethic and the way of life conditioned by it for the origin as well as development of modern capitalism as an economic system. But this importance is not asserted by enumerating some prescriptions of economic ethic and then inferring the way of life and juxtaposing it with the characteristics of the industrial economy, as one might gain the impression from some critical discussions of it, but by making it part of a general sociological question on the relations between certain historical economic forms and the ultimate religious attitudes in those societies. In so far as Weber's interest in non-industrial economic forms or systems is autonomous, and he considers their causal connections, the logical structure is the same as in the specific question of the historical explanation of modern capitalism in terms of its individual characteristics. The whole analysis serves, thus, to explain, with as much certainty as it is possible, the *individuality* and the degree of development of the industrial

---

* It is one of the sad weaknesses of contemporary sociology that such minor, though factual, questions are mistaken for fundamental problems.

† i.e. studies of Confucianism, Hinduism and Ancient Judaism as well as parts of Agricultural History of the Antiquity (untranslated) and General Economic History; cf. von Schelting, op. cit., p. 283.

economic system as well as to clarify many of the problems of sociological generalization.

He first analyses the entire process, which leads to the historically unique result of modern industrial capitalism, in order to make each component analysable, further, in a mental experiment, as the 'possible' cause of the rest of the contents of the process. The 'controlled' component is the special economic sentiment, the hypothesized causal factor in the individuality and the high degree of development of modern capitalism.

The hypothesis may have been formed intuitively, but since, for Weber, intuitive hypotheses are only raw materials of explanation, the task is not simply to exemplify a hypothesis but to test it.

In this test, the first step is to determine the meaningful correspondence, the adequacy of meaning and the 'elective affinity' which have obviously existed between the capitalistic economic behaviour and the practical maxims of the Protestant ethic.[8] Then, a valid proof has to be given that this ethic is the real cause of the *individual characteristics* of the Western industrial economic system, by answering the question 'whether by imagining the continuation of the ethical qualities the development was as hypothetically expected or not?'

Weber, besides answering this question, makes use of another logical operation: he compares this complex entity of ethic and empirical reality with other developments in world history, in which if comparable situations and processes differ in some elements they are the same in others. Weber could indeed have constructed comparable entities theoretically, which would have been logically valid, but empirically useless, fictions.* As such fictional, speculative constructions would make empirical explanations of these historical developments impossible, and defeat the whole purpose of sociological analysis, it is not surprising that Weber rejected the dubious exercise of 'hypothetico-deductive' construction, i.e. of putting together speculative fragments of empirical reality, to illustrate the

---

* This is what ideal types have been expected to be by recent theorists, who, it seems, are unable to distinguish the formal elements of a concept from its substance, because the form of a concept for them depends entirely on the degree of *fictitiousness* of contents, and not on its consistency with the principles of validity. It is no wonder that they cannot see why their theories should be considered speculative in substantive relations and invalid in form. Cf. Parsons.

hypothesis, and making generalized inferences from them as *theoretical* explanations.

The significance of this judgment of Weber's has not even been discerned by any of the 'hypothetico-deductionist' or the inductionist or the intuitionist sociologists today—for the validity of the relation between his methodology, theory and empirical analysis—however much they protest their various allegiance to Weber's thoughts and ideas. Is it any wonder, then, that they cannot relate theory and empirical research in sociology except in pious assertions?

As a consistent development from the principles of sociological knowledge—and it is on this point that the validating analysis of Weber's researches is to be judged—Weber looked for those real processes and situations which differed from the particular historical entity of Protestant ethic and modern capitalism to the same degree as theoretically postulated. In other words, Weber sought *in all times and among all peoples* historical developments, which in a number of components are comparable to those components—which he has already analysed—which contributed to the historical *result* of modern capitalism, but lack the *particular* factors which *seem* decisive for the Western development: that is, a theoretical and empirical answer to the question: Have the analogous historical developments shown the specific, economic practical ethic?[9]

It is obvious that Weber was not the first to use this method of causal analysis, but it is also obvious that he did not use his historical-experimental analysis to illustrate his methodological doctrines. Yet, there is no contradiction between them—an achievement which would seem slight only if one were unaware of the extreme complexity and the subtle meshes of historical phenomena.

This consistent relationship between his methodological principles and substantive analysis is evident in the definition of capitalism itself. He does not deal with a general concept of capitalism, but with a directly opposite one, that of the specific uniqueness of the modern Western capitalism. A general concept of capitalism, as a preliminary to empirical analysis, must necessarily be non-empirical and defined in *a priori* deterministic or, at best, hypothetical terms; thus preventing an empirical causal explanation of the correlation as well as confining the empirical reference of general or abstract concepts to fragmentary allusions, and creating a theoretical sociology with no empirical validity.

29

The analogical analysis, therefore, is of fundamental importance for the empirical validity of sociology by providing a more conclusive answer than hypothetical constructions, to the central question of causal imputation: what kind of development is objectively possible when the alleged causal factor is eliminated?

It is in this way that Weber's intention of finding the cause of the *uniqueness* of Western capitalism leads to a clarification of the whole basis of sociological knowledge, and to a series of empirical generalizations from which many theoretical concepts developed by him come and implicit generalizations from which many others can be developed. The hypothetico-deductive formulation of sociological theory is *thus* seen to be a *subsequent* possibility rather than an *a priori* thought, which makes an effective and precluding rejection of Parsons's notion that Weber should have developed systematic theory more fully than he did.

The uniqueness of the economic life of modern times lies in its historical isolation as a form of development, in the sense that it has not originally existed anywhere but in the West, or at best only in rudiments.*

It is this problem, therefore, that Weber analyses: the origin of the uniqueness of the modern technological industrial and rational system—which has impressed itself on the present-day economic life of all nations, whatever their particular ideological orientation and size—in order to clarify both its historicity and its general sociological implications.[10] Although this quality is at the centre of his sociology, the problem cannot be explained without the specific economic ethos of ascetic Protestantism, i.e. without its practical effect on everyday economic life; and it would be illogical to consider the generality of the implications as a justification of the notion of *a priori* theoretical formulations being part of Weber's sociology.†

* This does not mean that it cannot exist anywhere else, given the circumstances. The possibility that it can exist will only be realized if one works out the factors of the historical isolation as Weber does, and not with the possibility as an *a priori* assumption.

† The idea is becoming increasingly acceptable to the current interpreters of Weber that, in his later 'phase', he abandoned the individual ideal typical explanation in favour of the general abstract definitions. This literary criticism of Weber, in terms of various influences on an author and their periods, could be interesting if accurately based on biographical information; but the conclusion that these commentators derive from such a critique, that Weber did not realize that general definitional concepts were what he should have

For the logical basis of the Protestant ethic thesis—which was discussed above—and the justification of Weber's claim that the probability* of a causal relationship between them is really great are both to be clearly seen in the arguments which Weber uses. In criticism of this thesis, it is said that modern capitalism could have the same characteristics without the special ethical element. In Weber's view there is no ground for this supposition, because it is contradicted by every attempt to construct an objectively possible development without the ethic and by every analogous but historically different process of development.

The other constituents of the historical development which led to modern capitalism can be included in general categories of events or categorized by general concepts; but this does not mean that these historical constituents would automatically lead to the modern economic structure, as it may be supposed by those who believe that science is defined by this kind of categorization. For example, one of these constituents is technology, through which it could be said that the traditionalism of the previous economic structure was overcome—because it was one of the components in the historical formation of modern capitalism. But, Weber points out, it cannot be taken for granted that, historically, technological advance causes the breakdown of traditionalism by itself or technological inventions as such are conducive to the formation of a new economic structure. The correct inference would be that the development of industrial capitalism became possible because it set a premium on discovery and invention. Similarly, although the increase of precious metals was significant for the change in the Western economic structure, it cannot, on historical and empirical grounds, be said to have created it. A third historical correlation in the formation of the industrial economic structure could be said to be the development of rational law, but the history of legal development in the Western civilization shows a long and complicated process before the beginnings of

---

formulated in the first place, till late, is absurd, because the most obvious question on the validity of sociological definitions—how would it be possible *a priori*?—seems not to occur to them; cf. my editorial introduction and contribution with Rex's in *Max Weber and Modern Sociology*.

* 'Probability' in Weber's work is not naïvely used as a technical, statistical concept, as, for example, Peter Winch implies in *The Idea of a Social Science*, Routledge & Kegan Paul, London, 1958.

modern capitalism. Therefore, the fact that it has been influenced in its later rationalization—thus the historical correlation—by the existence of modern capitalism has to be set against the pre-existing fact of the progressive rationalization of the law, which makes any inference of causal connection between them illegitimate.

These correlations and influences in the formation of the modern economic system are undoubtedly important, but they do not answer the primary question of causal imputation: 'how did the system come about?' The question is not to be faced by attempting to show the complete irrelevance of these historical constituents— because it would be absurd to do so—but by *determining* whether any of these components could objectively lead to the historical result *on their own*. It is in this form that Weber's argument as well as experimental analysis works; and the conclusion, from this analysis of the objective possibility of each historical factor in the development of capitalism, is that none of them are capable of originating something like the special characteristic of modern Western capitalism. The ethical implications of the profit-motive, which seem to contradict Weber's thesis on the uniqueness of this economic form, are discussed by Weber from a variety of points of view. For example, it is true that there was a widespread desire for gold at the beginning of capitalism and even before,[11] but Weber points out that modern capitalism was carried on by people who were hostile to colonial plunder and other kinds of political capitalism; and, further, a comparison with the development of a limitless pursuit of gold in other times and places shows that an unrestricted lust for gold is not suited to the creation of an economic structure like modern capitalism. In fact, Weber further argues, the universal dominance of absolute unscrupulousness in money-making has been a characteristic of those countries where the growth of modern capitalism has remained backward by Western standards.[12] An absolute and conscious recklessness in profiteering has, in fact, gone together with the strictest traditionalism, without in any way breaking or changing the prevalent economic structure. Thus, the change of European economy cannot legitimately be attributed to profiteering; nor can it be said that the change over to the industrial economic structure was desired by the particular group or class of people known for such a motive.[13] It could be argued, further, from a contemporary point of view, that the practices of monopolism, diversification of interests and high profit on individual products rather than on the volume of sales are indications of a *reassertion* of traditionalism in this modern economic form.

All these and other examples derived from an analysis of the historically composite factors are logically related in terms of their objective possibility, based on the principles of explanation inherent in the ideal typical analysis. The traditional view of experimental analysis would suggest that Weber should have made a *positive* logical construction on the objective possibilities of these components, with the ethical element in 'control'. But the objective possibilities of the remaining factors would have led to some other form of economy, rather than to modern capitalism. This empirical restriction on the hypothetico-deductive experimentation is one of the most significant indications of the correctness of Weber's methodological principles. Thus, to overcome this divergence between actual historical-social processes and the hypothesized development, Weber turns to historical analogy, without in any significant way modifying the structure of causal analysis.[14] The analogical analysis is both of certain historical examples which had positive factors and of others in which unfavourable factors were less numerous or less intensive than in modern times, i.e. in both positive and negative forms. Analogies are found—and developed in varying detail—by Weber in different historical and cultural areas and periods, e.g. in the Greek and Roman antiquities, the Ptolemaic Egypt, and in Ancient Judaic, Islamic, Chinese and Indian civilizations. Logically, the ideal case would be to find a historical development with all the necessary factors except the specific economic ethic of ascetic Protestantism. Weber did not, of course, find such an ideal situation, not even in China.* His use of these analogies shows, however, that the existence of an extensive or intensive surplus of unfavourable factors could not have stopped the development of modern capitalism in those places where the specific economic sentiment, that of ascetic Protestantism, prevailed.

For example, in certain phases of Chinese economic history Weber finds a considerable number of favourable factors, e.g.

---

* This point shows the clarity of Weber's concept of sociological rationality (see pp. 46-8). The rationalism of the Chinese civilization is so similar to the Western rationalism in content that it becomes difficult not to believe that rationality can be defined substantively or to judge any differences from such a definition as imperfect rationality.

orientation to worldly life, high regard for wealth, obvious acceptance of the profitability of money, free choice of occupation, lack of status privileges by birth, lack of any limiting laws on usury, etc., and, further, considerably favourable economic politics, freedom of choice in production methods, absence of slavery, a relatively high number of technical skills and of new inventions, intensive inland trade, at least periodically considerable export trade and peace.[15] All these factors helped the development of various kinds of political capitalism—there and in other similar circumstances. The importance of the Protestant ethic thus becomes obvious; but the logical significance of this conclusion for the problem of causal imputation, by experimental elimination of the factors according to their causal importance to get a picture of the objectively possible development, is realized when we find that even a surplus of favourable factors and a scarcity of unfavourable factors could not have brought about this particular result in any other way. In fact, the remaining historical factors of the Western development itself could not have produced the special characteristic of modern capitalism. Many of the favourable conditions of European development were lacking in China and other historical examples used as analogies, and some favourable factors contradict unfavourable ones; but, on the other hand, the areas where modern capitalism arose lacked some of those favourable factors and had limiting factors not found elsewhere. The logical conditions of his analysis are revealed by Weber in the following sentence: 'In spite of the various superficially favourable circumstances, modern capitalism developed as little in China, in Western or Oriental antiquity, in India, or in the Islamic regions; although in each of these areas other conditions as favourable would seem to be helpful to its rise.'[16]

It cannot, however, be denied, Weber goes on to say, that the basic peculiarities of the sentiment, i.e. the practical attitudes to life, are conditioned in their development by political and economic circumstances, but the force of their own laws of development has also been part of this conditioning.[17]

The central question of causal imputation—'what kind of development is it possible to think out if the alleged causal factor is eliminated and whether by elimination or change in the causally relevant factor the result would remain the same?'—is not asked in analogies to determine the logically possible result of the mental elimination of the factor, but for the alteration in the possible result; as all historical analogies will have some economic sentiments, but that they will be different from the modern ethic. So, if empirically and analogously, the actual result, i.e. 'modern capitalism', could not be considered objectively possible on the experimental alteration or variation of the economic sentiment, then we can justifiably say that the Protestant economic ethic was not causally insignificant for the actual historical result of modern capitalism. Indeed, in the mental experiment it should be possible to relate the eliminated or altered factor with the actual result in a positive sense as well. If it is impossible, then it has to be accepted that the analysis of the course of events into individual factors was faulty or that our knowledge of historical events was not enough.[18] The positive connection between Protestant ethic and modern capitalism is shown by Weber most clearly in his comparison with the kind of connection other economic ethics, especially Buddhism and Confucianism, have with the economic life of the particular society.* In these comparative analyses it is seen that this connection has either a less positive or directly negative character, both where economic activity is disapproved of and where it is approved of. In all these areas of different economic sentiments one finds the rise of political capitalism, but not of industrial capitalism.

In the Protestant economic ethic the positive value is concentrated on the economic calling (*Berufsarbeit*) as such, on economic management and the profitable continuation of the economic process (*Betrieb*). Management and industry acquire a special meaning, their own life, while their ultimate end and meaning remain transcendental.[19] This makes a clear analytic separation between means and end, as the economic ends, although empirical, only serve as sociological means to transcendental value-ends, and allows a sharp perspective on a whole range of economic, social and metaphysical relationships. It shows, in fact, the clear simplicity achieved by Weber in his

* This comparison may seem imbalanced if one does not consider that the Protestant ethic is an analytical ellipsis of the Protestant way of life and of societies in which the Reformed doctrine prevails. The comparison is, therefore, between ideal types of different societies, Protestant, Chinese or Indian, and the degree of detailed description of any particular society, necessary for adequate information, varying according to what can be assumed as already known to the reader. Cf. my 'Hindu Reformist Ethics and the Weber Thesis: An Application of Max Weber's Methodology', 2 vols, University of London Ph.D. thesis, 1969.

methodology without any over-simple assumptions on the existential processes of social reality.

It is, however, on this point that von Schelting believes[20] Weber to have reached the end of his own interpretation, for the relationship between transcendental world of religious meaning and empirical reality of economic ends and their own independent meaning lies beyond reasonable causal explanation. But, in Weber's work, this particular relationship is of the utmost importance: how, for example, could the understanding of psychological motives be based on an ultimate ideal relationship, like that of a religious or philosophical explanation of the world with one's life?

The whole of Weber's methodology is centred on the theory that the historical knowledge of actual individual events, especially causal interrelations, is inseparable from knowledge generally, because the individual ideal-typical abstraction from reality has the same logical form as a rational concept of knowledge. This is not simply an attempt to unite 'history' with 'theory'[21] or the individual with the general, but to bring together, in the ideal-type concept itself, the whole of the functional relationship of theory and empirical material in an individual causal imputation.

Besides the historical-causal ideal types and the general ideal types, in which complete rationality is assumed both from the subjective and the objective points of view, there are ideal types of non-causal relations and of a particular kind of understanding.[22] The historical-causal ideal type is a straightforward form of analytical description, and the general ideal types are abstract definitional concepts or objectively possible representations of the general conditions of reality. Both these ideal types are causally related—and often with interchangeable elements—in causal imputation. Since the individual historical ideal type is governed by the rules of causal imputation and the general definitional ideal type serves individual causal imputation as a means, their construction must obviously be entirely consistent with each other in form and substance. They are both causal, therefore generalizing, ideal types; and the concept of understanding is important to both in the same measure, in so far as the causal meaning depends on understandable motives.

These two kinds of ideal types have been taken as the dichotomy of the empirical and the theoretical in Weber's thought; and, in the traditional manner, the general definitional ideal types have been made the theoretical *a priori*, part of Weber's sociology.[23] But the connection between the individual-historical and the general-definitional ideal types is a methodological one, as the general definitional concepts are a means of individual causal explanation in Weber's work. The causal explanation, as we are aware, is undertaken by Weber in order to make individual historical statements validly generalizable, i.e. sociological. Since the historical ideal types have both general and individual elements, and the logical inevitability of the methodological concepts of individuality, value-relevance and understanding determines the validity of the relationship of the general elements and individual characteristics in them, the functional relationship between 'history' and 'theory' becomes a crucial question of validity: *How is this relationship to be realized?* The individual historical ideal type, far from being the complete empirical, substantive element of sociological analysis, becomes only a partially clear form for this purpose. The other kind of ideal type, to be found in Weber's sociological analysis, the acausal, which von Schelting believes 'breaks through' the limits of his methodology,[24] becomes in the realization of this relationship an extremely important and logically necessary concept. The acausal ideal type is another form of analytical description: of ideas, ideals, life-meanings, spiritual attitudes, motivations, codes of conduct and institutions into a 'unity of "spirit" '.[25] This unity has nothing to do with causality, although there is the same complete assumption of rationality. In an analogical analysis, for example, the acausal ideal type may be used when one needs to define an idea and its purely rational consequences as distinct from the causal relationships one is investigating. This kind of definition requires the inclusion of all the value-relevant and significant points which express it most clearly, not in order to realize its causal adequacy as the means used, but to achieve a complete consistency of meaning in all its elements.[26] Therefore such an ideal type would only include those ways of behaviour as well as motivations which are not contradictory but form a unity in terms of ideas and meaning rather than of experience. This kind of rational description allows the actual realization of such phenomena, which could not have this degree of rational consistency, to be compared and judged. This is the point of confusion, as von Schelting rightly mentions,[27] between a highly consistent meaningful, but acausal, ideal type and an abstract definitional, but causal, ideal type. There

37

is not only the difference of significance, in the assumption of complete rationality in both cases, but also of purpose. The significance of the causal ideal type lies in the rationality of end, while the rationality of the acausal ideal type is achieved in a pure ideality. The purpose for which they may be constructed can also seem to be the same, if one does not realize that an imaginary, value-relevant, meaningful description is not the same as empirical, understandable explanation of the contents of reality which it embodies. But an explanation inevitably includes such analytical descriptions, because without them it cannot contain the complete form of an historical and cultural phenomenon and its ultimate meaning. It is on this relationship that Weber's sociological analysis seems to be so ambiguously causal in its methodological form and intuitive in its connections. If, however, one considers all the ideal types together, in relation to the form of causal imputation which Weber applies in the Protestant ethic thesis as a whole, one finds that Weber's belief in a complete agreement between his methodological ideas and empirical research is fully justified.

The acausal meaningful ideal type and the general definitional ideal types, as we have seen, are abstract and highly rational in content: they are both, in Weber's special sense, ideal. But, they both serve the principle of causal explanation as means, and are not explanations themselves. A third dimension in judging the validity of Weber's methodological concepts is formed by the abstract generalizations which the causal explanation is aimed to provide on the relations of actual historical values, interests and action. These are inductive or empirical generalizations arrived at by applying the logic of causal analysis. What, one may ask at this point, have they in common with the general abstract definitions and the abstract and rationally consistent idealities? The answer lies in the primacy of the causal interpretation or explanation. Logically, therefore, the construction of the 'historical individual' must have the same form for all its elements, and all its relationships, *actual and experimental.* To fulfil this requirement, it is necessary that a complete rationality should govern all the substantive elements. Obviously, it is the ambiguity of the statement that all substantive elements of description should be completely rational that leads to a confusion of meaning, because, as we have seen, the rationality of various ideal types is governed by at least two senses of the term, causal and ideal.

These two forms of rationality are related to the two kinds of understanding, empirical and aesthetic, which Weber's work attempts to unite under sociological knowledge, since the contents of sociology are understandable—or knowable—only in those terms, not separately but together. This point, although it raises the most complex philosophical problems, is important for sociology, because all attempts to use one or the other form of understanding as its exclusive basis leave a residue of insoluble elements.

The resolution which Weber attempts of this philosophical duality of knowledge is given in his concept of understanding. Although von Schelting finds the validity of this concept problematic, paradoxically, it is in his detailed and precise discussion that we find the point of Weber's originality and simplicity of approach most accurately presented.

This point, however, eludes us when we confine ourselves either to the methodological essays or to the theoretical-empirical analysis, for it is realized—as Weber must have known when he claimed a complete consistency for his work—in the whole of his contribution to sociology. However, in von Schelting's view,[28] Weber's concept of understanding becomes problematic because historical research material first of all does not adapt itself to the formal categories and structures of historical and sociological knowledge. For, although the factual elements of historical knowledge would seem to be easily contained in the process of understanding, they come in the end to the action and behaviour of individual human beings.

This makes their inclusion in the logical structure of knowledge impossible, thus making the objective validity of understandable knowledge as such partially questionable. This, he says, does not seem to have occurred to Weber, who, in his methodological discussions, considers understanding unproblematical. Second, Weber's formulations betray 'an inner division', and irreconcilable descriptions of understanding are put together without any clear decision. Most of his formulations on understanding and situations which are related to psychological motives and causal explanation, and his undifferentiated use of the term for all 'sympathetic' understanding of inner reality, show that Weber tends to use both Dilthey's definition of understanding (as an important force in the actual psychological experience) as well as Rickert's (i.e. understanding being confined to the accretions of meaning to objects) without

39

judging one against the other. Thirdly, for Weber, it is possible to have knowledge of: (i) the non-understandable phenomena, (ii) the understandable actual reality and (iii) the 'ideally understandable unreality'. The last two categories in Weber's methodology, von Schelting says, are not clearly differentiated. The emphasis is always on reality: that is, the meaning attached to the psychological reality is not separated and, as such, immediately acknowledged by Weber as it is by Rickert. For Weber understanding means knowledge of the psychological reality or the actual relations brought about by it. We comprehend them with the proof of our own inner experience. But, von Schelting points out, Weber's material researches exceed this definition of understanding and reach *a pure intellectual* understanding of the meaning of an experience. This kind of understanding Weber calls causal understanding, which von Schelting finds unexceptionable because it concerns psychological reality and its interrelations with the external observable phenomena or actions, and their actual objective effects. The opposite of the intellectual understanding of meaning is the pure reactive understanding or re-experience, but for Weber such an understanding is also knowledge because of its proof in the inner re-experience; and, as knowledge itself is always rational, objectifying and conceptual, understandable knowledge must also be so. So, the accompaniment of understandable knowledge, re-experience, can either be intellectual or emotional. Emotional re-experience is also knowledge, therefore rational. The historical and sociological researches proceed in a philosophical opposition between the meaning, the ideality, of psychological experience and re-experience itself, both of which are fused together in the subjective meaning of an individual, who does not separate the meaning and the psychological act. That is, a subjective meaning can be present even in a 'pure' psychological reality. And the understanding of such subjective realities is possible when one finds the specific proof of its reality in one's own subjective or 'inner' re-experience.

It is this 'naïve' unity of an individual psychological reality that is decisive for a *sociological* concept of understanding, which Weber applies in his material researches. Von Schelting discusses and demonstrates the empirical validity of this application,[29] but does not conclude that in application Weber has made a decisive selection, from the characterizations of understanding by Dilthey and Rickert, which becomes in reality an empirical as well as a philosophical resolution of the problem of understanding. This is primarily because, in von Schelting's view, the other aspect of Weber's causal analysis of the Protestant ethic and the spirit of capitalism remains a residual element in the problem of understandable knowledge, that of the pure ideal roots of the contents of the religious motives. These contents refer to other meaningful contents of a comprehensive spiritual world with an inherent unity, which, through its peculiar religious meaning of the world and human life, creates practical consequences. These conditions have a definite form based on actual ideally-founded motives of everyday life of the time. It is for such phenomena that Weber uses the term 'adequacy of meaning (*Sinn-adäquanz*)', as distinct from 'adequacy of conditions'—for an explanation on the basis of inner re-experience alone, even when a valid causal explanation, with this motive as cause, is lacking—in the same way as the term is used for constructing the meaningful ideal type. In von Schelting's view,[30] the term 'adequacy of meaning', as applied to the ideally-founded motives and their consequences, does not achieve the same significance as it does in the case of rationality and logical consistency of the two forms of ideal types, causal and acausal. Weber is always inclined to change pure affinities of meaning into actual psychological causal relations or re-experience and to explain them as ideal types. He was convinced, nevertheless, of the realizability of pure ideal motives and their historical consequences,[31] and von Schelting points out that we are not concerned at this point with the historical consequences of such idealities—which is what the causal analysis of Protestant ethic and capitalism is about—but with the question of their understandability as knowledge. That is, how, when and where the individual elements or the *normative* consequences of ideals have been realized in the historical reality, through human motivations, as practical maxims?[32]

The actual historical causal processes in no way need to correspond ideally to the contents of the ideal motive or the cause. This means in effect the determination of the ideal, not causal, interrelations of the motives or ways of behaviour which have historical consequences. But Weber always means causally explicable understanding when he mentions understanding of historical phenomena, i.e. the causal explanation of the behaviour of individual human beings, their collective actions and their actual results, through recurrence of motives as actual psychological components of the subjective reality, be the motive material or ideal.[33]

From the above résumé of von Schelting's critique of Weber's concept of understanding, it is not difficult to deduce that Weber was developing a sociological concept, rather than a philosophical definition, of understanding. However, von Schelting's objections to the concept are not answered entirely by this point, because a positive decision on the validity of Weber's concept of understanding can only be made if the relationship between the acausal, meaningful rationality of the analytical descriptions of idealities and the causal rationality of the historical as well as the definitional ideal type is clearly demonstrable as being logically derived from Weber's methodological principles, which have been accepted as valid.

The point which would answer von Schelting's criticism is centred on the validity of the meaningful ideal type as a part of the causal analysis which leads to empirical generalization, for the meaningful ideal type cannot be treated as simply a problem of understandable knowledge. It must be consistent with knowledge generally. The second point which von Schelting makes in his critique, on the relationship between idealities as spiritual wholes and their practical consequences, is of direct relevance to the first, more logical, criticism. This point is of the degree of rational consistency which can be reached in the description of such ideas and the practical maxims based on them when it is neither meaningfully nor causally rational, but can only be taken as an intuitive whole. Thus, before one can relate the meaningful ideal type to the causal ideal type in methodological terms, the second point must be satisfactorily answered.

The situation which von Schelting envisages is simply that of the relationship of the doctrine and the ethic in a religious system of ideas; or, in more general terms, that of the premise and inference. The realizability of practical maxims, not as historical consequences but as psychological and subjective reality, is given in the inevitable defining relationship of an ideal system, for no religious system presents a set of doctrines and a set of ethics without any kind of relational argument. Indeed, neither the doctrines nor the ethics would have any meaning if no relational arguments were given or were allowed to be made by the believers. It is immaterial whether the doctrines are mystical or rational and ethics ritualistic or empirical.

Since both doctrines and ethics must inevitably have meaning, their rationality can be judged on the basis of the relational arguments of the system, which can be found either in the form of the doctrines (or of the ethics) or in the justifications which make them into a system of ideas. It is their developments which make intuitive ideas or perceptions understandable. Any such development must always be in terms of the meaning of the idea or perception, and, as such, it is its realization. The subjective variation of its realizability makes no difference, for the question which von Schelting raises is: how the realization, as practical maxims, of the individual elements or the *normative* consequences of ideals, through human motivation, is possible as understandable knowledge?

Therefore, the Weberian conviction that pure ideal motives and their historical consequences are realizable through psychological motivation is fully justified and demonstrable,[34] although historical consequences cannot, even in a generalized form, be attributed to the pure ideal motives and their subjective consequences simply on the basis of their internal analysis. They can be theoretically inferred and empirically *predicted* if there is an adequacy of conditions in the historical situation.

This is, in fact, the final sequence of Weber's sociological thought and analysis. But, before it can be achieved, the place of the analytical description of ideas and their meaning within the framework of causal analysis has to be seen.

To recapitulate the process of causal analysis: the first step in the construction of the 'historical individual' is the clarification of the value or the point of view. This clarification is, in fact, the determination of the theoretical premise of description, analysis and explanation. Values are primarily ideas which give significance or meaning to the sequence or correlation of facts or events.

The clarification of values, therefore, entails analytical description of value-ideas, with the highest internal consistency of meaning necessary for fulfilling the logical requirement of 'adequacy of meaning'. This analytical description of value-ideas covers the real problematical case of von Schelting's critique: the relationship between ideals and practical maxims without historical consequences. It is through the clear internally consistent description of doctrinal and ethical ideas as well as relational arguments that the 'adequacy of meaning' is achieved; and the intuitive wholeness of such systems

43

of ideas is turned into a rational and consistent description, to serve as the ideal-typical norm of comparison in the analysis of the varying actual individual psychological reality which is formed by the ideal system.

Therefore, the internal consistency of meaning, as one of the primary forms of rationality, determines *without exception* the analytical description of idealities, whether they have only subjective consequences or both subjective and historical consequences. This is indeed a confirmation of the validity of Weber's methodology; but the problem that may still arise with acausal ideal types and 'adequacy of meaning' is related to the fundamental point of von Schelting's criticism, that of the limits of understandable knowledge.

For Weber, understandable knowledge is synonymous with causal explanation of psychological reality and its subjective and historical consequences, in so far as such reality is re-experienceable. Therefore, the primary concept is that of causality.

One can no longer, after Weber's entirely consistent definition and use of the concept in analysis, regard it as the irreconcilable antithesis of meaningfulness. Moreover, the implications of his characterization of causal understanding, after the resolution of von Schelting's serious doubts on its validity, are far-reaching. First, since the analytical description of meaning which the acausal ideal type makes is governed by the causal relationship of means and end in a given, specific or individual situation—because explanation is always individual—it can only be a variant of the descriptive form of ideal type. The 'historical individual', therefore, cannot be just a rationalized history of events, or a causal ideal type, but must include a consistent description of relevant ideas. Obviously, the relevance of both events and ideas, which characterize an historical individual, must be to a value, for the meaning or significance of these events and ideas lies in it.

In the construction of an historical individual, however, it would be impossible not to have elements which do not have a general, universal meaning. It is these general elements which become problematical now. How are they related to the value-relevant description of individuality?

General elements, in fact, are the means of isolating the individuality of social phenomena. These general elements can be ideal or existential, subjective or objective, since the criteria of Weber's concepts are both the 'certainty' of re-experience and the objective rationality of internal relationships; but causal explanation is achieved only when both coincide. The definitional concepts are, therefore, general hypotheses on the basis of an assumption of complete subjective and objective rationality. But objective rationality is not possible if the subjective reality of experience is ignored. This necessary knowledge of the subjective reality of the variety of experience is sociological and empirical, and not *a priori* or purely psychological. For psychological reality must be expressed, to be known or understood, in terms of other known experience; that is, it must be 're-experienceable' both ideally and causally.

This inevitable unity of the ideal and the causal in psychological reality is thus the basis of Weber's concept of causal understanding and, indeed, of the whole of his sociology. It still leaves the validity of both the abstract definitions and empirical generalizations in doubt. Where do the general concepts, definitions come from? They are clearly hypothetical generalizations. On the other hand, the process of making empirical generalizations is clearly set out in his theory of causal analysis and its application in the Protestant ethic thesis proves the empirical validity of the methodology. In other words, they are empirical inferences which transform a hypothesis, through a thesis of individual causal imputation, into a theory.

The clarification of the inherent value of an historical or social phenomenon, action or event, leads to a description of both the value-ideas and their relationship to the sequence of action or event. The criteria of meaningfulness and of causality, instead of being the philosophically irreconcilable antitheses of social-historical reality, form together the concept of descriptive individual ideal type, which allows a substantive analogical analysis of historically unrelated sequences of human experience—a term which combines the conceptual reality of ideas, culture and society with the objective reality of events—in order to understand the causes of such combinations, as they form the social reality of human existence. These specific analyses, thus, become generalizable in terms of ethic and action, values and facts or ideality and reality. The role of hypothetical generalizations, or general definitions, begins to emerge in this analytic process. They are not *a priori intuitions*, but *general inferences* on the possibilities of experience; their validity as general propositions depends on their rationality and objectivity as elements

45

of knowledge. The presupposition of rationality in hypothetical definitions is not, however, their justification as empirical knowledge, but simply a proof of their internal logical consistency, because the structure of social reality reveals an intricate relationship of ideal and causal rationality, i.e. of re-experience and objective proof, of meaning and cause. Therefore, hypothetical generalizations in sociological knowledge can neither be judged on intuitive certainty nor on objective proof—as in other varieties of knowledge—but on the validity of causal understanding, which includes—what, in von Schelting's view, 'breaks' through the limits of Weber's methodology —the pure intellectual understanding of idealities. For only when a re-experience is translated into a pure intellectual understanding is it possible to relate re-experience to cause, through rational description and analysis, as Weber attempts to do in methodology as well as in empirical analysis, and succeeds.

The beginning of causal understanding, therefore, on the basis of Weber's work, must lie in the definition of rationality in sociological terms. Substantively, as we have seen, it is basically of two kinds: causal and ideal. What relates them as rational is their structure—not their common origin in the individual psyche. The structure of rationality is seen in the relationship of end, means and condition or of premise, inference and conclusion, i.e. in the logic of the situation or the interpretation *on the basis of experienceability.**

It is thus the structure of a situation, experience or thought which determines their sociological rationality, not their causal or ideal relations; and it is Weber's definition of sociological rationality which reveals the inadequacies of categorial thought in relation to social reality. For instance, the analytical concepts of ideal-typical description and causal understanding would have been impossible if Weber were unable to define sociological rationality in the way he did; and the categories of rationality† make this distinction between the form and content of sociological knowledge clearer by showing how knowledge depends on the validity of form rather than of content. That is, how the analytical or formal concepts must, without exception, be applicable to all the contents of the reality

* Experienceability is, obviously, not the quality of an individual's experience or re-experience, but of all intellectual perceptions of ideas and emotions.

† End-rationality, value-rationality, affectual-rationality and traditional rationality. For their respective definitions see Weber, *Theory of Social and Economic Organization*, pp. 115ff.

for which an explanation is being sought; and how the categories of objects of explanation must have formal validity, i.e. have the same structure when their characteristics are different; and, finally, how categories systematize the objects in question in terms of their irreducible actual characteristics. These points are impossible to deal with if the characteristics of one category of objects are formalized and all other categories are judged by them. This has been the fundamental restriction in social scientific knowledge—since the formalized characteristics of either causal or ideal rationality has been used as the form of explanation of all the contents of social reality—which Weber overcame in his work by correctly defining the nature of scientific explanation itself.

As scientific explanation is a kind of rational explanation—which is more definite than all other forms of explanation—its form is not derived from the nature of its objects of study—only its concepts— but from the form of rationality itself; on the other hand, its concepts are. The form of scientific knowledge, therefore, is subservient neither to individual perceptual differences nor to the characteristics and manifestations of reality: it is only bound by the unknown limits of reality or experience, while concepts must always be specific and contextual.

Many of its concepts will, however, remain irreducible to other more comprehensive concepts or categories because the characteristics of reality are not in *any* rational sense reducible to one general substantive concept. Objections may be raised, however, as to how it is possible to say that they are scientific, if they are not so reducible, especially when many concepts and theories are constantly becoming reducible to more and more general concepts and theories. The answer is that they are scientific—whether they are reducible or not—because the formation of all concepts is consistent with, indeed determined by, the form of scientific explanation. For example, the concept of sociological rationality, i.e. consistency of means-end relationship in a context, although a more comprehensive concept than other concepts of rationality—primarily derived from a culture-bound philosophical concept of rationality—does not modify the structure of rationality itself. It further gives rise to four irreducible categories, because the characteristics of social reality are themselves not reducible to any one of these categories.

The concept of sociological rationality, in fact, resolves the whole

47

problematic nature of definitional concepts, hypotheses and theory in sociology. As one cannot validly judge or hypothesize on social reality in the dogmatic framework of any one of its categories, it becomes necessary that all the categories be taken into account in relation to the object of study. Definitions, hypotheses and theories thus, instead of being intuitive, obvious and repetitious statements which they seem to be and often are in sociology, become inferential generalizations from primary concepts to be empirically and analytically tested. It is only the explicitness of Weber's concept of sociological rationality which makes this extension of scientific knowledge to social reality realizable.

3 Pareto's analysis of sentiments and tradition in society

Vilfredo Pareto's achievement lies, above all, in extending the applicability of the principles of scientific knowledge into areas which would seem to lie beyond it, without introducing the kind of discussion on which Weber's work depends for clarifying the principles of sociological knowledge. The most important points in judging Pareto's work are: first, that the complexity of his theory is not inherent in its structure but in the material with which it deals; and, second, that the analysis of the primary elements of action justifies his descriptive concepts, like 'equilibrium', 'social system' or 'the circulation of élites'. Therefore, to take any of these concepts out of the theoretical structure—as has been done in contemporary sociology—and to claim any kind of analytic value for them is, to say the least, absurd. This kind of eclecticism betrays a complete incomprehension of what is involved in scientific-analytical thought. Let us see why they have no value for analysing social reality and are simply descriptions in a hypothesized form of reality, which depends on the validity of the concepts of analysis.

Pareto discusses a general form of society, of which these descriptive concepts are parts, in chapter 12 in the fourth volume of *The Mind and Society*. In this discussion he first deals with those elements which serve to constitute society. Then, the state of equilibrium; the composition of 'residues' and 'derivations': various sorts of 'interdependences' (or correlations); utility: maximum utility of an individual or community *and* for a community. This is followed by examples analysed in terms of these various concepts: the writing of history; the use of force in society, the relations between ruling

49

and subject classes in society; stability and change in society and forms of government and how they are founded in consent and force, and how their efficiency depends upon their utilization of residues—for efforts to modify residues themselves are likely to fail.* Fluctuations in doctrines prevailing in a society are related to fluctuations in the sentiments of the people. Such fluctuations are in the form of waves. Here, examples of how they are inter-dependent lead to his ideas on 'the science of society as a whole'. Even in this abstracted form his conclusions are not in any way recognizable as an *a priori* conception of social reality, which his interpreters see when they praise or criticize these ideas, but on the correctness of his empirical generalizations and, before it, of analytical concepts. That is, if we take any of the descriptive concepts we notice that it simply describes a relationship between certain sets of facts. The whole discussion centres on the validity of methodological principles and concepts which govern the analysis. For instance, the concept of equilibrium is quite meaningless without an empirical knowledge of the forces which can be said to be in equilibrium. These forces are not recognizable purely by defining the concept of equilibrium as an element of an *a priori* theoretical structure or by re-defining it through an analogy with its use in other sciences. Similarly, the concept of social system is equally meaningless unless one knows what the actual elements are going to be which can be designated altogether as a system. Thus, such concepts can only describe what is analytically known or can be hypothesized. If they describe only what is hypothesized, the necessity of an empirical analysis to validate them as concepts is quite obvious. This means that the principles on which such an empirical analysis can be undertaken must be validated at some stage. It is not at all important which sequence is followed, but only that the sequence is logically related.

Finally, however, even if such concepts provide a valid description, what analytic value can they possibly have? How does the knowledge that social forces equilibrate or that they form into a system, lead to a knowledge of, first, what they are, and second, how they are formed, and, third, how they interrelate?[1]

* Residues, derivations and derivatives are in simple terms (a) the sentiments, (b) their justifications and (c) theories in which sentiments play a significant part.

Pareto's discussion of the problem of the succession of recurring social movements[2] is aimed at a conclusion on the form of movement which societies have, and it shows the clear absurdity of taking a set of descriptive concepts as an analytical framework; or, in other words, as a theory which allows empirical analysis. For example, Pareto considers the phenomenon of 'oscillations in derivation in correspondence with social oscillations'[3] of extreme importance as a manifestation of ideas and doctrines. It appears in conflicts between various 'sentimental, theological and metaphysical derivations' as well as in conflicts at various times between them and scientific methods and arguments. As a manifestation of the forces that operate in society, it appears in conflicts between various residues— chiefly conservative or innovating—and, therefore, between logical and non-logical conduct. This movement is very general, and in one way or another pervades the whole history of human societies. The first problem which this conflict between ideas and doctrines—i.e. 'the problem of interdependence of waves'—sets is 'why experience has a different effect in sentimental, theological and metaphysical "derivations" or justifications from that in scientific reasonings?' And, second, how and why certain derivations persist century after century, even though by an objective standard they are false or absurd.[4] These problems must lead, as a first step, to an ordering of forces in terms of their *intrinsic* and *extrinsic* aspects, i.e. a classification.[5]

The intrinsic aspect obviously refers to the degree of adjustment between theory and reality. That is, one has to determine to what extent, if at all, there is any difference between the sentiments and the results of experience. In the extrinsic aspect one has, therefore, to determine the influence of, for example, economic or political conditions or of class-circulation, which may modify sentiments.[6]

The 'oscillation' of derivations—e.g. between reason and intuition —is caused chiefly, according to Pareto, by a confusion between the 'social utility' of a theory or doctrine and its consistency with experience.[7]

The point which Pareto makes in considering the extrinsic aspect is that the majority of people 'adopt residues and derivation under the direct impulse of sentiments'. This is because if one only considered the intrinsic aspect one is liable to assume that derivations

51

are always accepted as logical inferences from certain sentiments. The intrinsic aspect is important for understanding theories, but not very significant for social movements, because such movements do not result from theories, but rather theories depend upon social movements—which have, therefore, to be correlated with other facts.[8] But merely describing these correlations will not yield any inferences or generalizations,[9] the thing to remember is that the general sentiments—or residues, in Paretian terminology—vary slowly and slightly over centuries, but justifications—or derivations —change rapidly and widely.

The concept of classes of residues corresponds to the general sentiments, whose existence Pareto *inferred* from his analysis of theories which have been accepted in society. This is an extremely clear indication of how Pareto would analyse social phenomena, and how, also, residues are not part of a 'psychological' theory of society.* The recognition which his analytical conclusions allow of certain general sentiments in society, and his subsequent classification, are, obviously, a necessary completion of the account. What, in fact, underlies the whole theoretical account is obviously more important. For example, if it were possible to identify the general sentiments—which are, according to Pareto, the source of socially accepted theories and the arguments and justifications inherent in them—within the theories themselves, there would be no need for analysis, simply because the internal relationship of the elements of the theories would be strictly logical.[10] From this point of view, which is Pareto's and not his commentators', it would indeed be ridiculous to formulate a framework of analysis, and further, as Pareto does, to analyse examples to show how the framework works. It is clearly an absurd supposition that Pareto had no idea of what he was in fact formulating, especially when the first chapter, 'The scientific approach', of his treatise has not been surpassed by even the most recent philosophers of science—who are presumably aware of the latest advances in scientific epistemology and analysis—in its comprehensive and unambiguous statement of what is involved in scientific explanation.

The distinction which Pareto makes between logico-experimental

* This is because there is a logical completeness of explanation at the level of sentiments *before* they are seen as originating in any hypothetical individual psyche. This can be the only basis of *any* 'psychological' theory of society.

reasoning and derivation is not a distinction in the *form* of reasoning, but in the *substantive values* of the elements of reasoning. For example, in the logico-experimental reasoning one may say that given the circumstances A, B, C . . . X will occur. In this A, B, C . . . are proven facts and the reasoning associating them with X is strictly logical. This is a scientific forecast which, although *inferred* from the connection between A, B, C . . . etc., is independent of it, because, even if X does not materialize, it does not mean that the connection between A, B, C . . . and X is wrong, but that the forecast on the recurrence of A, B, C . . . in future was wrong. On the other hand, if within this form of reasoning A, B, C . . . are given characteristics which are not 'experimental' or factual, or if they are associated with X, in a way which is not strictly logical, we get a 'derivation'. This process does not make the probability, that X will occur, in any way greater. But, if this derivation is believed in, it becomes a social fact because this belief will have consequences. This statement again leads us back to the problem of how to understand the relation between the social fact of a derivational belief and its consequences. This is where the distinction between the intrinsic and extrinsic aspects and between the experimental truth and social utility of the theories plays a significant role, because it allows one to see the need for comparison on the basis of the form of logical reasoning, to see what substantive connections there are between derivation or justification, facts of existence and what can be inferred from recurring patterns of such correlations. Residues as inferences on the nature of general sentiments prevailing in a society thus become possible.

It will be noticed that the structure of Pareto's analysis is in fact the same as Weber's, i.e. based on the comparison of an actual reasoning with a logically constructed reasoning—both the actual and the logical theory having the same substantive elements. None the less, the substantive context of an analysis brings with it a problem of judgment: 'should one judge the "derivational" argument on the basis of its intrinsic deviation from the norm of comparison alone or should it be judged as modified by other considerations?'

First among these extrinsic considerations is the relationship of the sentiments with other forces in a society; and, second, the *utility* of these sentiments, their justifications and theories which contain and obliquely reflect them—i.e., of the 'residues, derivations

53

and derivatives'—as they appear in any particular society and, for sociological theory, in their general form.

The two aspects are obviously related, if one judges them on the basis of their acceptance by people, sociologically the most important point of view. Although a few individuals may accept derivations as the logical consequence of certain sentiments, the vast majority—according to Pareto—'adopt residues and derivations under the direct impulse of sentiments'. Therefore, an intrinsic analysis of socially accepted theories is important only for a theory of doctrines and not for a theory of social movements, as Pareto's entire work so impressively demonstrates. Social movements—which are obviously more important than doctrines for any sociological theory on the role of ideas and sentiments, or of reform, revolution or reaction—do not result from doctrines but rather give rise to them; and what the intellectuals, i.e. the producers of social theories and doctrines, say or write about mean nothing in themselves for society as a whole except when they enjoy popular acceptance. These are very reasonable assumptions to make, even though they may not be emotionally acceptable to those who attribute intrinsic powers of realization to intellectual creations. Thus, the popular acceptance of an author's works must inevitably serve as an index of social movements. But, one may ask, how does the extrinsic aspect of such theories and doctrines affect their analysis?

There are obviously *direct* and *indirect* effects of the elements which act and react upon society. Of these elements, residues a; interests b; derivations c; social heterogeneity and circulation of classes d—in Pareto's language—are sociologically most important, and one can say that (i) a acts upon b, c, d; (ii) b acts upon a, c, d; (iii) c acts upon a, b, d; and (iv) d acts upon a, b, c. The combination (i) is at the basis of human history, since residues, or, rather, sentiments, vary slightly.[11] One of Pareto's examples is of the second century B.C., Rome, when two 'concomitant facts' are to be observed: (1) a quickly increasing economic affluence and (2) a decline in the residues of group-persistence in the masses, and to a greater extent in the upper classes.

Then comes a reaction, which differed from other cases—which Pareto deals with later—only in its nature and intensity, not its form. 'The action and reaction appear therefore in conjunction and it is their sum as a whole that is to be viewed as correlated with variations in wealth and in class-circulation.'[12] The question to ask about this situation is whether it is just a series of coincidences or a *correlation*.[13]

A further example which Pareto gives may perhaps indicate more clearly what an extrinsic analysis involves. The Renaissance occurred in a period of economic prosperity and of quick price rises as the result of the inflow of precious metals from the Americas. Old institutions could not bear the strain of such a rapid change, and everything seemed to need reforming. The modern world was being born, but a religious reaction set in—as usual, from the masses. For the leaders religion served only as a means of government, but the masses were deeply concerned with religion and tried their best to enforce it one way or another. Yet economic conditions which were behind the social change persisted and regained the ground from the masses for the leaders. ' "Reason" again set to work to demolish the edifice of "superstition".' The demolition of 'superstition' occurred, for the upper classes, towards the end of the eighteenth century. In England it occurred perhaps fifty years before it did in France. There was recurrence in this period of the pattern shown in the sixteenth century, and one can say it took two hundred years to complete the work. The philosophers of the eighteenth century were, as Pareto says, the heirs of the Humanists and, like them, inclined towards paganism.[14]

The point of these examples is that one cannot take the theories prevailing in society as straightforward reflections of either the static state of society or of great historical changes. The logical analysis of social theories and doctrines has to be related to the external conditions of change, if one is to decide whether the connection between theories and social reality is simply coincidental or correlational.

Pareto's theory of utility adds the decisive point to the hypothesis of correlation between theories, doctrines etc. and social reality.[15] As a preparatory step, he introduces the notion of 'two extreme types of abstract societies,* the first type being a society based entirely on sentiments, and the second, based on logic and reasoning.

* This may seem like an implicit typology of societies, similar to those found in contemporary sociological theory, but it should be quite clear that this notion is—as all such notions should be—just a device to simplify discussion. Any typology based on such notions is an expression of utter naïveté.

55

Thus, the form of the first type is determined if the sentiments and external conditions are given, or if sentiments are regarded as governed by external conditions.

An extreme version of social Darwinism would give, in Pareto's view, a complete solution to the problem of environment and sentiments with its theory of the survival of individuals best adapted to environment. In the second type, where logic and reasoning prevailed, the form of society would remain indeterminate when the external circumstances were given. It would need an indication of the ends which 'logico-experimental' reasonings served as means. This is because 'the data of the problem' which has to be solved by logical reasoning are entirely unknown.[16] In other words, what various individuals in society conceive of as good for them and good for others are essentially heterogeneous, and there is no way of reducing them to unity.[17] This is why the notion of utility remains vague, and becomes difficult to define. For example, social reformers who ask 'What is the *best* form of society?' are in fact asking a subjective question: 'What form of society best fits my sentiments?' They turn it into an objective—therefore the former—question by assuming that their sentiments will be—in Pareto's words—'shared by all honest men', and that they are not merely excellent in themselves, but are also in the highest degree beneficial to society.[18] Actual societies are to be found in between the two extremes; their form is determined—apart from external environment—'by sentiments, interests, and in a secondary way, by derivations, which express and sometimes intensify sentiments and interests'.[19] But logico-experimental reasonings become important when the objective, or the end, of action is explicit *and* when the best means of achieving it is needed. This is a significant point to be put against classifying societies by assuming either sentiment or reason as the determining principle—that is, human beings necessarily do not choose, or do choose, the most logical means for achieving their ends—for logico-experimental reasoning can be used in pursuit of ends which may themselves be 'sentimental'.[20]

The whole mystery is not about the choice of logical or illogical means to given ends, but of ends themselves, because unless ends are explicit it cannot be decided which means could or could not be logical. Pareto's theory of residues is an attempt to discover why certain phenomena which persist in society are not understandable by a deductive analysis from general assumptions about human nature and social reality, because the pursuit of certain objectives by human beings is logically devious and, moreover, success in such a pursuit is not objective but a matter of feeling. Therefore, *a priori* assumptions on both human nature and social reality become impossible. This does not mean that the interrelation of human objectives, the means used, and the feeling of success, is not analysable. Indeed, it is sociologically the most important interrelation, for it contributes to the formation of social reality. It is in relation to this that Pareto makes the point that almost all the reasonings used in social activity are 'derivations'. It means that although in a minority of cases the relationship between objectives, the means used and the feeling of success in social action may be logical, and immediately understandable, the majority of social actions are in fact based on a psychological satisfaction for proof of success. Derivations—non-logical or sentimental reasonings—are, therefore, directly linked to the notion of utility, of good and bad, beneficial and harmful. If one tries to discover the principles on which conclusions may be logically based, one may in many cases 'succeed in discovering the sentiments and interests that explain the *acceptance of the conclusions to which* the derivations pointed the way' by leaving the most important element, i.e. the proposition which defines the phenomenon in terms of feelings of good and bad, beneficial and harmful, of utility, inexplicit.[21]

The character of derivations is understood through such propositions because the motives which determine the opinions of men and women are, in fact, contained in them. As an example Pareto analyses the famous controversy between Bastiat and Proudhon on the legitimacy of interest on capital.[22] The derivation appears in the question itself, whether interest on capital is 'legitimate' or not. They both agree that the loan of capital is a service, but they draw different conclusions from this premise. For Bastiat, 'a person who renders a "service" has a "right" to a remuneration.' For Proudhon, 'the individuals in a society render mutual "services" and their "rights" therefore offset one another's'. Bastiat—Pareto adds further —uses the very common derivation of giving a hypothetical example as proof. If, however, an example is to serve as proof it must be demonstrated as being equivalent or similar to the real situation, but Bastiat reduces the parties to only two: the capitalist and the

E   57 worker, or 'the man who has a saw and a plane and another who wants to make boards'. In the real situation, on the other hand, there is the consumer, i.e. the one who uses the board while the other two produce them by putting capital and labour together. This necessity of introducing a third party in an empirical example completely changes Bastiat's proposition, for one can clearly see that the problem is not how the capitalist and the workers are going to divide the fruits of their labour, but how they *ought to*, since, without the consumer, the worker has no use for the boards he produces. Similarly, although Proudhon offers a 'practical' way of achieving a balance between 'services' and 'rights', the implicit assumption is, again, a moral one.

This problem of 'ought'—or moral legitimacy—cannot be resolved unless the term is given a specific meaning, since there will be as many solutions as there will be meanings of what *ought to be* in the circumstances. Furthermore, if one adds to these meanings the consideration of social utility, defined as the realization of certain social purposes, there will be still more solutions. None of these solutions, obviously, can be intrinsically 'true' or 'false'.

Thus, such solutions, which appear in answer to questions of 'what ought to be' presented as 'what is', are obviously related to sentiments and not to the logical necessity of such conclusions from the ostensibly given empirical premises. Implicit in such phenomena is the concept of utility, for social reality cannot be distinguished and defined by taking moral propositions as logically empirical and by disregarding the relationship of moral choices to underlying sentiments.

'When we know, or think we know, just what thing is advantageous to an individual or a community, we say that it is "beneficial" for both individuals and communities to exert themselves to obtain it, and judge the utility they enjoy the greater, the nearer they come to obtaining it.'[23]

This is the simple definition of utility; however, within this definition, Pareto would include what the metaphysicists mean when 'they speak of the "purpose" or "end" a human being is made for', and one could add 'towards which individuals and communities tend or "ought" to tend'. This 'end' or 'purpose', besides being metaphysical and absolute, could be relative, if individuals determined it for themselves.[24]

However, the various utilities for the individual or a given community in different contexts[25] may stand in opposition to each other, and what we get as a result is net utility.[26] Both in the case of an individual and a group,[27] we find that he or it may suffer some direct harm, on the one hand, but gain indirectly, on the other, as a member of a community.

In so far as an individual acts logically, he tries to gain a maximum of individual utility; but a government—generally speaking—may compare all the utilities it is aware of. For example, in the case of population increase, if we think of the utility *of* the community in terms of prestige and military power, a high population increase becomes advantageous. If, on the other hand, we consider the maximum utility *for* the community, the limit of population increase is much lower. In this situation, population increase has to be considered in the light of the advantages that various social classes may or may not enjoy with the increase in prestige and military power. If, for example, the lower classes say that they refuse to have children because children merely increase the power and profits of the ruling classes, they are, Pareto says, dealing with a problem of maximum utility *for* the community. The arguments—or derivations—they happen to use may be of one religion or another, of Socialism or pacifism, but the underlying motivation relates to their response to a problem of maximum utility *for* the community. The ruling classes, on the contrary, often confuse between a maximum of individual utility with a maximum utility *for* the community. That is, they try to make the lower classes believe that the indirect utility turns their sacrifice into a gain for them. This may sometimes be true; but when it is not, non-logical impulses, or sentiments, can make the subject classes forget their individual advantage and work for the advantage *of* the community or the ruling classes.[28] If, however, there is reason to believe, for example, that forces which may prevent a clash between established authority and a revolutionary group, operating by themselves, would increase utility, it does not follow that in opposition to other residues and modifying circumstances, their effect will also be an increased utility. The variation in utility depends on the actual effect of these circumstances and not on the hypothetical result envisaged in the derivation. The real resultant of various forces in society indicates the direction in which the individuals are moving much more accurately than a particular derivation or a utility might lead one to suppose. This is especially true of those societies in which the activities of individuals are aimed at real goals and in which prosperity is increasing. It is unimportant whether the derivations used by individuals are fantastic or not, because derivations only show the *direction* in which an individual (or group considered as an individual; cf. Weber's 'historical individual') may be carried, not the limit of his movement. On reaching the limit, the movement may show an increased utility; beyond the limit, the utility may diminish, and the derivation may become detrimental if the individual pursued it further.[29]

It follows, in Pareto's view, that, sociologically, the problem of utility, or of good and bad evaluation, is quantitative, and not qualitative as commonly believed. One has to determine in what proportions the consequences of a given derivation, or its underlying principle or sentiment, may, when combined with the consequences of other derivations, prove beneficial to society; and not, as usually done, try to decide whether the derivation is in itself beneficial or detrimental to society. In other words, to decide on the intrinsic qualities of a moral problem is without meaning.[30]

Pareto illustrates this point by taking history as an example in which ideal and real are mixed together in order to discover compound utilities.[31] If history designates those compositions which have factual observations of one kind or another supplemented by derivations and ethical considerations, without any distinctions being made between ideals or myths and real facts, it serves its purpose of influencing the sentiments of human beings—through exhortations interwoven with facts. It becomes, then, a history of concepts rather than of forces which these concepts reflect.[32] If, on the other hand, ideals and myths are considered intrinsically, we get systems of ethics, metaphysics and theology in the name of history; or if real facts alone are considered, with ideas, ideals and myths taken as objective facts, we get *scientific history*.*

In Western countries, in our times, theological histories have fallen into neglect, but metaphysical and ethical histories are still fashionable. In these the basic assumption that the conduct of human beings is a consequence of their beliefs is rarely stated categorically, rather, the reader is allowed to infer it. That is, they are convinced

---

* These terms are not necessarily used in the sense of one being morally superior to another, but as designations of varying forms of history.

that the ideas which people have immediately govern their conduct and form their social reality.[33]

When one analyses such writings, the immediate question is about the validity of such an assumption. If a writer, for instance, ascribes a supernatural origin to religion or morality he is at least logical in regarding religion as the cause of social phenomena. But if he ascribes a natural origin to religion or morality he must, to be at least logical, show how and why religion is a cause and not an effect— or simply coincidental. He must state what relationship exists between observance of certain religious, moral or other norms and social utility or benefit. On the other hand, no such statement is necessary when one is only examining either cases of conscience or social phenomena independent of conscience or moral choice. If the two things are inseparable, then, one has to specify what relationship there is between them—this relationship is not given or axiomatic.[34] To separate the various elements in the social reality is essentially an analytical exercise, but to assume solutions for the elements not considered allows a writer to take the element by itself and develop a logically easy conclusion. Such conclusions are more readily accepted by the public in so far as they take for granted certain generally accepted relationships between moral ideas and human conduct.[35] Further, such writers make ethical and legal judgments on the conduct of public individuals, without making their norms explicit. For example, considered by the norms of private law and morals, the morals of Catherine II of Russia were reprehensible and her activities to gain her throne criminal. But such a judgment, Pareto says, has very little relevance to the question of whether it would have been to the advantage of Russia for her husband rather than her to be on the throne. Such facts as the morals of a public individual are historically relevant, not through their intrinsic ethical value, but as circumstances related to certain events or as determining certain others.[36]

The main reason for the ethical method in history is twofold. On one side is the essential subjectivity of moral judgments, or interpretations, on facts; and on the other, the use of the same phraseology by each of the contending parties in an event.[37]

Included in the subjective aspect are not just the personal ethical judgments of the historian, but also what may be considered 'extrinsic ethical values',[38] the judgments of persons participating in

61

the event. This may be severe or mild according to the sentiments of the particular person. In politics, particularly, scandal only harms the weak, as can be seen every day. The objective aspect, that of similarity of language in contending points of view, leads to 'identical derivations disguising different residues'.[39] The result of this is that, if one only looks at the justification of action or interpretations of facts, one can know nothing of the forces which really brought about the event.[40] In some cases, however, inconsistencies between interpretations and facts are so glaring that they do not escape the historian. The problem itself can be seen as that of sincerity or insincerity of the individual and judged as such; or it can be seen as a far more significant problem of history, that is, 'how and why the sentiments and interests covered by the derivations in question were successful'. The personality of an individual, therefore, becomes less important in itself and the sentiments and interests which he represents are seen as prevailing over the sentiments and interests of other individuals.[41] What happened is thus seen as the resultant of all the social factors, which include the derivations.*

In his discussion of the use of force in society, which follows, Pareto makes the point that societies in general subsist because in the majority of their constituent members there are strong sentiments of sociality. But there are also individuals in whom some of these sentiments are weak or may even be lacking. This mixture of strength and weakness in sentiments has two interesting, apparently contradictory, effects. One part makes for a society's progress in civilization, and the other threatens its dissolution. Underlying it, however, is not a static separation, but a continuous movement which can take almost any direction.[42]

It is obvious that if the demands of uniformity were so strong in all the individuals in a society as to prevent them from breaking away from such norms, there would be no internal causes for dissolution; but neither would there by any causes for change, either in the direction of individual or social good or of detriment. On the other hand, if the demands for uniformity or conformity were to fail, each individual would go his own way and society

* Specific derivations are products of both the personality as such and social forces like sentiments and interests that the personality may be said to possess. The question of pure psyche and social elements of individual action is discussed in relation to derivations, and elsewhere in the book.

would dissolve. Societies that persist, therefore, are situated between these extremes. It is possible to envisage a homogeneous society in which demands for conformity may be the same in every individual, and so such an intermediate state can be reached. But actual societies are essentially heterogeneous: with some individuals strongly conformist, some moderately so, some weak and some completely non-conformist. The average is to be found not in each individual, but in the group formed by all of them.

In view of the relative strengths of sentiments of uniformity or conformity, one can easily forecast that two interpretations—or 'theologies', as Pareto designates them—will appear: one glorifying the unchangeability of one or another uniformity, and the other, movement or progress, in one way or another.

In this respect, the question of the use of force is not whether it is beneficial or not, but whether force is used by those who wish to preserve certain uniformities, and by those who wish to oppose them; 'the violence of the one stands in contrast and in conflict with the violence of the others.' So, in the solution of the problem of the use of force, there is more to it than the solution of the problem of its utility; it is essential to compare all the advantages as well as disadvantages. But this only leads to the solution of it as a scientific problem,* it does not lead to an increase in social utility or advantage. Social utility is often best gained if the ruled—whose function is to act and not lead—choose one of the two 'theologies', according to the situation.[43]

This particular discussion shows, and Pareto points out why, apart from theoretical difficulties, solutions to general problems have so little bearing on realities. 'Practical empiricism implicitly takes account of many circumstances that theory, until it has been carried to a state of high perfection, cannot explicitly appraise.'[44]

The use of violence in enforcing conformity, within modern societies, is more readily condoned when it is a case of individual deviation for individual advantage, than when the deviation appears as a collective act aimed at collective advantage, especially when it seems to be directed against general norms. The conformity could be either material or intellectual, and, in Pareto's view, at the present

* Incidentally, this may interest only scientists or certain members of the ruling class, according to Pareto.

time intellectual conformity is less vigorously enforced than in the past.[45]

What are, then, the correlations between this distinction of 'privately' and 'politically' motivated crimes made in modern societies, and other social facts? There is, as usual in Pareto's view, a sequence of actions and reactions in which the use of force or violence may appear on some occasions as cause and at others as effect. Concerning the governing class, there appears to be mainly five facts to take into account. 1. A handful of people, willing to use violence, can force their will upon a public authority reluctant to meet violence with equal force, and if their reluctance is due to humanitarian sentiment, that result will be quickly achieved. 2. If, however, they are unwilling to use violence for other reasons, then the result will be of the governing class resorting to 'diplomacy', fraud and corruption, while ostensibly surrendering to the violence of the small group. This manoeuvre will have a far-reaching influence on the recruitment of individual members into the governing class. 3. Thus, the third effect comes about in the intensification of the residues of combination or innovation and weakening of the residues of group-persistence or traditionality. 4. Such a change makes the governing class more satisfied with the immediate and less concerned about long-term policies and aims. Sentiments of individualism begin to dominate over the sentiments of the family, community and the nation. Material and immediate interests prevail over the ideal interests of the community and nation and of the future. 5. These phenomena become observable in international relations as well: wars become essentially economic and regarded as speculations and expected not to get out of control and change into armed conflicts; but such a country may be forced to go to a proper war by more traditionalist peoples.[46]

Regarding the subject class, we get certain corresponding correlations between use of force and other social facts. 1. When the subject class has a number of individuals inclined towards the use of force, they can, in many cases, with capable leaders overthrow the governing class—especially when it is inspired by humanitarian sentiments but excludes the entry of exceptional individuals from the subject class into its ranks. 2. It is, however, far more difficult to overthrow a governing class skilled in the use of 'chicanery, fraud and corruption', especially when it is successful in assimilating those individuals in the subject class who share their qualities and may have led their class against them. 3. Thus the innovating sentiments or combination-residues become to some extent weak in the subject class. This should not be supposed to mean that the circumstances of the subject class are in effect the same as the governing class, which, with its small number of individuals, shows these changes much more quickly than the population at large. There always remain many innovating individuals in the subject class, but their energies and talents are applied to non-political activities—which makes for stability in their society. However, the 'differences in temperament' between the rulers and ruled become stronger, and leads eventually to revolution. 4. Revolution brings about a change of rulers, who are more traditionalistic than their predecessors, a change of aspirations from the immediate to an ideal future, and a change from scepticism to faith. 5. These general notions are applicable to international relations as well. If the innovating, individualistic sentiments are reinforced in a country beyond a certain limit, compared to traditionalistic and conservative sentiments, it is easily defeated in a war by a country in which 'instincts of group-persistence' remain relatively stronger— mainly through the strength of their faith in an ideal or tradition.[47]

The point of this discussion of the interrelated effects on the governing and subject classes of changes in the proportion of the two main sentiments—found in every society—at different times is that a governing class is found everywhere, from a despotism to a democracy. There are always people who play a very important role in actual government.[48] But this governing class is not a homogeneous body; it too has a select band of people or a leader who 'effectively and practically exercise control'.[49] Ruling classes, like other social groups, act 'logically' as well as 'non-logically', and the main factor in what happens is 'the order or system, not the conscious will of individuals, who indeed may in certain cases be carried by the system to points where they would not have gone by deliberate choice'.[50]

The last sentence is the key to the whole of Pareto's theory— indeed to sociological analysis itself.

It raises two questions: (i) whether all action can be said to be determined either by the personality of the individual or by social forces; or (ii) whether there are elements of personal choice and decision as well as elements of social norms and expectations in any individual's action, one set of elements dominating the other in certain contexts. It becomes obvious, on analysis, that the second question is the more pertinent, for it distinguishes the nature of human action much more accurately than the first. Pareto's theory of sociological analysis—like Weber's—is concerned with the second question. It effectively refutes, first, the notion that the 'psychological' and 'sociological' are extensions of each other, and, second, that any sociological concept which may reflect a psychological reality— e.g. the concept of residues—is reducible to a 'psychological' theory of society. The 'psychological' and the 'sociological' are only aspects of human action; they form neither its determinants nor its contexts.*

Before, however, one examined the primary concepts of Pareto's theory in relation to this assumption, it would be necessary to acquaint oneself with his ideas on the scientific approach. Indeed, his exposition of what is involved in scientific analysis, apart from clarifying his own approach, corrects a whole range of mistaken notions which have accreted to science and experience.

In his discussion of what the definition of sociology should be, he says: 'Let us keep to our quest for the relationships between social facts . . . and let knowledge of such relationships be obtained by any method that will serve.'[51] Further, he distinguishes between two approaches that a writer may choose: (a) he may seek his principles to be accepted as demonstrated truths; or (b) he may put forward his principles as hypotheses or simply as 'indications of one course that may be followed among the many possible'. In the case (a), if the principles or general statements are considered demonstrated as truths, then all their logical implications must also be regarded as proved. In the case (b), since the principles are in no sense 'demonstrated in the concrete', all their logical implications remain as hypothetical as the premises they are drawn from. In the second case, however, it often becomes necessary not to make such deductions, for empirical relationships can only be inferred from facts alone.† To show how the two approaches work, Pareto takes the example of Euclid's geometry. He says that if we accept Euclid's premise that a straight line is the shortest distance between two points, then his whole system has to be accepted as true. We have in such a circumstance nothing to 'set against it'. On the other hand, if

---

* The implications of this statement are discussed in the next chapter.

† This point clearly shows where theorists go wrong when they do not distinguish deductive generalizations from empirical ones. Cf. chapter 6.

the premise is taken simply as a hypothesis, then there is no need to dispute the premise as being true or false.

The mathematician can develop its logical consequences, and one's task then is to accept only those implications which correspond to reality and reject others. The most important result from this point of view is that other geometrics become possible, and we can make use of them empirically without, logically, losing our freedom of choice. In other words, we have then something to set against the Euclidean geometry.

All the sciences therefore have progressed in this way, i.e. when they have related hypothetical inferences to reality or concrete cases—and not 'quarrelled over first principles'—or treated them as simply assumptions and not demonstrated truths. 'Profiting from this experience'—Pareto adds—'we do not posit any dogma as a premise to our research; and our statement of principles serves merely as an indication of that course, among the many courses that might be chosen, which we elect to follow. Therefore, anyone who joins us along such a course by no means renounces his right to follow some other.'[52]

Pareto wrote that sociology had 'nearly always been expounded dogmatically',[53] and one should not be deceived by the word 'positive', which Comte applied to his philosophy. Comtean philosophy is a religion, similar to those found in the writings of Spencer, De Greef, Letourneau and many others; since they are based on a belief in the absolute truth of their propositions, they must of necessity exclude the possibility of other truths. In contrast, Pareto's sociology is an attempt to develop a 'purely experimental' science, like chemistry, physics and other such sciences.*

Thus, the beginning of Pareto's theory lies in the following sentence: Current in any group of people are a number of propositions, descriptive, perceptive, or otherwise.[54] Such propositions connected, logically or pseudo-logically, and enlarged by a collection of various facts,[55] without being interpreted, organized or thought out, are experimental facts for sociological analysis in Pareto's theory. They are to be considered 'objectively and without

---

* Such a statement has led to a great deal of trouble for social scientists for they invariably take it to mean an adoption of the actual processes involved in these sciences, rather than an application of *the principles of experiment* involved in them.

67

regard to any intrinsic merit they may be credited by faith'.[56] The justification for considering them as such is that it is often only through them that we can know the various forces, i.e. 'the tendencies and inclinations of human beings', which create the reality of society.[57] The first step in this objective examination is the classification of these propositions and theories, for without classifying them it would be difficult to grasp the variety of such interpretative statements in any society at all adequately.

One should, however, consider before going further a few general points on *a priori* and experimental reasonings made by Pareto. He says that if one is guided mainly by sentiment—or *a priori* belief—there can only be 'true' or 'false' theories. When it is added that every 'honest' or 'intelligent' man must accept such 'true' theories, they are given an absolute character, 'independent of the minds that produce or accept them'. Further, if every theory which is 'true' is also considered 'beneficial'—and vice versa—then the reality of a theory being beneficial to some and detrimental to others is made illegitimate. If one were to answer such an *a priori* reasoning by asserting contrary axioms, it would be similarly *a priori*, and experimentally, or scientifically, both sets of assertions would be equally without significance. On the other hand, if one were guided by experience—and would speak of experimental or scientific facts— the first thing to decide would be whether the terms of these assertions correspond to some aspect of experience and reality and whether the assertions themselves are corroborated by facts, or not. In this decision we cannot be certain that these propositions are categorically true or false and we have—unlike *a priori* thinkers— to accept the possibility that they can be either.[58]

From the objective point of view, the theories have to be distinguished on the basis of whether they are entirely experimental or are, in some respects, beyond experience. This is a qualitative difference and not a question of degree, as each category has its own method of reasoning and its own standards of 'true' and 'false'. The terms 'true' and 'false' are logically applicable to both categories of propositions, but their meaning depends entirely on the standard of truth chosen. In the experimental category the standard is experience and observation; in the non-experimental field, it has an absolute meaning and lies beyond objective experience—for example, 'in concepts that the human mind finds in itself, as some say, without the aid of objective experience'.[59] But it may seem paradoxical to those who associate logic with objective experience, and emotion with subjective experience, that the notion of logico-experimental truth in Pareto's theory is not given a similar absolute character. He says: '. . . not even logic supplies *necessary* inferences, except when such inferences are tautologies. Logic derives its efficacy from experience and nothing else.'[60] It is an important point, which clearly shows—by correctly defining the relationship of logic to experience—why his distinction between the experimental and the non-experimental is neither a distinction of form nor of merit. It is commonly seen as a distinction of form—e.g. in philosophical discussions of science—when form is confused with abstractly general but *substantive* characteristics; and as a distinction of merit —e.g. in sociologists' discussions—in the assumption of the 'inherent' superiority of logico-experimental or 'scientific' truth to other standards of socially accepted truth. The term 'logico-experimental', thus, distinguishes precisely—on general substantive characteristics—the propositions and theories which only have elements of objective experience related strictly according to the rules of logic from those which include elements of non-objective experience which may or may not be logically related. It is made clear in this way that logic by itself can neither be a basis of classification of descriptive or perceptive propositions nor be synonymous with rationality, since it simply allows one to identify their actual form, or in the case of rationality to designate it. Further, rationality itself is a result of experience not of logic. Thus, rationality is a matter of progress in experience and, therefore, of content of thought and reality. Logic is made separate from rationality by sociological analysis, because human perceptions whether social or individual are heterogeneous and no assumption of true perception, based on a particular context of rationality, scientific or otherwise, can be justified as a criterion of the ultimate truth of social reality in which the form and content are inevitably merged together. On the other hand, justifications and interpretations of human perceptions, whatever the social or individual context, are always in a form which is logically recognizable. It is for these reasons that the logico-experimental category of theories or statements has to be considered not as a norm of ultimate truth, but as a norm of analysis. Any judgment of logical consistency is only possible through

69

experience, and experience itself is progressive and objectifying both in its individual or subjective and objective or social-cultural-civilizational sense.

This description of logic and experience in sociological analysis is inevitable since social reality transcends all specific contexts of perception. This point, though a simple one, seems to elude a philosophical solution for those who argue on the basis of generalized but nevertheless specific contexts of science and dogma, since they pursue what is essentially the reasoning of sentiment, by assuming that certain substantive notions are necessarily primary and self-evident.

It should now be possible to see why Pareto's classification of theories on the basis of the three aspects: (i) objective, (ii) subjective, and (iii) of utility, is not a ritual tribute to the scientific method, but a necessary step in the complete analysis of all the dimensions of the given material. He says, on the objective aspect, that the theory be considered independently of both the person who produced it and the person who accepts it; and to account for all possible combinations that may arise from the character of the *matter* and the character of the *nexus*, we must distinguish between the following classes and sub-classes:

Class I   Experimental matter
   Ia   Logical nexus
   Ib   Non-logical nexus
Class II   Non-experimental matter
   IIa   Logical nexus
   IIb   Non-logical nexus[61]

This classification is not, of course, a description of actual theories, which will be blends of such types and can also be logico-experimental in appearance but non-logico-experimental in reality.[62] The subjective aspect of theories includes: (a) reasons for an author in asserting a proposition; (b) reasons why another person accepts it. These questions are applicable as much to societies as a whole as to individuals. The aspect of utility concerns the action of 'certain individuals evolving a theory because they have certain sentiments' with the reaction of the theory which may produce, intensify and modify certain sentiments in other individuals.[63]

These are questions of experience and cannot be answered *a priori.*[64] Only after objects have been classified can one examine them, and it would be instructive to follow Pareto's analysis of the varieties of theories which 'reflect social activity' to see whether his work provides an adequate view of sociological analysis, both in its form and content. In chapters 4 and 5 he considers theories with special reference to 'their accord with experience and observation'. In chapters 6, 7 and 8 he studies the sentiments in which theories originate. In chapters 9 and 10 he considers the ways in which sentiments are reflected in theories. In chapter 11 he examines the characteristics of these elements. And finally, in chapters 12 and 13 he shows the social effects of the various elements and arrives at 'an approximate concept of variations in the forms of society', which is the principal aim of his work.[65]

One of the points that he makes about the validity of scientific analysis and theory is 'the necessity of analysis in studying the various aspects of a concrete phenomenon—the analysis being followed by a synthesis in getting back from theory to the concrete'.[66] Without this relationship of analysis and synthesis, of empirical research and theory, one can easily be led into denying the truth of a theory because it fails to account for every aspect of a fact, or insisting that all other similar, even irrelevant, theories should be included in one theory.[67]

In his discussion of the difference between Hegelian metaphysics— which Hegel's French translator, Vera, calls absolute science—and science, Pareto says: 'While metaphysics proceeds from absolute principles to concrete cases, experimental science proceeds from concrete cases, not to absolute principles, which, as far as it is concerned, do not exist, but to general principles which are brought under principles still more general and so on indefinitely.'[68] In a knowledge of 'essences' one aims at demonstrating particular facts through general principles, instead of inferring general principles from facts. This leads to a confusion of the proof of the fact with the proof of its causes. For instance, we observe a fact A; we then hypothesize B, C, D, as its probable causes. If the 'essentialist' finds later that they are not its causes, he draws the conclusion that A does not exist. But this conclusion would only be valid if the existence of B, C, D, had been observed and the existence of A inferred. It cannot be valid if A is the observed fact and B, C, D are hypothesized.[69] This, again, is an important distinction which Pareto makes in the

71

validation of hypothetico-deductive conclusions. By showing how the role of hypothesis-testing can be falsely extended to reject the observed fact and replace it by an entirely hypothesized 'reality' he raises the whole question of the status of hypothesis in scientific analysis, which is another of the elusive, unresolved questions of philosophy of science, and gives a simple and obvious answer. How far, as it is sometimes assumed, are scientific conclusions based on this misplacement of the actual by the hypothetical? Pareto's answer—i.e. in so far as experimental thinking is replaced by sentimental thinking—is not the opposition of the contents of 'scientific' work or the eminence of scientists to the 'non-scientific' but the difference in the logical relationship between experience and theory in the two categories of thought and action. Although authority plays a great part even in scientific propositions, though it has no status as proof, the essential point that Pareto makes is that experience and observation remain powerless against faith, and vice versa.[70] They cannot supersede one another, however much one may exalt logic and experience over faith. It is for this reason that Pareto sees them as two kinds of thinking, for the aim is to find *what distinguishes them*, not 'to compare and much less to pass judgment on the relative merits and virtues of those two sorts of thinking'.[71] They are both social facts; but logico-experimental thinking is not problematical in itself in terms of his work, i.e. 'how beliefs arise and develop and in what relationships they stand in terms of other social facts'.[72] Pareto's statement, that 'experimental science has no dogmas, not even the dogma that experimental facts can be explained only by experience',[73] is valuable, first, because it defines the central aim of scientific analysis, and second, because it makes it possible to analyse all actual theories, whether designated 'scientific' or 'non-scientific', in exactly the same way, i.e. in terms of their logical consistency with experience and their subjective validity and utility. As he says, it is difficult really to find anyone—although it is logically possible to do so—rejecting the criteria of logico-experimental truth; for even when the truth is of extra-experimental nature, as in religious doctrines, there are almost always proofs included which are pseudo-logical or pseudo-experimental, with, of course, proofs of utility to individual and society.[74]

In both logico-experimental and non-logico-experimental theories one finds certain general propositions, or principles, from which theories can be logically deduced, but it is the principles which differ in character which make the inferred theories of one category or the other. The principles in the logico-experimental category are only abstract propositions summarizing the common characteristics of many different facts. The principles, thus, depend on facts, not facts on principles. They are accepted hypothetically only as long as they are consistent with facts, and rejected when they become inconsistent.[75] But in non-logico-experimental theories one finds principles that are accepted *a priori*, 'independently of experience, dictating to experience'.[76] In other words, if there is a discrepancy between the principles and experiences, facts have to be made consistent with the inferences from the principles, rather than the other way round. In historical reality, such *a priori* theories often come before experimental ones,[77] which again shows that Pareto's discussion of scientific approach is concerned with the clarity of analytic concepts, rather than the promotion of scientific thought to a higher moral-historical position.

Returning to the use of the hypothesis in scientific analysis, Pareto points out that one does not depart from the experimental field simply by making use of hypotheses, especially if they are used only and strictly 'as instruments in the quest for consequences that are uniformly subject to verification by experience'.[78] When one begins to treat hypotheses 'as instruments of proof without reference to empirical verification', as defining 'essential' properties of objects, then one is turning scientific statements into dogmatic truths. The validity of scientific principles only extends as far as one finds that inferences from them correspond to facts; but if a considerable number of inferences from a given hypothesis have been justified by experience, it becomes increasingly probable that a further inference would also hold true. There is always a temptation to treat new inferences as being true without verification, which explains the blurring of the distinction between 'hypotheses subordinate to experience' and 'hypotheses dominating experience' in many minds. This does not, of course, mean that in practice one may not accept any implications of a hypothesis without proof.[79]

Regarding the philosophical debate on Nominalism and Realism, Pareto's view is that it would be presumptuous to decide whether only the individuum or only the species existed, for the good reason, among others, that one could not adequately know what the term 'exist' meant. He intends to study 'things and hence individua, and to consider species as aggregates of more or less similar things on which we determine ourselves for specified purposes'.[80] But this does not mean that a number of individua are a simple aggregate; 'they form compounds which, like chemical compounds, may have properties that are not the sum of the properties of their compounds'.[81]

A final point that should, however, be made in this discussion is in his word of caution to the reader of his work:[82]

> In general, when I call attention to some untoward consequence of a thing A . . . in no way do I mean to imply that A on the whole is detrimental to society; for there may be good effects to overbalance the bad. Conversely, when I call attention to a good effect of A, great though it be, I do not at all imply that on the whole A is beneficial to society.

This caution is necessary if one is to understand Pareto's work in any constructive way. The material he deals with presents an inherent difficulty of interpretation: sentiments or moral beliefs, judgments and values, and their consequences, cannot be analysed in a neutral language, even though they are postulated as objective, social facts and separated from one's own individual values. The concepts of sentiment and moral value are dependent on the autonomous, interrelated and conflicting meanings they have in specific subjective and social contexts. They preclude, therefore, a mechanical explanation implied in a neutral language.[83] They, in fact, make it necessary to use the language of moral statements, judgments and criticisms to make these meanings explicit.[84]

Any lack of neutrality of language in Pareto's work should not, therefore, prejudice one in understanding it, for it neither weakens the continuity of his analytic argument nor the objective truth of his theory. As we have seen, this is evident in the first part of his theory in which he establishes the distinction between the logico-experimental and the non-logico-experimental categories of thought and action. We can now turn to some of the examples he analyses to see some of the implications of this distinction.

As a preliminary to the analysis, Pareto says that if one were to discover that all human actions were logico-experimental or the majority of them were and the rest could be treated as pathological,

74

one's approach would obviously be different from the reverse situation, in which one found that all, or the majority of, actions were non-logico-experimental.[85] But, he cautions, one must not be misled by the terms used. In reality both categories are subjective, since all human knowledge is subjective, and the terms designate an action only on the basis of greater or less fund of factual knowledge that we have.[86] It is on this basis that he classifies actions 'that use means appropriate to ends and which logically link means with ends' in one category; and those actions in which these traits are missing, into another.[87] The most obvious example of the second category of action, the non-logico-experimental is, of course, magic, which Pareto describes as those 'actions in which words act upon things'.[88] At one extreme of magic there is the unknown power of certain words or acts to produce certain effect; then, a logical connection is made with the interposition of gods, ending, at the other extreme, with a completely logical action, e.g. the medieval belief that one could acquire power to harm by selling one's soul to the Devil. However, instead of there being no substance to this belief, the only cases one knew were of successful magic due to a belief in the Devil, then, of course, one would have to accept the logical interpretation that men believe in magic because they believe in the Devil. This would not be substantially different if we found the Devil replaced by some other divine power; but if we found cases in which there was no divine intervention at all, the interpretation would not be true. Since these phenomena themselves are accepted even though a logical interpretation is not true, it is obvious that the essential element in them is that which associates certain words, invocations or practices with certain desired results. The introduction of the Devil, or other gods or spirits, serves only to give a logical form to these associations. If the substance remains the same in an individual, he may entertain several such logical forms in his mind.[89] Logical interpretations assume the forms which are most general in the ages in which they are found. There is, however, no direct evolution of these forms from the pure non-logical association of words and acts into a pure logical action; it moves along with other actions derived from it. It is impossible to say that it could have been a succession from the 'mere association of acts and facts' or fetishism to a theological interpretation, then to a metaphysical interpretation and, further, to a positive interpretation.

75

All such interpretations are bound inextricably together and an individual who accepts them would most probably be unable to separate them; for him it may be enough that certain acts must have certain results.[90] Moreover, even though gradual enlightenment does have an influence on such non-logical, associative conduct, there is no definite correlation between them. For example, the Romans burned neither witches nor magicians as the Italians, the French and the Germans etc. did in the seventeenth century, even though their scientific development was substantially less. Belief in the non-logical conduct is not a result of the logical interpretation that might be given of it by a church or a government or any other authority; but such interpretations are believed in because of the original belief in the associative conduct. This does not mean that such theories or interpretation do not have the effect of stimulating the belief and giving rise to it in other places.

The point of the several examples of magic, witchcraft and popular superstition which Pareto analyses is that they have something in common, the feeling that there are certain means by which certain facts can be influenced—which remains constant in all of them; and the means and justifications of their use—which are variable, and differ in almost all of them.

If the whole case of non-logical associative conduct were judged from the logico-experimental point of view, the ritual-ethics of religious and metaphysical systems, for example, would appear insane and childish. But to infer from this that these systems are equally insane and childish and therefore harmful to society, as it is sometimes done, would mean that the greater part of the history of human societies was absurd; and, further, if everything that is not logical and scientific is harmful to society, and therefore to the individual, we should not be able to observe that certain non-logical behaviour—like instinctual behaviour in animals, or habitual or traditional behaviour in human beings—proves beneficial, even highly beneficial.[91] Therefore, Pareto asks: 'Since the inference is wrong, the reasoning must also be wrong. Where is the error?'[92] The error lies in not relating the conclusion to the actual circumstances, i.e. non-logical theories are not always detrimental to society. But, Pareto adds, in order to establish this relationship we need a theory 'of doctrines and of their influence on individuals and society'.[93]

Another case which Pareto examines is that of the logical form which the Romans gave to their relations with the gods. It was, generally speaking, the form of 'a definite and unambiguous contract interpreted according to the rules of law'. He adds that if that were all, we would merely find an illustration of what is considered the legal-mindedness of the Romans. There are similar facts to be found among all peoples, but what makes the Romans different is the intensity of this state of mind among them, 'the wealth and precision of detail, the subordination of substance to form—in a word, the powerful cohesion of one act with others'.[94] For the Roman statesmen especially, the whole relationship of men and gods was an exact science of asking and giving—which Plato had dismissed as a ridiculous definition of holiness, although it was defined as such by a great number of Greeks.[95] It means that in spite of the similarity in the contents of Greek and Roman beliefs, the difference in the intensity of the state of mind that these beliefs created made them what they were. The significance of this conclusion is shown by Pareto in some further conclusions he draws from examples of the scrupulousness and circumspection of the Romans in the duties of life. If one logically analysed the substance of their beliefs and practices, it would seem ridiculous that in making an offering to the gods they should choose their words carefully and always add explicit conditions and qualifications to their statements so that they may not be bound by any tacit obligation. But if one granted their premise that certain acts were related to certain ideas, their scrupulously exact and explicit behaviour becomes rational. As Pareto says, 'if the sting of a scorpion is really to be avoided by pronouncing the number 2, is it not evident that when one comes upon an insect and would avoid its sting, one must know exactly whether it is a scorpion, or not, and then the number that has to be pronounced.'[96] The point of their correct ritual was that if it is the act that is important above all else, one must do it exactly as it is and not something else; and, for Pareto, the thing to note is that whatever the value of this reasoning, it 'occurred *a posteriori* to justify conduct in itself non-logical'.[97]

This trait was noticeable in their systems of divination as much as in their religion. It depended on a strict 'yes' or 'no' answer to the question whether the gods favoured or did not favour the thing about to be done. What the Romans could not find in new forms of

77

divination at home, they borrowed from Greece and Etruria—where imagination was freer than in Rome. One of the most extraordinary rules which the Romans had for divination and which is explained by their intensity of feeling for certain association of ideas and acts, is that they treated an unauthenticated augury with the same respect as those which had been observed. The augur could have it announced as a fact—which became a regular practice as it was more trustworthy than observation of a real sign—according to a sacramental formula and it *became* equivalent to a real sign.[98]

Pareto remarks that the Romans dealt with facts as they chose but adhered strictly to forms or rather certain associations of ideas and acts; the Athenians modified both content and form, and the Spartans were reluctant to change either.[99] It shows the various uses of tradition which different people make and how it is not the contents of their tradition that have sociological consequences but the 'intensity' of their feelings towards it or the sentiments it gives rise to.

Ancient Roman law shows the same characteristics of solemnity of words and the subordination of facts to words as in religion and divination. Pareto quotes the historian von Jhering's comments on this and adds that certain associations of ideas—or 'words, acts and effects'—had arisen over time and the Romans were reluctant to dissolve them, and developed their law accordingly. Anything legal had to defer to the forms in the various *actiones legis*.[100]

The most interesting characteristic of ancient Roman law was not its strict adherence to the word, but the progress it made in spite of it.[101] This particular trait is noticeable in all aspects of their law and in many aspects of their politics.[102] Pareto remarks that in their long constitutional changes from kingdom to republic and return to monarchy under the empire, through a division of the functions of magistrates and their recombination, the Romans preserved the forms as much as possible, even though the substance changed; while in Athens forms were made consistent with the changes in substance.[103] Another trait which defines the psychic state of the Romans was the powerful influence of *religio* on their consciences. The Greeks had no term which corresponded exactly to at least one of the meanings of the word, 'painstaking, conscientious, diligent attention to duties', which suggests, if nothing else, that the feeling described by this term was not as intense among the Greeks as it was for Romans.[104] The *religio* of the Romans was manifested in the many facts which show them as a 'conscientious, exact, scrupulous people, devoted—even too much so—to orderliness and regularity in their private lives'.[105]

One might get the impression from the religion of the Greeks, in which reason and imagination were more prominent, that it would be more moral than the religion of the Romans, which seems to be nothing more than 'a series of fictions in which reason played no part whatever'.[106] If we consider not the antics of gods, but the influence of religion on the conduct of daily life or ethics,* the performance of ritual was everything without any concern for intentions. The Greeks passed through this phase, in which murder was expiated by a ritual, but soon they, or rather their thinkers, 'outgrew their materialistic formalistic morality';[107] and one would expect to find a morality comparable to their exalted thoughts, but in fact we find the opposite. On the other hand, Romans remained moral until comparatively recent times, mainly because of their respect for a word given solemnly.

Further, Athenian law which attempted to decide questions on broad lines without ritualized formalism or too many fictions, and was essentially logical, resulted in a chaotic application mainly because—Pareto quotes Sumner Maine's *Ancient Law* at this point —'the Greek tribunals exhibited the strongest tendency to confound law and fact' and to arrive at an ideal decision on the facts of particular cases.[108] Pareto disagrees with Maine when he ascribes the superiority of Roman law to Roman theory of natural law, because that theory was added to the traditional collection of laws at a later date; and is inclined to accept von Jhering's description of the Roman psychic state as the 'rigorous logic of the conservative spirit', combined with 'logical and practical inferences that entail the fewest possible modifications in certain associations of ideas and acts' as an explanation of the causes of the superiority of the Roman system of jurisprudence.

The most important point that Pareto makes on this phenomenon

---

* This part of religion is the only one which has much sociological significance, but it is not often analysed in the so-called sociology of religion. For an analysis on the basis which Pareto proposes, but through an application of Weber's methodology, see my Ph.D. thesis, 'Hindu Reformist ethics and the Weber thesis...'

79

is that the moral disinclination of the Romans to violate any principle, once it was recognized, stimulated them to devise ways and means for reconciling logic and practical necessity.[109] Finally, on Roman politics, Pareto remarks: 'We can only wonder how a system so absurd from the standpoint of logic could ever have survived . . . Yet it did function for century after century, and gave Romans dominion over the Mediterranean world'; and when it finally broke down it broke down because it had been worn out by a new people that had lost the *religio* of the old. 'Thanks to ties of non-logical conduct and to forces of innovation, Rome found a way to reconcile discipline with freedom and strike a golden mean between Sparta and Athens.'[110]

> Among the modern peoples [Pareto remarks] the English have more than any other people resembled the Romans in their psychic state. English law is replete with fictions. The English political system keeps the same antiquated forms, whereas in substance it is constantly changing . . . English political organization is adapted to the needs of the English people, just as the political organisation of ancient Rome was adapted to the needs of the Roman people, and all modern people have sought to copy it more or less faithfully. That organisation . . . had secured Englishmen greater liberties than the majority of European peoples have enjoyed.[111]

Pareto's analysis of classical societies is by no means an antiquarian study, for by analysing past societies he is able, first, to provide the detachment necessary to understand the implications of his theory and, second, to draw parallels with the characteristics of modern societies. The detachment, thus, works to discipline one's interest in contemporary facts and to reveal the hidden relationships of continuing sentiments and seemingly important immediate changes in a society. Second, his theory shows the basis on which generalizations are possible about value-facts, without turning them into an absurd collection of social indices of pseudo-scientific appearance. Although his conclusions on modern England—that is, till the end of the nineteenth century, but in many respects still true—agree with what has been observed by many people, they make an original contribution, with the background of his analysis of classical societies, in two respects: first, by showing what makes a particular society, e.g. England, different from other societies; and, second, by revealing the importance of sentiments or certain persistent associations of ideas, acts and things in creating this difference. The significance of this analytic insight lies in demarcating exactly the unique and the general in the formation of social reality and, also, how they relate to one another, in empirical terms.

Incidentally, this point shows up the naïveté of certain common criticisms: that Pareto confines himself to the facts of Western civilization and other civilizational notions would not be understood through his theory, and also, paradoxically, that he is not historical;* or, that his theory is élitist and cyclical; and the most naïve of all criticisms, that his theory is tautological. The main point of his theory is, as mentioned earlier, that it enables one to see what makes one people different from another even when they share the same civilization, let alone peoples of other civilizations or non-civilizations. The second important point is that historical facts are an inevitable part of sociological analysis, and sociological theory must as inevitably replace conjectural theories and philosophies of history. Third, the analysis of the thoughts and actions of élites of a society is also inevitable, because no one can justifiably claim a direct knowledge of whole populations, especially when they are dead! Pareto has amply demonstrated the relationship of élites and the general population in his analysis, and also how they can be established in any actual context. The criticism of cyclicism would have been justifiable only if the analytical part of the theory was derived from an *a priori* notion of cyclical change in society. As it is in Pareto's terms, it is just a general description of what form societal or civilizational changes seem to take. It has no analytic value, and none is claimed for it by Pareto. As for being tautological, if one is unable to see—like almost all the commentators till now—how a theory works, then it is bound to appear circular in its reasoning, since its descriptive relations are taken as analytical or empirical relations. In other words, since a logical description is necessarily tautological, it can only break the circularity of

---

* This criticism is not true. Various examples from other civilizations and cultures are to be found throughout his book. Even his brief comments have an incisive quality which is wholly lacking in more comprehensive studies of non-Western sociology.

logic if the description is judged by what it refers to and not by its form.

Therefore, to judge the objectivity or the truth of Pareto's theory, one has to examine the analytical part, the theory of derivations,[112] which centres on the question, 'How is non-logical conduct rationalized?' We have in the literature of thought, in Pareto's words, 'an image in a curved mirror; our problem is to discover the form of the object so altered by refraction.'[113] For our purposes, we should ignore those writings in which due consideration is given to the fact that environment, climate, race, occupation, temperament, etc. have some effect, at least, on the conduct of human beings, in so far as they state things as they are, as behaviour from such causes cannot obviously be a product of pure thought, or, in other words, non-logical. But when a writer insists on all conduct being logical beyond such causes, then he usually means what in his opinion *ought* to be.[114] The controversy between Herbert Spencer and Auguste Comte, which Pareto takes as an example, brings out a number of interesting facets of non-logical conduct.[115] Pareto quotes from Comte's *Lectures on Positive Philosophy* where he speaks of social reorganization of civilized nations. Comte assumes that 'ideas govern and upset the world'; and if a unanimity of opinions existed on a common social doctrine, appropriate institutions would necessarily arise from it.[116] Herbert Spencer, Pareto continues, put forward a theory opposed to the notion of ideas governing action, and substituted the dictum that 'the world is governed or overthrown by feelings, to which ideas serve only as guides'; and, further, 'all social phenomena are produced by the totality of human emotions and beliefs'.[117] But —Pareto comments—in the course of their arguments Comte and Spencer reverse their stands. In his *System of Positive Polity* Comte makes sentiment the more important instrument of social change; and Spencer eliminates the influence of non-logical actions altogether by making temperament the premise and assuming that people make logical deductions from it and act accordingly. This reversal came about, in Pareto's view, because Comte began by hoping to convert people, and ideas were the accepted means for doing so in his time, but ended by concluding that there was no hope of conversion except through a religion imposed by force. In the achievement of this aim, only sentiment could obviously have any important part to play and to speak of ideas governing or upsetting the world would not be possible.[118] Regarding Spencer, Pareto comments that by assuming that human beings always infer logically from the knowledge they have and act according to their inferences, he puts himself in the position of having nothing but logical conduct, and one must conclude that ideas do govern or upset the world and there is no place for sentiments in such a world of 'experimental facts, however badly observed and, of logical inferences derived from such facts'.[119] Pareto comments further that this Spencerian principle makes sociology very easy, especially if combined with the other two principles of unitary evolution and 'identity, or quasi-identity, of the savages of our time with primitive man'.[120] In general terms, therefore, the procedure of the Comte-Spencer reversal of ideas and sentiments could be described as follows: we have two things, P and Q, that need to be considered in determining the social order R. We begin by asserting that Q alone determines the order; then we assert that P determines Q. Thus, Q is eliminated and P alone determines the social order. If we substitute 'ideas' for Q and 'sentiments' for P we get Comte's argument, and if we make Q stand for 'sentiments' and P for 'ideas' we get Spencer's.[121]

In this description of Comte's and Spencer's theories we can see the nucleus of 'derivational' reasoning. Formally considered, the relationship of the derivation to logic gives rise, first, to the question of logical soundness and, second, to the question of its relationship to experience. A derivation may be strictly logical, yet because of some element in the premises may not be experimental; or it may apparently be logical, yet, because of some indefinite term, have no—or very remote—experimental meaning. Apart from these, the other two aspects on which actual derivations need to be examined are their subjectivity and social utility. If only their substance were to be considered, the whole problem would be resolved by classifying primary and secondary residues.[122]

Since derivations account for the creation and acceptance of what may generally be called 'social' theories, their subjective analysis becomes more important, in terms of Pareto's theory, than others.[123] Such an analysis involves 'the subjective character of the "explanations" that are given, through derivations, of certain behaviour, certain ways of thinking'; and 'the persuasive force of such explanations'.[124] If there is no such explanation or justification there is no derivation, for a derivation is inherent to such elaborations.

83

Even in the pure precept there is 'a germ of derivation', for it is an appeal to a sentiment.[125]

The most sophisticated derivations are those in which we find proofs 'that are primarily verbal, explanations that are purely formal, but pretend to pass as substantial'.[126] The study of derivations is the most important part of Pareto's theory, as it allows the basic question of sociological analysis—i.e. how can what is theoretically recognized, or hypothesized, be found in reality?—to be answered. One should remember Pareto's point in this connection that the only things we can claim to know directly are the actual reasonings, interpretations or theories accepted in a society. From this direct knowledge Pareto analysed two elements in them: one constant (a) and the other variable (b)—or residues and derivations. His hypothesis is that residues are more important than derivations in creating or maintaining the social equilibrium. When a person is influenced by a derivation, he usually makes a decision according to his sentiments rather than, as he imagines, on logical and experimental grounds. In other words, agreement or conflict between two derivations is, in reality, agreement or conflict between residues, rather than of facts. If one stopped at derivations—as often happens in studies of social phenomena—one would only know the reflections or manifestations of social activity, not its causes; and instead of a history of social or political institutions we would have a history of social or political theories or interpretations; and instead of a history of religions, we would have a history of theologies.[127] Derivations, in fact, are universally used, the difference lies in whether or not an *intrinsic* value is attributed to them, that is, whether they are used as social determinants or as *indications* of the actual forces or determinants in society. They are social determinants when the purpose is to induce people to act in a certain way, since the language of derivations is the only one 'that reaches the human being in his sentiments and is therefore calculated to modify his behaviour'.[128] It is, therefore, easily seen that if one is to understand the language of derivations one must logically separate their use as social determinants from their indication or manifestation of the actual reality behind them; for even as social determinants derivations are not independent causes of action, they work in relation to the sentiments of their audience. They are, thus, from the point of view of understanding and explanation, indications of reality even when they are active as social determinants.* Pareto refers to John Stuart Mill's *System of Logic* to show a certain correspondence between their notions on the causes of this difference.[129] Apart from logical fallacy, Mill mentions intellectual and moral 'sources of error'. The intellectual source is approximately the same as Pareto's distinction between the inferential descriptions and principles of logico-experimental theories and the logical reasonings, fallacies and sophistries and inferential manifestations of sentiment.† The other source of error, moral, is of two kinds: (i) 'indifference to knowledge of the truth' and (ii) 'that in which we are biased by our wishes';[130] the second kind being what Pareto means by sentiments corresponding to residues. Since Mill was dealing with logic, he did not, rightly, go into these matters in any detail; but, in Pareto's view, he handled the moral error rather badly, mainly because of his assumption that 'only logical behaviour is good, beneficial, praiseworthy, whereas non-logical conduct is necessarily evil, harmful, blameworthy.'[131]

An important distinction in the analysis of derivations is that a person who is trying to prove something is almost always conscious of the purpose of his derivation, but not often the person who accepts the conclusion of his derivation. When the purpose is to justify some rule of conduct, it will be associated with certain residues by more or less logical arguments. Thus, the procedure can be formulated in order of importance as: (i) the purpose; (ii) the residues with which one starts; (iii) the derivation.[132] This order is not, according to Pareto, usually accepted by 'theologians, metaphysicians, philosophers, theorists of politics, law and ethics. They

---

* Cf. my comments on the impossibility of using a neutral language in explanation of such phenomena, above p. 74. This means that even though the form of 'derivational' language is separable logically from the form of explanatory language and their contents are the same, *their respective logical structures will be different*. The logical structure of a phenomenon is neither synonymous with the formal structure of logic nor necessarily common to similar phenomena simply because their substantive elements are the same— as mistakenly assumed by many philosophers and theoreticians—*because it depends entirely* on the way in which the form and the content of the particular phenomenon are related, and not on formal or substantive generalities of logic or philosophy.

† Cf. Pareto's distinction between the element *B* of logico-experimental theories and the element *b* of non-logico-experimental theories. He always signifies the fundamental distinction by his use of capital and small letters.

85

place derivations first and consider residues as axioms or dogmas, and *the purpose* becomes just the conclusion of a logical reasoning'.[133] This difference, Pareto says, allows some significant conclusions on the 'logic of sentiments'.[134] First, if the basic residue, from which a derivation develops, is no longer there, then obviously the purpose should also disappear; but in non-logical theories the residues are replaced as premises by others. This change does not eliminate the purpose, it only weakens it. In other words, 'the ideal remains but is accepted with less fervour.'[135] This relationship between premise and conclusion also, at times, occurs in logico-experimental theories, but, generally speaking, if it can be shown that the conclusion is not logically deducible from the premise, the argument is rejected. In non-logico-experimental theories, on the other hand, the general case is that if the reasoning which connects a given residue (the premise) with a given conclusion (the purpose) is shown to be unsound, then a new derivation is produced to replace the one rejected. The reason for this is *that the residue and the purpose are the fundamental elements* and the derivation is secondary, unlike logico-experimental reasoning, in which the inference or argument is the important element. For example, the various Christian sects have differing, even contradictory, doctrines on good works and predestination, yet—Pareto says—'there is no difference between them as regards practical morals': it shows the operation of the connection between the same residue in all of them and the same conclusion they all accept, through a variety of derivations.

An important point about derivations, as distinct from logical inferences, is that the strongest conclusions are those which directly relate to powerful residues without any derivations.[136]

Further, the proof of a derivation is frequently different from the reason for its acceptance.[137] The causes for the acceptance of the simplest form of derivation, i.e. by assertion, are three kinds of a feeling (a) that a person who expresses himself assertively *must* be right; (b) such a form itself is authoritative; (c) that this authority is justified.

Although it may seem that these kinds of the feeling which leads to the acceptance of an assertion are parts of a general feeling of justification of some authority in certain circumstances, they are, in fact, frequently independent; if (b) and (c) categories are related in certain circumstances there is a priority of the authoritative form over the justification. That is to say, 'a person first has the sentiment of authority and then goes looking for ways to justify it'.[138] The second form of derivational reasoning, by authority, provides both proof and persuasion through it. An extreme authority-derivation would be one strictly logical, for evidently, in such a case, the opinion of an expert has a greater probability of being confirmed by experience than the opinion of one less knowledgeable; but in cases where the expertise is not experimental, the authority may be assumed to exist from misleading or fictitious evidence.[139] The residue or sentiment of authority can also be present in devices which are used to discredit authority of individuals or symbols (divine beings, personifications, metaphysical entities, etc.)—as one can find in any theological, moral or political debate or conflict.[140] Apart from the authority of individuals or groups of individuals and symbols, Pareto also distinguishes the authority of tradition, usages and customs—'such authority may be verbal, written, anonymous, or of a real or a legendary person',—which can allow an 'explanation' of things through a certain resemblance of ideas and accord of sentiment.[141] Traditions can become residues in themselves, if powerful enough, but they often serve merely as derivations to reinforce other more powerful sentiments or residues.[142] Traditions show the same variability as derivations inasmuch as they are interpretations of certain basic ideas. Different and contradictory doctrines have been based on books like the Bible or the Gospels, but one cannot decide which of them are true experimentally—except as to whether or not they depart from the literal meaning—since the belief in them comes not from experience but faith. One can, nevertheless, show what exactly is their influence on the action of believers in its various aspects, through the different interconnections of logical and non-logical action which Paretian analysis has revealed.

The third form of derivation, by accord with sentiments or principles, also has three ways of realization: (a) a person conforms in his conduct with sentiments simply out of reverence for the 'opinion of the majority or of experts of "the mind" '; (b) he may do so from fear of consequences; (c) he may be impelled to do so 'by a mysterious force' or a form of imperative.[143]

In the first means, there is no explicit attempt to relate the conformity to any aspect of objective reality. The basis lies in the feeling that if a thought occurs in the minds 'of all men or of the majority of men or just in the mind', it is objective, self-evident or axiomatic.[144] Sometimes this agreement of minds is presented explicitly as proof, or it may be demonstrated by reference to another metaphysical principle—which, in Pareto's opinion, 'serves primarily to satisfy the demand of educated people for logical explanations'.[145] In almost all derivations this article of consensus in some form or another is always present—as 'proverbs, adages, sayings or generalities'.[146]

In the second means of realization, the appeal to individual interest, there are many devices used which are not all derivations. If a person, for example, does not know that it would be to his advantage to act in a certain way and he is shown that it would be, then it is not a derivational demonstration; it is a 'function of experience, of the trades, of science'. Similarly, if a person is made to act in a certain way through the exercise of actual powers by a real and external authority or through custom and usage; or if his own temperament makes him act in the given way because otherwise he will feel remorse or sorrow; there is no derivation.[147]

Derivations come into play when the real connection of advantage through knowledge, actual sanction or personal feeling, is replaced by an imaginary one. All such derivations are, Pareto says, of great significance for human societies: they are aimed at avoiding or harmonizing possible conflicts between the individual and society. One of the ways of achieving this goal is to confuse the two interests through derivational reasoning, by making them identical.[148] This identity is achieved automatically by a pseudo-experimental proof, as in the case of the violation of a taboo and its physical remedy or in the violation of religious precepts and its spiritual remedy by confession and penance. In both cases the derivational reasoning is concerned with the restoration of individual integrity.[149] On a more intellectual level, Pareto takes the example of Bentham's philosophy as typical and examines it for derivations which show 'the outstanding trait of reducing to the principle of individual interest conduct which seems to have no bearing whatever upon it'.[150] For Pareto, Bentham's principle of 'utility', or of pleasure and pain as felt 'by the peasant as well as the prince, the plain man as well as the philosopher', raises the question, which relates to all theories of this kind, how should the principle of absolute selfishness be reconciled with the principle of altruism?—which Bentham, however, is unwilling to give up.

In some theories the reconciliation is achieved by verbal subterfuges—which Bentham rejects; in others, concessions made on one principle are withdrawn on the basis of another—which he uses. Bentham, in Pareto's view, includes the altruistic principle through public approval or disapproval. It still leaves the first principle, that of absolute selfishness, unreconciled; Bentham, then, points out that the disapproval of others is harmful to the individual, therefore it is to his advantage to avoid it. Bentham's second proof, through the use of another principle—that of 'the greatest happiness of the greatest number'—eliminates the ethical problem of finding a way of reconciling individual utility with the utility of the greatest number, but does not solve it. It has a certain intuitive truth, Pareto adds, in so far as there is a 'maximum' of happiness or advantage for both the individual and the community, but, like all intuitions, leaves the subject unclear.[151]

The logico-experimental value of Bentham's philosophy is very slight, because he tries to reconcile logically contradictory principles by logic, and, further, by making all conduct logical he loses touch with reality. Nevertheless, this weak logico-experimental value has little relevance for the subject of derivations and sociological analysis. The reason for the success of Bentham's philosophy lies in its combination of 'residues of personal integrity with residues of sociality'; the derivations or the interpretive reasoning or connection is not, as has been said earlier, at all important for social acceptance.[152]

The final form of derivation, by providing verbal proofs, has more sophisticated devices than others because it uses the varied resources of language itself.

Verbal proofs are part of all forms of derivation, but in this specific form the predominant trait is that an abstraction or a concept is endowed with reality through a number of linguistic devices. In fact, it is a form of derivation which is related primarily to the use of language and meaning in society in all its complexity.[153] A verbal derivation depends specifically, however, on the characteristics of the terms of a syllogism. Pareto says: 'when a term that can have more than one meaning is used in a syllogism, the syllogism may come to have more than three terms and so be fallacious. Very often it is

G

the middle term that vitiates the syllogism by its indefiniteness.'[154] In specific reasonings the danger is simply minimized, not eliminated, in so far as the terms used serve as designations or labels; in other reasonings, designations or labels can progressively become, through an accumulation of meanings, metaphysical entities.[155]

It is the characteristics of language, through its variety of meanings and concepts, from the descriptive to the metaphysical, that make verbal derivations sociologically significant. Basically, as has been said above, verbal derivations arise when a term with several meanings is used in a syllogism, which accounts for its logical fallacy, but, derivationally, it is precisely the possibility of transferring to the term another meaning that is important. For example, if in the argument 'A $=$ X and X $=$ B, therefore A $=$ B' X has two meanings that cannot possibly be confused, we get a mere pun; but if X means a large and vague collection of sentiments, and certain sentiments are meant in A $=$ X, and certain others in X $=$ B, we can see that the possibility of a verbal derivation is immediately created.

The various kinds of verbal derivation which Pareto distinguishes, he cautions, appear in combination with each other as well as with other forms of derivation. The analysis and abstraction of simple varieties are meant only for understanding and explaining the concrete derivation which is a compound of the simple derivations.[156]

The varieties of verbal derivations show two procedures: (i) from the thing to the term and (ii) from the term to the thing, real or imaginary. In actual cases these two forms of connective argument are mixed and often lead from the term to something else. This is a way in which a logico-experimental argument can change into a non-logico-experimental one; and theories in which the nature of an object is derived from the etymology of its name is an example of the second procedure and what it can lead to.[157] In this kind of derivational reasoning indefinite terms may designate real things or indefinite things may correspond to terms;[158] or terms which designate things can also arouse incidental sentiments or incidental sentiments can determine the choice of terms. The second type of derivation is usually evident in legal and political rhetoric, as techniques of persuasion. Pareto's quotation from Aristotle's *Rhetorica* illustrates this derivation well: 'If one would favour a thing, the metaphor must be chosen from what is best; if one would harm it, from what is worst.'[159]

A term like freedom, for instance, can be used in a derivation in three different senses: (i) vaguely, as a personified abstraction; (ii) definitely, as a capacity to act or not to act; and (iii) such capacity in a given individual or in others. These meanings are often contradictory, and derivational reasoning brings the other meanings into use by including them in the first notion of personified abstraction. The practical conflict between an individual's freedom and others' freedom is not, however, formulated by derivations such as: 'Given certain ends, is it desirable to favour an individual's at the expense of others?'—or vice versa; but as attempts 'to exploit the agreeable sentiments that the term suggests in general', by transferring them to its specific senses. This shows the limit of logico-experimental reality in relation to derivations;[160] and the use of metaphors, allegories and analogies as proof reinforces the agreeability of sentiments they serve by explaining or conveying conceptions of the unknown through the known and the familiar.[161] In his discussion of non-logical theories, Pareto found and dealt with two problems: (i) the relation of a theory to experimental fact and (ii) means of arriving at pre-established conclusions, persuasiveness. That is, he analysed the structure of the derivation as well as the manner of its acceptance.[162] The one common characteristic of all derivations is the arbitrary use of non-experimental entities; but the important fact of the whole Paretian analysis is that this arbitrariness *has its limits in the sentiments associated with words and in certain conventions on their use*.[163] The acceptance of the derivation is also limited, to the extent that animal fables have never been taken as literally true, mythologies are believed by a certain number of people, 'but much more numerous among educated people are those who believe in a more or less mitigated Realism.'[164]

Another very important consideration on which derivations have to be judged is their relations to reality. Reality is not simply what is experimentally true, but *includes individual and social utility*,[165] for a theory may be altogether fantastic as objective-factual statement, yet 'correspond to subjective facts of great moment to society'.[166]

Finally, Pareto makes the most important point on the subject of derivations, that the fluctuations in social beliefs and opinions result, theoretically, from a clash between the factual truth of derivations and their social utility. 'If the truth and the utility of social

91

beliefs and opinions harmonized, then it would not be difficult to imagine a continuous progress in society; but since they are in reality discordant, antagonistic, and since both a complete desertion of reality and a complete disregard of social utilities remain if not impossible, at least difficult, it necessarily follows that in regard to social matters theory oscillates like a pendulum, now swinging in one direction and now in the other.'[167]

It will now be realized that the whole of Pareto's analysis of social beliefs and opinions, of logical and non-logical theories and derivations, and the role of facts and utility in the formation of social reality, leads to a discernment of a persisting sum of feelings, actions, facts and ideas which in their particular configurations identify a society in distinction to others. These configurations are designated by Pareto as residues or manifestations of sentiments. It is an *inferential* concept: it does not describe or classify any form of actual reality. It allows one to make a substantive assumption on the nature of social reality, which depends for its validity not on certain axiomatic feelings but on analytical conclusions.*

The theory of residues forms the second volume of *The Mind and Society*, after the distinction between logical and non-logical conduct had been made. In fact, the recognition of an instinctive, non-logical element that was constant and 'a deductive element that was designed to explain, justify, demonstrate the constant element', in the analysis of observable social theories, leads to his postulating the theory of residues. The full analytical implications of this theory cannot be appreciated until the recurrence of the residual element in all the various analyses has been noted. Therefore, although the residue is identifiable, its complete definition cannot be judged properly until one is closely acquainted with the analysis of the variable element, the derivation.

Incidentally, Pareto's theory of residues illustrates an extremely important point about the nature of sociological theory. It shows that no substantive theory on any aspect of social reality can be either strictly inductive or strictly deductive; inductive in the sense

---

* The confusion between the process of making valid *substantive* assumptions and axiomatic premises, which underlies philosophical and theoretical dimensions of the subject of sociology, arises mainly because no clear distinction has been made *between* thought and experience themselves *and* when they relate to each other.

of being successively generalized from the increasing quantity of data, and deductive in the sense of being derivable from certain axioms on the character of social facts. In fact, it is, as Pareto's analysis shows, inductively based and the generalization is not successively quantitative but qualitative, since the qualitative difference in social facts comes not from changes in quantity of homogeneous entities but from the uniqueness of combinations of various substantive elements and values.*

Again, one has to take the composition of logico-experimental theories as a norm of comparison to see how the residue is related to the derivation. In logico-experimental form, the basic element—which Pareto designated by A—consists of 'experimental principles, descriptions and experimental assertions'; similarly, in the non-logical form there is a basic element—which Pareto designated by a—composed of manifestations of certain sentiments. There is also a certain correspondence between the elements B, i.e. 'logical inferences and experimental principles used for drawing inferences from the basic element A', and the element b, or 'logical reasonings, fallacies, sophistries, along, further, with other manifestations of sentiment used for drawing inferences from a'. The theories—or rather the conclusions drawn from the other two elements—are designated by C and c respectively.[168]

The main clue to the nature of residues is given by Pareto in the following words: 'Things that exert powerful effects upon the social order give rise to theories, and we shall find them, therefore, in the course of our quest for a's.'[169] In addition to these basic elements there are appetites (or instincts) and interests, which, altogether, contribute to the making of the social order, which also reacts upon them. There is, therefore, a correlation rather than a straight cause-effect relationship. It is the combination of instincts and interests which gives rise to theories and if human beings had no interests it is quite unlikely that they would have sentiments.[170] Further, it is the manifestations of sentiments that we observe in the theories; sentiments themselves are, obviously, not observable in any sense. Their existence can only be inferred; and, as such, it is only their manifestations that one can ever refer to. In other words, the concept of residue is formed through an analysis of the structure

---

* This point is developed in the next chapter in relation to both Weber and Pareto, as it is significant for sociological analysis in general.

of theories *about* socially powerful objects or activities rather than as a generalized observational statement.*

Two basic impulses are noticeable in the element *a* of such theories: (a) what Pareto calls 'an instinct for combinations', i.e. of certain things with certain acts, and (b) 'an instinct which inclines people to believe that certain combinations are suited to certain objectives'. The curious fact about this phenomenon is that one combination tends to persist over long periods of time and prevail over all other combinations that arise with it.[171] As these persisting elements constitute a 'multifarious mass of facts', they have to be classified in terms of similarities and differences but only for analytical purposes; for, in individual minds, the sentiments that operate correspond to whole groups of residues which are, in themselves, obviously simpler than the subjective feelings that make up these sentiments. There is, however, a logical limit to any analytical simplification, for if residues were simplified any further, they would only become meaningless generalities. There is, further, no linear progression between a derivative or theory *c*, derivation *b* and residue *a*, because a derivative may become a residue in certain circumstances, and vice versa; and derivations are closely related to residues, in their effects.[172]

Pareto has classified six groups of residues based on instincts for: (i) combinations; (ii) group-persistence; (iii) self-expression; (iv) sociality; (v) integrity of the individual and; (vi) sex. Of these groups, the first two are obviously the most significant factors in the formation of societies as recognizable entities, but in social reality as a whole, the other groups of residues have as important a role to play.

Pareto envisages the residues of the first group, of combinations, as one of the important forces in civilization. The scientist, for example, in the laboratory, makes 'combinations according to certain norms, certain purposes, certain hypotheses, for the most part rationally, but also, at times, randomly. His activity is, therefore, in the main logical, but other individuals combine things from analogies— often by chance, but, nevertheless, like the scientist's random

---

* Only if residues were reified as sentiments or located in the psyche of individuals as instincts—which are, incidentally, inferential concepts themselves—would Pareto's theory appear confused or confusing. Yet, invariably Pareto's theory of residues is either misunderstood or underrated in significance on these very grounds!

combination—in both it simply means that the causes of such acts are unknown.'[173]

There are passive as well as active sides to such inventive actions. Passively, human beings are subject to them; actively, they interpret, control or produce them. But if such actions or combinations did not persist, they would be ephemeral and without effect; thus, the instinct or impulse provides the material, but persistence of such association of things, acts and ideas make the structure firm. Then, the faith in the effectiveness of such combinations inclines people to use this structure; in many phenomena these instincts and impulses have a mixed result, of 'logical action, scientific inferences, effects of sentiment'.[174] The effect of the instinct for combination may at times appear in ridiculous and absurd ways, but its importance as a major force in social reality cannot be denied.[175]

The residues of the third group, of sociality, which account for the need to express sentiments by external acts, explain a whole range of activity from idolatry to symbolic action of all kinds.[176] These residues are those which impel individuals to conform, accept or enforce, and identify with a group of people in all their various manifestations, from the need for uniformity to asceticism.[177] Residues of individual integrity are in fact complementary to those of sociality. 'To defend one's own things and strive to increase their quantity are operations which frequently merge.' Interests, which are, in reality, a collection of sentiments, could be included in this group of residues, because of their similarity, but they are intrinsically too important for social equilibrium not to be treated apart from the residues as a whole. The main point of individual integrity is that if there are changes, whether real or imaginary, in the social equilibrium, the individual suffers, at least subjectively, and he acts to restore the equilibrium. This happens, though rarely, even if he may gain by the change.[178] This sense of integrity is among the most powerful sentiments of human beings, rooted in the instinct of self-preservation and reaching out into many aspects of life.[179]

The last group, the residues of sex, has little to do with the nature of sexual appetite;[180] they are concerned with theories and modes of thinking associated with sex because they reflect the sociologically important sentiments associated with the sex instinct.[181] Although these residues are associated with a great number of social phenomena, they are particularly active in literature, with religious and

95

moral overtones. The final point that Pareto makes on the sex-residues is that if one considers the immense power that the church held through the spiritual, moral, and material weapons it had at its disposal, and the insignificance of the results of its actions throughout history, one can realize the 'tremendous power of the sex-residue . . .'.[182]

It is obvious, therefore, that the study of the sentiments prevailing in a society, through Paretian analysis, is the most indispensable task of sociology. Without the discovery of such sentiments, much of the observable social facts—which, so far, have been the only kind of material that the sociologist has effectively concerned himself with—remain only superficially meaningful. For example, a study of 'social mobility', however impressive in its statistical volume and technicality, can only show certain descriptive correlations in the characteristics of sections of a population, i.e. in their educational attainments, income ranges, employment patterns and, perhaps, differences between the individual's circumstances and his parents'. Some studies may go further and compare these results with identical patterns in similar countries, and be designated cross-cultural. But the questions which factual studies immediately raise are: what value do people give to such patterns in their lives? and what would happen if the assumptions of their value fail to be meaningful? These are the primary questions of sociological analysis, since the first question refers to the sentiments which make the actual, realizable expectations that individuals may have in the context of their society a reality, and the second question refers to the nature of the sentiments themselves and their interaction with the material conditions of life both in the particular context and in general. Pareto's work is eminently an attempt to answer these fundamental sociological questions, on which the meaning of any systematization of social facts—which is what such studies at best are—depends. The explanation of social facts can only come from a knowledge of the actual sentiments and values that makes them meaningful, *and not from epistemological or methodological assumptions*—a point which is fully realized in both Weber's and Pareto's sociology and remains a philosophical and theoretical confusion in contemporary thought.

Sentiments and values, to use Pareto's and Weber's respective terms, are two theoretically distinguishable aspects of social reality and they both indicate its defining quality as well as its complexity—and, thus, determine the epistemological and methodological assumptions of social scientific knowledge. The whole aim of Weber's and Pareto's analyses of the observable or, more correctly, noticeable complex manifestations of social reality is, it should be evident now, to discover and state this defining quality in order to be able to reduce the complexity into validly explicable terms. What emerges from the whole of their respective methodological as well as substantive discussions on the two primary questions, is of the utmost significance for sociological analysis. Although it may seem obvious at first that the irreducible observable datum of analysis is the behaviour, action or conduct of the individual—and the debate in sociology has always been in these terms—it is not in fact, as we see in both Weberian and Paretian analyses, what one records or is confronted with. The individual does behave, act or conduct himself *but his behaviour, action or conduct is not separable from his account, justification or rationalization of what is designated as behaviour/ action/conduct.* That the contemporary sociologist is unaware of this particular point is glaringly obvious in the various doctrines of behaviourism, whether called positivism or neo-positivism or phenomenology. What has to be judged in this phenomenon of behaviour is its motive not its externally observable manifestations, but both the behaviourist and the phenomenologist impute a motive derived—though differently—from an external source, i.e. another individual's objective or subjective experiences. In both Pareto's and Weber's analyses the imposition of externally derived motivation is shown to be what it is: a subjective interpretation on the part of the 'scientist'. Much has been made also of the superiority of 'action' or 'conduct' over 'behaviour' as a unit of analysis in contemporary sociology, but what has not been noticed is that however the external manifestations of an individual's life are designated, the basic problem that has to be faced is: what do they mean? The meaning comes from *his* interpretation of behaviour/action/ conduct through a commonly understandable language and neither from the scientist's language of concept-formation nor from the philosopher's notion of linguistic norms.

4 Comparative analysis of Weber and Pareto

A comparative outline of Weber's and Pareto's methodological ideas[1] may perhaps be useful for drawing the general implications of their theories for social scientific analysis as a whole, as well as for realizing the complementary nature of their substantive conclusions on rational and sentimental aspects of social experience.

The theme of Weber's sociological analysis, as we know, was the process of rationalization of life, historically and not *a prioristically*. This process involves a change in the meaning of responsible action from subjective rationality to objective knowledge. The two factors responsible for this change, the need for rational knowledge and the use of such knowledge in meaningful action, are the basis of his methodology. We can see in this how intimately Weber's methodology is concerned with his sociological analysis. There is another point which, by removing it from the immediate confines of the subject-matter, makes it a significant methodology. One has become accustomed to expect that, since the immediate inference of a theory leads to a single explanation of action or behaviour, it is the only form of action or behaviour which can be significant for determining the cause of any specific action.

In Weber's case the immediate inference is that, as it is impossible to see the consequences of one's action, the only kind of action which is meaningful to us is responsible or logical action. But, as von Schelting points out,[2] Weber does not make such a conclusion. Although sentimental action, the alternative to responsible action, remains a formal or unanalysed category in Weber's work, it, nevertheless, plays an important part in his definition of action and its

98

sociological analysis. His method of causal analysis is applicable—as may be seen in the earlier discussion of his theory and methodology —to every situation, whether it concerns the subjective action of an individual, the development of an historical event or a 'meaningless' course of natural events. The centre of his methodology is not concerned with any substantive category of human experience, but with the logical structure of individual happenings; and the conflicting value-contents of various religious orientations and actions, the empirical context of its application. A methodology, in the Weberian sense, is concerned with the clarification of the logical structure of a particular kind of analysis or a particular science with the help of its contents, and not with new methods. It can be said, then, that historical or social sciences, like other branches of science, are entirely dependent on the analysis of the substantive elements of knowledge that they embody, through more or less explicit logical standards of objective validity. But, since the natural and social sciences are antithetical on the questions of individuality, values and understanding, and since all given reality is in itself individual, the obvious task of social sciences may seem to be the reconstruction of reality in its endless variety. Weber's argument against this is that the formulation of concepts is not to reconstruct reality in its endless variety, and that the peculiarity of historical-social situations lies in the existence and combination of different historical 'times' in one social setting or the same time period, and in the representation of contemporary as well as anachronistic forms in a single stratification, or in the ideals, of individual groups. It means the impossibility of validly explaining historical or sociological knowledge —i.e. in methodological terms—without the principle of value-relevance, unless one would resort to final metaphysical causes (which are, in any case, experientially unknowable). Besides value-relevance, there is another principle which is crucial for understanding Weber's ideas on sociological analysis, that of effectiveness. But effectiveness as such, i.e. what has happened or has an effect, cannot be an objective principle of selecting facts of analysis, because it has weaknesses similar to those of value-relevance in its literal or philosophical sense, i.e. as subjectively significant perception of reality as such. The argument for the interpretation of value-relevance as an objective principle of selection of facts is an entirely logical inference from the self-evident relationship between the conceptual selection involved in the scientific knowledge of historical-social reality and the actual effects of historical or social developments. Weber's argument is that the historical reality which becomes significant *through* its effects must be meaningful to us in terms of some value; the rest of the total effective reality always remains insignificant from the particular point of view. If this were not so, then we would have to include in an explanation of historical events everything that has happened before without exception—thus losing, so to speak, all sense of relevance. The point is that it is the meaning which a value gives to an action or event that makes it significant in effect, and not its mere existence as a fact. This notion of value-relevance thus has the quality of unlimited generalization for purposes of objective analysis of any action, or event, that is part of social experience.

Indeed, the whole of Weber's discussion of sociological analysis depends on this transferability of the analytical framework of value-relevance from history as description of events and developments—including ideas—to individual behaviour in an everyday context. It also makes sense of his notion of collectivities as individuals and not as a category, which it is in the traditional descriptive sociology. It shows, further, that the basic ingredient of historical-social reality is neither a self-perpetuating idea nor the material destiny of humanity in general, but the specific actions of individuals, either in momentous situations of history or in the confines of domesticity; what is, therefore, significant for sociological analysis is not the metaphysics of human life—which is only subjectively and individually valid—but a means by which we can understand the reality of existence, which includes the subjective reality of metaphysics.

This particular problem of social scientific knowledge would seem insoluble only if one did not understand that the two principles, of value-relevance and effectiveness, are essential concepts of analysis in the combination which Weber puts them. The stages of Weberian sociological analysis thus follow the principle of value-relevance quite logically. First, one analyses and determines the value inherent in a situation, or, to use a term of logic, one clarifies the premise; second, taking this value, or point of view, as the principle of selection, one organizes the facts and interpretations of the case into an ideal typical description. The third and the fourth stages of analysis, comparison of various ideal typical descriptions—whether as norm and deviation or as exploration of aspects—and generalization on interconnections of different elements of the descriptions, become possible only if the original descriptions are made in the ideal typical form, since it systematizes discrete fragments of reality in a meaningful and comparable whole.

Thus, it is obvious, that ideal types, whether abstractly general or empirically specific,* are always descriptive, whether they are constructed on the basis of an alleged causal relation between facts and interpretations, or on the basis of a meaningful relationship which highlights an idea. They cannot become ends in themselves, since they are only relatively valid because of the unconditional acceptance of the premise in their construction. The difference which Weber postulated between meaningful explanation and causal explanation is fundamental to ideal types, indeed to his sociological analysis as a whole. Causal analysis refers to the third and fourth stages, as it is an attempt to determine which one, or which combination, of the several possible value-relevant or meaningful explanations is the correct one. In other words: *which* subjective explanation establishes the causal relationship between the results of an action or actions—which may also describe an event—that we observe and the factors presented in this explanation? There is nothing new in this form of reasoning: we find it in legal judgments, in scientific experimental judgments; it is the form of all rational judgments. What distinguishes it in Weber's argument for social scientific research? It is that in Weber's theory of causal analysis no substantive principles or deterministic postulates are necessary in the way they are in legal and natural scientific experimental reasoning; nor in the way most of the social sciences have generalized the substance of their theories to such an extent that they resemble formal principles. In natural scientific analysis the generalization of substantive principle to a formal level does not matter, because all natural sciences assume a rational determinism of all natural processes and behaviour, an assumption which has not been refuted in their case. In legal analysis there are both substantive principles—like the definition of justice in actual contexts—and formal

---

* I.e. whether they are preliminary hypothetical definitions of types of action or descriptions of historical or contemporary correlations of facts of any kind. For the relationship between the various kinds of 'individualizing' or 'generalizing' ideal types see *Max Weber and Modern Sociology*, chapter 4.

requirements for specific cases to meet this definition, which are given for determining the judgment of validity. With sociological materials it is impossible to make any judgment of validity either by assuming a rational determinism of processes and behaviour or by imposing an *a priori* definition of social reality.*

It is this fundamental transcendence in the contents of social reality of the traditional assumptions of reality, and the indeterminacy of its *a priori* form, that provide the bases of Pareto's ideas on sociological analysis. We have seen that in the first chapter of *The Mind and Society* he rejects the *a priori* principle and chooses the experimental principle of hypothetical premises and inferences which are to be accepted only in so far as they correctly refer to or describe empirical reality. We have also seen that his analysis is threefold, corresponding to the three aspects of socially accepted theories or, in general, interpretations of social reality: objective, i.e. without reference to the author or interpreter; then, subjective, i.e. with reference to the author and the accepter or the subjective interpreter; and, finally, in terms of its utility, i.e. both individual and social benefit or harm accruing from such theories or interpretations. These aspects are always related to the specific contexts and not used for their general classification as an end in itself. We have also seen that, given this point of view, there can be no rigid categorical distinction of actual theories into logical and non-logical; they are distinguished only for analytical purposes. The subjective aspect of a given theory is revealed by the questions: 'Why does a given person assert that A = B?' and 'why does a given person accept the proposition A = B?' Both these questions can be extended from the individual to society at large, in the same way as Weber's 'collectivities' can be treated as individuals. The third aspect, of utility, which Pareto considers essential to his sociological analysis, allows one to keep the theory separate from the state of mind or the sentiments that it reflects. Certain individuals evolve a theory because they have certain sentiments; but the theory reacts upon them, as well as on others, to produce, intensify or modify other sentiments. There is an important proviso here: 'On all that we can know nothing *a priori*. Experience alone can enlighten us.' Pareto's

* This is why sociology does not have the same *apparent* precision as a natural or a legal science, even though the structure or the form is exactly the same.

sociological analysis is primarily in terms of logical and non-logical action. In reality, he says, the two categories are both subjective; they are distinguishable only in terms of whether they use means to appropriate to ends and logically link them together—on the basis of objective factual knowledge existing at the time—or not. Further, a distinction is necessary between such intrinsic, objectively knowable truth and subjective feeling of benefit from them, i.e. their utility, since objective, factual truth does not necessarily coincide with subjective individual or social feeling of truth and/or benefit.

There is a similarity between these points of Pareto's theory of analysis and Weber's concept of value-relevant explanation, which postulates that it is the values that give significance and meaning to facts of behaviour. Both Weber's and Pareto's distinctions go beyond the *a priori* descriptive theories in sociology which fail to distinguish between the objective truth and the social benefit of values. In Pareto's theory we may find ourselves going even further than in Weber's. Pareto distinguishes, first, between (a) logical (or strictly rational) conduct and (b) non-logical (or value-determined) conduct; and second, between (c) value-determined rational conduct and (d) value-determined non-rational (or sentimental) conduct. Weber's empirical research is concerned primarily with value-determined rational conduct, in which value is taken as given, and the analysis is confined in the first instance to the *inferences* which people draw from the value. But his methodological categories are similar to Pareto's. For example, (i) *Zweckrationalität* (end-rationality) is the same as Pareto's logical action; (ii) *Wertrationalität* (value-rationality) is the same as non-experimental action with logical nexus. The (iii) affectual and the (iv) traditional rationality of Weber's scheme would either fit into the logical or the non-logical categories or in the sub-categories of non-experimental with logical or non-logical nexus. These could be easily, and accurately, translated in Weber's terms as: value-determined rational or non-rational conduct/action/ behaviour. It is because of the exigencies of their respective substantive researches that there is any difference in the classification of social action. The basic distinction between the strictly rational, i.e. in which the means-end relationship is entirely logical, and those in which the relationship can be considered rational only when the premise is accepted as unconditionally valid, *is common to both*. The kinds of action, in which rationality in the given context is not in question but in which the relation of the value itself, or its social utility, is not distinguished, are not part of Weber's empirical research; but they form the whole of Pareto's. Thus, we find their theories to be complementary in their empirical contexts as well.

Another complementary point should also be mentioned before we go any further, as it is directly opposed to the contemporary use of reified concepts and indicates why this reification has become inevitable. The point is that the most important means of understanding the relationship between concepts and action is the orientation of action, which is never seen as a part of the material of analysis by contemporary sociologists because their descriptive framework already makes it a theoretical assumption or a fixed premise. Weber discusses the orientation of action as the ethics of responsibility and of sentiment (*Verantwortungsethik* and *Gesinnungsethik*),[3] and shows, specifically, how one should translate an actual action into scientific categories. In Pareto, the discussion of ends and purposes of 'rationalization' and their connection with underlying sentiments is clear enough to show the importance of actual orientations in the sociological analysis of action.

The question which should be decisive for the validity of Weber's and Pareto's theories is: are their methodologies interchangeable? In other words, can one apply Weber's methodology to the Paretian material and arrive at the same empirical conclusions as Pareto without having to modify the methodology; and vice versa? What we may have to modify, as we found in the discussion of the types of social action, are the definitional concepts. In Pareto's work we found the particular category of sentimental action both distinguished and thoroughly analysed. The value-determined rational action, which Weber's sociological analysis is specifically concerned with, can be a strictly logical inference or a 'derivation' for Pareto; but the most important point that becomes obvious is that, for both Weber and Pareto, the part of reality which is sociologically significant is concerned with sentiments, feelings or values as the premise of *logical* or *non-logical* interpretations, which describe, signify, express, or react to them—and not, with the purely rational perceptual description of the universe in which human beings are placed, if it is at all possible, opposed to what is not purely rational and perceptual. The perceptual description of the universe is enclosed in the sociologically important value-interpretations. It, therefore, does not allow one to treat the perceptual—or, in other words, the natural scientific—description of the universe as a substantive norm of perfect rationality, even though it has become a philosophical axiom. The only criterion of truth in sociological knowledge is the framework of rational analysis itself, which can be applied to all the varieties of experience, and no substantively perfect perception of truth can be treated as interchangeable with it. This is an obvious point to make (if it were not so consistently missed by philosophers, scientists, sociologists and dogmatists alike in their various arguments), since any perception of a substantive truth would be governed by the requirements of the form of perception and of the analysis of all perception as knowledge. This in turn would depend on the conviction of the truth of perception and analysis as knowledge. The conviction of truth, as Pareto has with such emphasis and continuity shown, can be either dogmatic or empirical. There is no valid way of reconciling the two, except by analysing the *experimental* truth of the dogma itself. Weber does not seem to go as far as this, since his interest is confined, substantively, to the sociologically significant inferences from the values which dogmas could be said to express, but it is quite clear in his work that values are considered unconditionally valid only for specific analytical purposes, and not as entities which they may be. Values—like Pareto's residues—are made up of ideas and beliefs on things and action and, thus, by their very nature changeable and not formed for all eternity. They cannot therefore be unconditionally valid as entities.

To return to a more specific comparison between Pareto and Weber, we find that the Paretian concept of the 'derivative' or—the more generally used term—'theory' corresponds only to the concept of meaningful explanation in Weber, and not to causal explanation. Pareto takes the rational inference from any kind of premise as immediately understandable, therefore unproblematic. In such cases Weber too considers a meaningful explanation to be a causal explanation. So, to translate Pareto into Weberian terms briefly, the 'derivative' is equivalent to the descriptive ideal type or meaningful explanation. The analysis of a derivative, by comparison with a constructed rational link between the means and the end apparent in it, would reveal either the real means and end or the actual relationship of the apparent means and end.

This is an important point in both of them, for the construction of a rationally possible hypothetical relationship, between the given means and end, allows a comparative analysis of the hypothetical with the actual case for the sole purpose of determining the real relationship of the actual structure of means and end; because interpretations, inferences or rationalizations are mental and not material connections. It raises the primary difference between social reality itself and the 'phenomena' of nature: social reality is created by these mental facts and the phenomena of nature are only recognized and understood by mental perception, i.e. in terms of mental facts and not as themselves. It thus shows up the mistakenness of the assumption that 'scientific' thought is the norm of rationality itself.

The question of values and sentiments is by no means answered by showing a correspondence between the 'derivative' and the 'meaningful explanation'. Weber would analyse the meaningful explanation further to see whether it is related or not, logically, to the given premise, and to what extent; in order both to examine the empirical validity of the value as a theoretical premise and to see, from the deviations that may arise, to what extent the meaningful explanation adequately imputes a cause to the result of the actual action or event.

The validation of the value as a theoretical assumption and the process of causal imputation are inextricably linked in the means-end analysis.[4] If the value-premise is justified in relation to the empirical explanation inherent in or derived from the subjective, meaningful explanation, then the immediate task is complete. If, on the other hand, the value-premise were not justified by the ideal typical or comparative analysis of causal imputation, then a Weberian analysis would seem only to go as far as Pareto's 'derivations'. The derivation in this case would be the same as the value-premise of the action or interpretation which was being analysed in Weberian terms, for the derivation is not simply an argument, it is also a belief or a value. But it would immediately suggest a source beyond the belief or value, to which the apparently illogical connection of action and belief referred. This is the area of Paretian analysis, where the dogmatic or sentimental reasoning opposes any apparent rationality of either beliefs or actions. But it can be analysed and a logically connected relationship shown for purposes of understanding and knowledge and not for intrinsic judgment, because such a relationship between sentiment and action is experimentally as valid as a direct, intrinsically rational one, i.e. between a validated value-assumption or belief and action or conclusion of an interpretation. The framework of analysis in either the case of direct rational relationship of belief, ethic and action and an indirect one of sentiment, values or derivations and interpretations of action* will have to be the means-end relationship; and it becomes immaterial whether one chooses the ideal typical norm of comparison or *the structure* of logico-experimental theories, for they are both based on the same rational relationship of form and content.

Before, however, one could conclude on the interchangeability of Weberian and Paretian methodologies, as the basis of their validity, one would have to examine the comprehensiveness of their material analyses. Weber deals, broadly speaking, with the relations of religious ethics and their social consequences. Pareto deals with examples of dogmatic belief in certain associations of ideas, acts and things with their social consequences. Neither of them finds the pure empirical rationality of certain actions which contribute, together with value-actions, to the formation of social reality at all problematical. They both treat the structure of such rationality as being present in different substantive relations in all human social experience; if this were not so it would be impossible to *explain* social experience, it could only be re-experienced or empathized, but without any communicable judgment of their experiential truth. The existence of languages, concepts and reasoning, and the possibility of their translation, justify their assumption of a *rationally explicable* structure of all social experience. Therefore, what is substantially the subject-matter of sociological analysis and explanation, that is, the problematic part of social reality, is all actions which are in any way value-determined. There are never, as one would readily agree after an acquaintance with their works, any social actions which are totally devoid in content of either the rational or the value element; therefore, an analysis can proceed in actual cases by taking the rational element as understood and translating the value-element (in terms of a rational framework) into a form consistent with the rational element—so that their relationship can be objectively understood.

* Action in this case would be directly reflected in the interpretation, as interpretation would come after action, in the Paretian material of sentimental action.

However, to assume the rational element as unproblematical, for the sake of analysis, is not the same as to identify it in a specific context. The rational element can only be determined *in relation* to the value-element, which brings us back to the inevitability of Weber's definition of sociological rationality and Pareto's insistence on the threefold analysis of 'theories'. In practical terms this means that, if a social action or an aspect of social reality is not immediately understandable in terms of its apparent means and ends, then sociological analysis becomes necessary in terms of the assumption of value or residue as a theoretical premise. Since Weber's work shows that the primary interpretations of life—or 'world-views' which have had social consequences—are directives of action, therefore ethical in nature[5] rather than purely aesthetic entities as systems of ideas, they create interests—material or ideal—which lead to action. Ideas themselves in religious, intellectual, social or political interpretations do not lead to action: a point which is exceedingly important for the development of the sociology of knowledge specifically, since in many ways a body of knowledge which prevails in a society is *its definition* of that aspect of social reality.* Pareto's analysis of sentiments and tradition in society is precisely about the connection between certain associations of ideas, acts and things *as aesthetic entities* and interests and beliefs which lead to action. It is a study of powerful conflicting, discordant factors which, paradoxically, create social equilibrium. The significance of Pareto's theory for the sociology of knowledge are even more obvious than Weber's: for he deals with the *images*—rather than the reality—of knowledge that societies have, and also with their consequences for the formation of the social experiences which create a society. It is a more formidable task to undertake than Weber's, but for sociology their contributions have equal importance because one without the other is an inadequate explanation. One can easily see that their substantive analyses cover the whole area of social interaction in human experience in its two distinguishable aspects; for the impulse of sentimental action is not governed by the circumstances or prevailing conditions, but creates them through derivations; while value-rational action is based on inferences which take account of the circumstances without being subservient to them. Neither of them would consider

---

* This may explain why linguistic philosophers and others take the language of natural-scientific description to be synonymous with knowledge.

the completely rational action, determined entirely by material circumstances, as being a *sociological* problem in itself—for self-evident reasons. Yet, the sentimental derivation which creates the circumstances of action, and the value-rational inference which takes account of them, have similar positions in the relationship of ideas, world view, interests, and action as the two sources of social action, rather than the circumstantially determined rationality replacing one or the other in either of their analyses of social action. The circumstantial rationality only provides a standard for judging the importance of sentiments and values in social experience and reality, for the intertwining of the rational and the sentimental (including value-rational) elements in human social experience is what one needs to understand. The recognition of the categories of rational and sentimental action obviously cannot provide any clue to the way in which they merge in reality: this is the simple beginning of their most complex achievements in sociological analysis.

The categorization of reason and sentiment as two sources of social experience has long been an axiom of knowledge, and the history of social thought contains full development of all that is possible to say in relation to them. The two most important traditions in socio-logical thought, Comtean and Marxian, contain all the ideas that we have been discussing in their discrete forms, but their compre-hensive analysis is to be found—as we have seen—only in Weberian and Paretian sociology because of their methodological clarity and comprehensiveness. The main concept which would designate their common methodological contribution is that of sociological rationality, based on the means-end relationship, applicable to all the contents of social action, from metaphysical ideas to everyday, interpersonal relations. The second contribution, which they both could be said to have made, is the context of meaning in which these actions must inevitably be understood; and the third concept would be their reference to the language of the interpretations which human beings give of their actions as the basic raw material of sociological analysis—not the words or things they use, but the *association* of words, things and acts. These three concepts which one can derive from their analyses—(i) the sociological means and ends; (ii) the context of meaning (the Weberian value-relevance or the Paretian individual and social utility); (iii) aesthetic entities of ideas and inter-pretations (the Weberian world-view or the Paretian association of

109

words, things and acts) constitute, as we have seen, the necessary elements of an adequate definition of social reality. But the adequacy of these primary concepts is not enough; they must also be seen in their various relationships to the basic process of social experience, i.e. in the formation of social actions. The relating concepts in Weber and Pareto, as we know, are interests (material and ideal) and residues and derivations, which mainly form the sociologically problematic actions. In the Comtean tradition we find the institutionalized part of social life fully described, and in the Marxian, the formation of institutions, changes and conflicts in them and in related beliefs and interests described at times with great insight. But the basic questions which are left unanswered in both Comtean and Marxian descriptions are not metaphysical, i.e. either (a) why do human beings institutionalize their social reality? or (b) why should their evaluation or consciousness of material circumstances make any difference to their institutionalization or changing of social reality? They are empirical ones: first, how exactly do the institutions connect with ideas and beliefs both in their static and dynamic states? and second, what is the common basis of institutionalization or change and ideas and action? In the Comtean tradition of descriptive comparison between social systems—historical or contemporary, primitive or civilized as standardized entities*—independent of specific movements or individual actions (in short, their history) which contributed to their formation as distinct entities—that is, between social structures in relation to the functions of their institutions or elements, one assumes that the common basis lies in the Comtean 'Religion of Humanity' or in humanity's duty to improve itself. The 'humanism' of the Marxian tradition seems much nearer to what social reality is made up of—in its notions of the role of material or class interests and of true and false consciousness. Obviously, the common basis of institutionalization or change is ethical in nature, but it is neither exclusively a moral imperative of better civilization, or progress, nor pursuit of one's interests in conflict with others. In the Marxian tradition, since the moral imperative is assumed and reality is seen as the dialectics of the conflict in interest

* What can be the history of a theoretically constructed 'social system' or structure? It is not surprising that in spite of Comte's exhortations, historical antecedents were not included in empirical studies based on his ideas on sociology, as, indeed, they cannot be logically related to the 'elements' of a social system or to the 'functions' of a social structure.

and consciousness, the form that this awareness of reality must logically take is, again, descriptive. It is, thus, invariably an historical description of social change and revolution. In neither of the two traditions can one discover the experiential basis either of the institutionalization of reality or of social revolutionary changes. In both it is a metaphysical *assumption*: i.e. either of man's moral progress in civilization or in man's 'alienation' from his nature. Thus, in neither of them can one draw empirical inferences which will be objective, because the descriptive and illustrative form strait-laces the inferences into speculative generalizations. On what basis, for example, can one ever justify the hierarchy of either the Comtean 'social systems' or the Marxian 'modes of production' as a logical progression of real forms, except by saying that in certain historical cases they may be true descriptions and, thus, generalizable to others. But their generalizability depends, in this case, not on their being true of some cases, but on the metaphysical assumptions of the rational—or dialectical—progress of all human experience. Incidentally, if one considered it a relevant point, 'rational' and 'dialectical' progress would be very similar, for logically the form is: premise (thesis)—formulation of contradictory inferences (antithesis)—conclusion by elimination of contradictions (synthesis). This should not be surprising, if one recalls that 'dialectics' was an earlier term for logical analysis: it simply illustrates the point that neither a change of terminology nor the use of a different illustrative material makes any difference to the conclusion as long as the fundamental premise remains the same. In both the Comtean and Marxian traditions the premise is of moral progress: in the Comtean tradition it is achieved through moral agreement, in the Marxian, through moral conflict; but if they both reach their conclusion of moral progress through a descriptive analysis of seemingly different kinds of data, then, obviously, the empirical materials must be related. It is, therefore, the relations of their respective materials that would allow empirical generalizations to be made on the nature of social systems or social movements and on the relationship between ideas, beliefs and institutionalization and change—and not the metaphysical assumption of moral progress, for the simple reason that what one may describe as 'moral progress' is the resultant of these connections not their *a priori* basis.

111

5 Mannheim and social conditioning of knowledge

Although Mannheim is well known for his sociology of knowledge, his work as a whole was an attempt to merge the Comtean study of institutionalized social reality with the Marxian analysis of historical movements in terms of true and false consciousness. He claimed—in the introduction to his *Systematic Sociology*[1]—that the main forms of 'living together', such as social contact, social distance, isolation, individualization, co-operation, competition, division of labour and social integration, can be 'described and explained on two lines and therefore we have two main sections of sociology'.[2]

These two main sections are 'systematic and general sociology' and 'historical sociology'. The systematic and general section describes 'the general forms and tendencies, as they may be found in every society, primitive as well as modern' and it 'does not deal with these factors of the living together of man in a haphazard way but in a systematic order, following the line from the simplest to the most complex and settled forms of integration—from transitory contacts up to the frame-group'.[3] Historical sociology is similarly sub-divided into 'comparative sociology' and 'social dynamics'. Comparative sociology 'considers a transition from general sociology to dynamic sociology', dealing mainly with 'the historical variations of the same phenomenon'; and social dynamics refer to a historical study of society dealing with 'the interrelations between various social factors and institutions in a certain given society'. It 'has also to answer the question as to where the driving force is to be found which brings about changes in the social structure in a given society':

'sometimes the main changes may be due to the transformation of the technique of production but sometimes a new kind of power organization or some other innovation is the starting point of social transformation and the related cultural changes'.[4] Although, in Mannheim's view, historical and dynamic sociology are 'two principal modes of inquiry in the study of the subject', there is an obvious connection—through the subject, i.e. the individual—between his 'systematic and general' description of psychological institutionalization of individuals and the historical analysis of social phenomena in his view of sociology as the central discipline of the social sciences, or 'a synthetic discipline, trying to unify from a central point of view the results of the separate disciplines' as well as 'an analytic and specialized description with its own field of research', i.e. 'the forms of living together of man, the sum of which we call society'.[5] However, when it comes to the factors of social stability and social change a considerable part is played by human valuation. He says, 'Custom, law, leadership, prestige, represent phenomena in which valuation is inherent, though we do not yet know what valuations are nor how they come about and change.' To the sociologist, he adds, they are 'functions of the social process'.[6] In 'any value-generating situation', therefore, there are: (i) an organism, (ii) a situation and an object; 'the organism is necessary to give meaning to the idea of value' and the situation is 'the immediate occasion for action'.[7] Although he quotes Cooley to distinguish between 'human nature values and institutional values', in his view the latter are 'much greater in number and can only be studied with reference to their social antecedents, that is, their history and the whole situation of the group'.[8]

In his criticism of the Marxist theory of class struggle as a theory on the causes of social change, he first mentions its virtue, that 'it tries to look at society as a coherent structure, as a mechanism, the rules of which, if they are found, can be consistently interpreted',[9] then concludes with a more 'elastic theory': 'everybody is guided by a set of various motivations and it depends on the situation which comes to the fore'.[10]

Perhaps the best statement of Mannheim's view of sociology is in his 1936 article on 'The place of sociology',[11] where he mentions that 'the centuries to come should be dedicated to the moral and social transformation of mankind';[12] and the co-ordination of social scientific problems 'should be made the specific task of a scientific discipline which has as its *raison d'être* the construction of a consistent general theory of society—and that discipline be *sociology* . . .'[13] He adds later that Max Weber's work is 'surely proof enough that a systematic sociology can be constructed on a plethora of empirical data'.[14] The only reason, in Mannheim's view, why it has not happened is that the empirical investigations have lacked a 'methodical basis', 'that the concepts we use are not clearly defined and that in our enquiries we do not keep the picture of the totality of the social process constantly before us'.[15] The special method which he proposes for sociology as the 'theoretical foundation of the social sciences' has three functions: (i) to 'retrace the variability of social phenomena' to certain basic or axiomatic concepts which make society at all possible; (ii) these axiomatic concepts of general systematic sociology should be developed from 'comparative sociological inquiry'; (iii) since the isolation and abstraction of general factors is only part of these 'functions of the social sciences', they should be shown not just in abstract but also in the 'specific, separate constellations which from time to time they assume in different societies in history'.[16] It is, in general terms, the task of Mannheim's 'structural sociology' to work out a 'simplified sketch of the circulation of events' (*Kreislauf*) in different societies (in feudalism, capitalism, etc.)—and not so much for answers to the question: 'What is the primary cause of historical events?' to elucidate such concrete problems as: 'How in certain given type of society, e.g. feudal, early-capitalist, monopoly-capitalist society, do certain factors and groups of factors exist side by side and fit in with one another?' 'How does each of these types of society mould its members (the burglar, the worker, the peasant, the functionary) in such a way that they acquire just those behaviour patterns which the smooth functioning of that particular social system requires?'[17]

The static aspect[18] of structural sociology deals with 'the problem of the equilibrium of all the social factors', i.e. 'what makes different societies work'. In this connection, Mannheim adds, 'even the working of the mind can be correlated with typical situations in the social structure'. Knowledge depends on the limitations of the social structure 'which can only bear a certain amount of rationalization', rather than just on increasing educational opportunities. In the dynamic aspect,[19] the emphasis is on 'those factors which are antagonistic in their respective tendencies' and produce a disequilibrium in the long run, bringing about 'changes which transform the social structure'. For example, he says: 'It is possible that the arrest of individualization in Germany today [1930s], with its regressions to more primitive mental patterns and standards, can be explained as a reaction against too great an increase of the former mental vitality of the people, which has become disproportionate to the absorbing capacity of the existing social order.'[20]

In his essay on 'German sociology (1918–33)', first published in *Politica*, February 1934, he summarizes some of the basic tenets of his view of sociology when he says that German sociology of 1918–33 owed three debts to the dynamic forces of the time:[21] (i) 'the awareness that every social fact is a function of the time and place in which it occurs'; (ii) 'the whole sphere of spiritual life appears in the new light of this constant variability'; (iii) 'besides this visible interdependence between objective facts and ideas ... social mobility and dissolution reacts upon the human psyche', as 'there is no social transformation without a change in norms.' It is this connection between the sub-conscious of the individual and of the group which for Mannheim has greater sociological interest than a description of social and cultural life; and it is—as the sociology of knowledge— a discovery of German sociology. Its significance does not lie in its treatment of these problems in isolation—as undertaken in France, England and America—but by the three approaches mentioned earlier. The study of this invisible dependence of thought on social forces has been studied, Mannheim adds, by Hegelianism, Marxism, by Dilthey and Simmel.[22] It is characterized by (a) 'the ability to master facts and to view them in a theoretical light'; (b) the recognition of history as the development of antagonistic forces—which Marxism owes to Hegel—by emphasizing the influence of the economic factor and class conflict in historical development; (c) the distinction by Dilthey between explanation (*Erklärung*) of natural science and understanding (*Verstehen*) or rather 'sympathetic intuition' of cultural sciences, and its application by Simmel in sociology. Such understanding allows one 'to grasp the meaning of a sentence or ... of a communicative act, such as a work of art, literature, music, etc.; in other words, 'to penetrate into the subject before us'.[23]

He refers to Weber's work as representative of German sociology of this period in his 'formulations of problems and manner of empirical investigation'; and concludes from his work as a whole that 'the manner in which the question was formulated by the materialists and the idealists was wholly wrong': 'we cannot separate spheres of economic and social change on the one hand from the sphere of a change in mental development on the other.'[24] His own interest lies in elaborating 'an accurate technique of situational observation': that is to make a psychological study of an entirely sociological character by watching 'the behaviour of individuals in relation to given situations, and to ascertain how that behaviour changed in response to the most unobtrusive changes in their social situation'.[25] This exact situational observation enables one to identify, according to Mannheim, the type of individual who is characteristic of 'the new era'; further, 'the same method of exact situational observation of mental phenomena led not only to the concept of an eternal super-temporal unity of the human mind becoming highly suspect but also to the notion of the immutability of human logic being challenged.'[26]

Even though Mannheim believed that sociology of knowledge 'purges' the implicit *Weltanschauungen* from scientific and philosophical theories, there remain 'important traces of the fact that our thinking is largely conditioned by our social status and that our logic is a particular and not a general one'.[27] In general, he concludes that 'the problem of the historical evolution of forms of life and types of inner experience' is dependent on this 'dynamic conception of human beings', i.e. the idea that historical and social evolution renewedly shape the individual and his spiritual life, which has made an historical examination of different aspects of spiritual life possible.[28]

In this rather synthetic collection of Mannheim's sociological ideas,* one can notice a traditional division of 'the aspects of sociology'; but the thematic notion is that since the social processes determine the individual in his psychological orientation to his situation, the social processes can first be designated in their *a priori* forms systematically, and then actual societies can be historically examined to justify these *a priori* forms both structurally and situationally. The situational or, more correctly, functional analysis of

---

* Mannheim's writings are not in any sense the development of an analysis or of an idea. One has to try to bring them together with the intrinsic connections that seem to link them.

historical changes reveals and justifies the social determinism of both individual psychological development and of thoughts and ideas as such.

Mannheim's sociology of knowledge—which embodies this fundamental concern with the social contextual analysis of *Weltanschauungen* or philosophical interpretations of life that he had in all his research endeavours from epistemology to education—is the centrepiece of his theory of moral reconstruction of the world through sociological knowledge. In *Ideology and Utopia*, it becomes more specific as 'the possibility of the scientific guidance of political life'.[29] He is concerned in this book with the problem of how men actually think; and how thinking 'really functions in public life and in politics as an instrument of collective action'.[30]

The assumption that is to be justified in this study of public thought is that 'there are modes of thought which cannot be adequately understood as long as their social origins are obscured'.[31] But for Mannheim the examination of an object 'takes place in a context which is coloured by values and collective-unconscious, volitional impulses';[32] yet, in his view, a new kind of objectivity in the social science can be achieved not by excluding evaluations but 'through the critical awareness and control of them'.[33]

From the sociological point of view, the decisive fact of modern times—for Mannheim—is the rise of a 'free intelligentsia',[34] in place of the monopoly of the priests, in the Middle Ages, and its consequence, the elimination of the 'ecclesiastical interpretation of the world'. The free intelligentsia is 'increasingly recruited from constantly varying social strata and life situations, and its mode of thought is no longer subject to regulation by a caste-like organization'. The results of this situation were the freely competing 'modes of intellectual production' and the pursuit by intellectuals of the favours of various publics in place of the earlier intellectually captive population. The opening of the intellectual market also created, in Mannheim's view, 'a profound disquietude' in the modern man and it led to 'those fundamentally new modes of thought and investigation, the epistemological, the psychological and the sociological, without which we could not even formulate our problem'.

Epistemology[35] was the first important philosophical inquiry that emerged with this freedom from the intellectual captivity of an earlier age—with the discovery that 'not only numerous world-views

117

but also numerous ontological orders' existed, and the solution of the problem from an analysis of the knowing subject, 'oriented within the polarity of object and subject'.[36] In periods when an objective world-view remains unchanged, the tendency is to base the intellectual capacity of individuals on objective factors; but in periods of breakdown, the point of departure becomes the subject rather than the object.[37] Then, in course of the development of historical and philological sciences, the necessity of such an analysis of thought 'drawing upon the historically evolving conceptions of the world' arose and it could be said that 'the structure of the subject influenced his world-view'. This led further to the development of a 'psychology of thought', and to the notion that 'the psyche, too, with its all inwardly immediately perceivable "experiences" is a segment of reality'; and these experiences can be known only through a theory of reality or an ontology.[38]

Finally, the full emergence of the sociological aspect of knowledge, in Mannheim's view, 'carries with it the gradual uncovering of the irrational foundations of rational knowledge'.[39] The 'three ways of stating problems', the epistemological, the psychological and the sociological, are parts of a whole situation, 'emerging one after the other in a necessary sequence and reciprocally penetrating one another'.[40] They provide the basis of Mannheim's sociology of knowledge, which may also be designated as 'the collective unconscious and its control as a problem of our age'.[41] The concept of 'ideology' reflects a discovery from political conflict: 'that ruling groups can in their thinking become so intensively interest-bound to a situation that they are simply no longer able to see certain facts which would undermine their sense of domination.' The concept of 'utopia' refers to the situation of certain oppressed groups who are 'intellectually so strongly interested in the destruction and transformation of a given condition of society that they unwittingly see only those elements in the situation which tend to negate it'.[42] The role of the collective unconscious is 'to disguise certain aspects of social reality from two directions'; Mannheim sees his task as indicating the significant phases of the role of the unconscious in the history of ideology and utopia.[43]

The method by which he would fulfil his task is, following Dilthey, 'the understanding of the primary interdependence of experience'.[44] For, 'in order to work in the social sciences one must participate in the social process, but this participation in the collective unconscious striving in no wise signifies that the persons participating in it falsify the facts or see them incorrectly'; and 'the type of participation which the thinker enjoys determines how he shall formulate his problems'.[45] There is, in Mannheim's view, 'a point where the movement of life itself, especially in its greatest crisis, elevates itself above itself and becomes aware of its own limits', which then becomes the object of the sociology of knowledge through 'scepticism and relativism'.[46]

The sociology of knowledge is 'the *systematization* of the doubt which is to be found in life, a vague insecurity and uncertainty':[47] in order, first, to refine the meaning of terms and concepts in thought, and, second, to perfect the reconstruction of social history in such a way as to make the whole social structure perceivable through 'the various modes of observing and thinking': i.e. 'a combination of meaning-analysis and sociological situational diagnosis'.[48]

Although Mannheim claims that his essayistic-experimental studies in the sociology of knowledge are 'a new way of looking at things and a new method of interpretation', and while contradictions prove discomfiting to a systematizer, his repetitions and contradictions play a positive role in one's understanding of his work;[49] his most fundamental idea has been the 'systematization' of concepts. Before, however, we examine this notion, in its context,[50] it will be worth while referring to Alexander von Schelting's main criticism of the sociology of knowledge as 'a new method of interpretation'.

In his comparison of methodology with sociology of knowledge,[51] von Schelting makes the point that the characteristic of Weber's theory lies in his simultaneous view of the absolute validity of the logical form as the inherent norm of valid knowledge and the relativity of interests, directions, the selection of facts and underlying values. The subject, before becoming knowledge, is psychologically, historically and sociologically differentiated and relativized; but *within* these relativized premises, the basis of objectivity is to be found in the formal structure of empirical truth. With this indication of the basis of objective-valid truth, the limits of validity are also made explicit. 'Sociology of Knowledge' deals, in general, with meta-scientific patterns of thought (*metawissenschaftliche Denkgebilde*) and as such has certain parallels with Weber's theory, but the point is that in any objective and intellectual understanding of the world,

119

there are many important questions which cannot be answered by single elements and determinants. There will, of course, be no logical contradiction within such a theory till one makes the assumption that the practical or existential meaning of scientific or a valid theory—or its dependence on real interests or ideological relations with a world-view—has any significance for its validity or invalidity as scientific or valid knowledge. Such an assumption means that factors like the social structure or psychological determinants lead not to a factual truth but to a *normatively valid* truth. Every attempt to make substantive knowledge relative—either through the evidence of its empirical dependence or through the proof of the empirical origin of its categories and formal bases in the mind of a particular person in a particular place at a particular time—is quite meaningless; for the formal, categorical and axiomatic bases of validity belong to the given premises of the investigation itself.

This is a definitive criticism, especially when Mannheim himself admits to this criterion.[52] Today, its interest does not lie as much in Mannheim's confusion about sociological knowledge as in the widespread influence that his notions have had in the last thirty years or so. One can easily detect many of them presented as self-evident truths in much of contemporary writing, variously called structuralist, existentialist or phenomenological contributions to sociology, which are, however, understandable only when one puts them against the background of Mannheim's arguments. In these notions those of 'irrational basis of rational action' and 'systematization' are intimately connected with the use of his concept of ideological and utopian thought. But a concept of rationality underlies all his preoccupations. In his Hobhouse Memorial Lecture (1934), 'Rational and irrational elements in contemporary society',[53] he describes what he means by rational and irrational. Rationality, in his view, is used by sociologists—and in common language—in two senses: 'substantial' and 'functional'. Substantially rational is 'an act of thought which reveals intelligent insight into the interrelations of events in a given situation'; substantial rationality, thus, lies in the 'intelligent act of thought' itself, and everything else 'which is either false or not an act of thought at all (as for example drives and impulses, wishes and feelings, both conscious and unconscious)' is 'substantially irrational'. Functional rationality is determined not by the fact that a person carries out acts of thinking and knowing, but when 'a series of actions is organized in such a way that it leads to a previously defined goal, every element in this series receiving a functional position and role'. It is not necessary in functional rationality that the goal be rational or the optimum of 'co-ordinating the means most efficiently' be attained. The two criteria which determine, in Mannheim's view, whether a series of actions is functionally rational or not, are: '(a) functional organization with reference to a definite goal; and (b) a consequent calculability when viewed from the standpoint of an observer or a third person seeking to adjust himself to it.'

At first sight, Mannheim adds, this distinction does not seem significant, 'as a functionally rational series of actions must in imagination be planned out by somebody and during its execution it must be also thought out by the person executing it, consequently both forms are only different aspects of the same rationality.' But such a rational action includes both plans made by persons 'far removed from the actors' as well as those determined by 'traditionally inherited regulations'. Everything that disorganizes this relationship between a definite goal and action is 'functionally irrational'.[54] 'Self-rationalization', consequently, is the 'individual's systematic control of his impulses';[55] reflection and self-observation being more radical forms of the 'rationalization of the acting subject'.[56]

If the distinction were considered carefully, Mannheim thinks, one would be forced to the conclusion that 'functional rationalization is, in its very nature, bound to deprive the average individual of thought, insight, and responsibility and to transfer these capacities to the individuals who direct the process of rationalization'; i.e. those whose actions can be said to be 'substantially' rational.[57]

Thus, we see that for Mannheim rationality is either an act of intelligence—rather, 'the capacity to act intelligently in a given situation on the basis of one's own insight into the interrelations of events'[58]—or the pursuit of a defined goal—i.e. 'the organization of the activity of the members of society with reference to objective ends'—through self-rationalization.[59]

In order to understand the Mannheimian notion of rationality—as it is, in his opinion, 'indispensable in sociological analysis'[60]—we have to examine his theory of knowledge, formulated early in his intellectual career and presented in his doctoral dissertation 'The structural analysis of epistemology'.[61] He referred to it in the first of his Ideology-Utopia essays, when he said that 'all epistemological speculation is oriented within the polarity of object and subject'.[62]

His fundamental premise is—on the basis of Croce—that every mental, intellectual or cultural field has a structure of its own. Logical analysis cannot even begin until one decides 'what we are to think of the systematic connection among the different branches of logic itself': i.e., whether the method of a discipline determines the form of its concepts or that 'the conceptualization explains the method.'[63] Thus, his main assertion is that the 'primacy among logical forms belongs to systematization': simple forms can be understood only in terms of this concept.[64] The unity of sciences in Mannheim's view is derived from 'quite superficial considerations', methodological and practical; one must, therefore, find their ultimate presuppositions—or 'their constitutive principles'.[65] As the correlation of form and content constitutes the unity of logic, and the correlation of subject and object constitutes the unity of epistemology, the 'correlation of the constitutive concepts' can be regarded as 'quasi-axiomatic postulates' of the particular discipline.[66]

'Systematization' is distinguished[67] by Mannheim from 'system' on the basis of the former being a 'constitutive form' and the latter 'a reflected, methodological form'. From the point of view of the subject: a 'systematization' is created by the transcendent–logical subject and a 'system' by an empirical one. The constitutive character of 'systematization' is defined by the idea that any given thing, any fact of experience, must already be part of an existing systematization if it can at all be grasped theoretically, for the simplest or the crudest way of 'objectifying' an element is 'to range it, to fit it in, with one of these inevitably presupposed orders'. An 'element' is only identifiable, in Mannheim's view, by its 'adopting the structure of the series to which it belongs, and this series in turn consists in nothing but the identity of structure, shared by certain elements that belong together'. 'Systematization' is a 'still to be completed chain of interdependent concepts belonging to the same level'. A system, on the other hand, is 'one of the possible solutions predetermined by the logical structure of the prior systematization'.

The contexts of systematization are called by Mannheim 'the different levels of theoretical systematization', forming a hierarchy. Some of these levels are primary, e.g. ontology; but in others a 'methodical pluralism' may be necessary as even the 'less exact disciplines' constitute a systematic unity in their basic concepts.[68]

The possibility of the existence of a variety of epistemologies is *a priori* for Mannheim because of the 'characteristic structure of epistemological systematization which commits us in a certain way but does not determine our conclusions in a unique fashion'. A structural analysis must ultimately aim at showing the affinities and interrelations among individual systems of epistemology typologically, for epistemology both looks for all ultimate presuppositions and attempts to determine their value. This combination of 'an analytical and an evaluative tendency' is based, according to Mannheim, on two formally distinguished objectives: '(1) to ascertain the ultimate presuppositions of any possible knowledge and (2) to evaluate the cognitive achievement as such on the basis of the evaluations underlying it.'[69]

There is, finally, 'no such thing as pure and independent epistemological analysis; epistemology always makes use of the concrete analyses of logic, psychology or ontology, and adapts them to its own purposes.' The types of epistemology are thus dependent on their respective auxiliary disciplines which contain the ultimate presuppositions of knowledge; and 'construct' rather than describe an object. Nothing but the mode of presentation of ultimate presuppositions, therefore, can explain 'why different solutions of the epistemological problem are possible'. 'For it is characteristic of the constructive disciplines that, although in both only one of the several suggested solutions can be true, the wrong solutions in the descriptive sciences are always impossible as well, whereas in a constructive discipline a wrong answer can be, not true . . . but nevertheless possible.'[70]

The theory of knowledge that Mannheim formulated in the beginning, thus, formally connects the systematic and general conceptual descriptions of 'man's living-together' with the specific, historical and reflective essays, which altogether make up his life-work. He suggests a revision of the thesis—while discussing the positive role of the sociology of knowledge—*'that the Genesis of a Proposition is under all circumstances irrelevant to its truth.'*[71] The duality between 'validity' and 'existence' or 'meaning' and 'existence' or 'essence' and 'fact' is the 'most immediate obstacle to the unbiased utilization of the findings of the sociology of knowledge'.[72] Although the separation of the known from the act of knowing 'in the "idealistic" epistemology and noology' had great value 'in the struggle against

123

psychologism'—and it can be demonstrated that the psychological processes which create meanings are irrelevant to their validity—such a separation in the sociology of knowledge—in which 'the existential position and the corresponding point of view' is a meaningful as well as a genetic relationship—is, in Mannheim's view, a false one.[73] 'A position in the social structure carries with it . . . the probability that he who occupies it will think in a certain way': it signifies not a 'factual genesis' but a 'meaningful genesis', because of the orientation of social existence to certain meanings. In Mannheim's view, 'if a model of this sort had been kept in mind in stating the relationship between being and meaning, the duality of being and validity would not have been assumed as absolute in epistemology and noology.'[74]

Thus, one of the tasks of epistemology is to incorporate within it 'the multiplicity of relationships between existence and validity as discovered by the sociology of knowledge', thereby transforming the traditional notions of epistemology into a new theory of knowledge 'which will reckon with the facts brought to light by the sociology of knowledge'.[75] There is, further, in the sociology of knowledge a recognition of 'the fundamental intent of the mind' which affects one's perspective; in other words, 'what the sociology of knowledge seeks to reveal is merely that after knowledge has been freed from the elements of propaganda and evolution, it still contains an activist element which, for the most part, has not become explicit, and which cannot be eliminated, but which . . . can and should be raised into the sphere of the controllable.' It should be considered, in Mannheim's view, 'as right and inevitable that a given finding should contain the traces of the position of the knower'; the problem is not 'to arrive at a non-perspectivist picture, but how, by juxtaposing the various points of view, each perspective may be recognized as such and thereby a new level of objectivity attained'.[76] From the point of view of the phenomenology of thought—which Mannheim takes—it is not necessary to consider 'knowledge as though it were an intrusion from the sphere of actual happenings into a sphere of "truth in itself" ': knowledge is conditioned by 'the nature and structure of the process of dealing with life-situations, the subject's own make-up (in his biological as well as historical-social aspects) and the peculiarity of the conditions of life, especially the place and position of the thinker'.[77] This 'relationalism' becomes relativism only when it is linked to 'eternal, unperspectivistic truths independent of the subjective experience of the observer'. The problem of relativity is solved, according to Mannheim, by the fact that 'different observers are immersed in the same system' and that 'they will on the basis of the identity of their conceptual and categorical apparatus . . . arrive at similar results.'[78]

Mannheim's new theory of knowledge also emphasizes the 'neutralization of situational determination' by attempting to rise above it through 'continuously broadening basis of knowledge, continuous extension of the self and of the integration of various social vantage points into the process of knowledge', and a search for an all-embracing ontology, in short, through 'group contact and interpretation'; and, eventually, by 'substituting in place of the qualitative and configurative description of phenomena a purely functional view modelled after a purely mechanical pattern'.[79] Formal sociology is the result, in Mannheim's view, of this 'neutralizing and formalizing operation'.[80] But 'the most elementary facts in the social sphere surpass in complexity the purely formal relations, and they can only be understood in referring to qualitative contents and meanings'—and thus one has to refer to the 'perspectivism' of the sociology of knowledge—for 'the problem of interpretation' is, in Mannheim's view, a fundamental one.[81]

The most important task of the sociology of knowledge, however, still remains; that is, 'to demonstrate its capacity in actual research in the historical-sociological realm'. 'It must emerge'—in Mannheim's own words—'from the stage where it engages in casual intuitions and gross generalities' and learn from the methods and results of philology and history of art, especially 'stylistic succession'.[82] Specifically, researches in the sociology of knowledge should 'determine the various viewpoints which gradually arise in the history of thought and are constantly in process of change'. This is a problem of imputation, involving 'a clear conception of the perspective of each product of thought' and relating it 'to the currents of thought of which it is a part', which in turn 'must be traced back to the social forces determining them'. This is going beyond what has been achieved, according to Mannheim, in the history of art itself.[83] Imputation, first, deals with general problems of interpretation, i.e. of reconstructing 'integral styles of thought and perspectives, tracing single expressions and records of thought which appear to be related

125

back to a central *Weltanschauung*, which they express.'[84] Second, it assumes that 'the ideal types built up through the process above described are indispensable hypotheses for research.' Every accessible author, then, must be compared to the ideal types, and 'the imputation in each case must be made on the basis of the blends and crossings of points of view which are to be found in his assertions.'[65] This is 'the reconstruction of intellectual development' aimed at by Mannheim's sociology of knowledge. It is achieved by reducing the first impressions of intellectual history into explicit criteria, which in turn makes a reconstruction of reality possible 'through the controllable determination of facts'.[86] The sociological imputation has, Mannheim believes, still to be worked out after the structure and tendencies of a style of thought have been determined.[87] It has, first, to be derived 'from the composition of the groups and strata which express themselves in that mode of thought'; and, second, should be an explanation of its 'impulse and direction of development through the structural situation and the changes it undergoes within a larger historically conditioned whole'.[88] This sociological imputation—or the sociology of knowledge—means for Mannheim, then, a 'systematic comprehension of the relationship between social existence and thought'.[89]

The whole of Mannheim's sociology is based—as we have seen—on a comprehensive notion of 'the social context'. It replaces all the ideas of valid knowledge, form of analysis and description, relationship between concept and fact, or between theory and reality, indeed the need for a definition of social reality itself, which Weber and Pareto were concerned with in their works. Alexander von Schelting has specifically criticized the theory of *Ideology and Utopia* in his review article[90] on its lack of epistemological as well as empirical viability—without in any way underestimating the importance of the sociological analysis of knowledge, thought and ideology—especially Mannheim's presentation of the hierarchy of ideological stages from a 'simple lie' to the 'whole manner of thinking' being inescapably linked with the thinker's social position—who himself is personally honest. This suspicion then becomes a suspicion of his total world view, including his fundamental categories of thought. From the 'laying bare' of socially determined sources of the individual's misconceptions, it becomes the social function of the forms of thought themselves, then the 'functional' thinking of a social class.

It corresponds to the development from simple distrust to a 'methodical' analysis of the opponent's thinking and, finally, to a general distrust of all points of view, including one's own. In other words, the concept of ideology culminates in the complete *inability* of the representatives of a social class to think in any way except ideologically. Von Schelting also notes that, for Mannheim, the whole area of consciousness is unified, coherent and dynamic, but its bearer is not the absolute epistemological subject of transcendental philosophy, but the social stratum or class. This makes this concept of ideology particularly suitable, Mannheim believes, for a real science of ideologies—the sociology of knowledge. This view of ideologies, as Mannheim himself makes it clear, originated in practice. Von Schelting agrees that it is an important object of sociological analysis, but he considers it extremely doubtful whether it can be simply taken over as a scientific concept and made the central and fundamental principle of the sociology of knowledge; for, if the *total* structure of consciousness is 'ideological', then even scientific thinking—especially social scientific thinking—becomes a function of social factors. If it also means that its objective validity is completely destroyed (according to Mannheim himself) then, astonishingly, how does he manage to offer scientific truth in this theory? If his analysis is more than mere ideology, then it must, as a minimum condition, postulate some possibility of objective validity for the achievements of knowledge. Mannheim does, however, make efforts to establish new criteria for the validity of his *own* ideology, but they necessarily imply the traditional concept of truth which Mannheim claims to have destroyed by his theory—i.e. the total, absolute and universal concept of ideology is at the same level of value as his own ideology—through his 'sociological' logic and epistemology.

These criteria lie in his finding an active principle in the social process, i.e. ideas fulfil a function in that process, and, in the other sense of function, their existential dependence (*Seinverbundenheit*), which rises from being a principle for destroying the truth of the earlier epistemology into becoming a constituent of new truth; the final criterion is almost a principle of inherent truth.

Mannheim's thesis, according to von Schelting, can be formulated as follows: the process of history is a gradual realization of an inherent meaning; thinking participates in this realization and certain 'structures' of thought have a function at every stage of contributing to the next stage of development in the meaningful process. The value or the 'truth' of social conceptions itself makes for their relative validity. It is not clear to von Schelting why the validity of scientific statements should depend on their function in social reality, even though the function may give them some practical[91] value. The traditional assumption of truth underlies Mannheim's view that the function of realizing an inherent meaning can be determined after the event, because without the inference that the evaluation of such 'active' ideas must depend entirely on such a verification, it becomes meaningless. Yet, this 'sociological' theory of knowledge has two implications which the 'traditional' epistemology would never assert: i.e. (i) that the meaning of history or at least the direction of its realization, can be known, or (ii) that it is possible to verify an actual historical change as the 'next step' of the historical development.

The notion of 'function', however, becomes apparently more precise in the concept of 'utopia': a 'true' utopia is distinguishable by the degree to which it enables a social class to break down an old order and establish a new one. In this as well, there is an underlying assumption of 'traditional' truth, the empirical evidence of successful utopias; otherwise, it too becomes meaningless. Finally, it becomes impossible to know, in von Schelting's view, what is the criterion of a 'true' utopia: the 'explosive force of ideas', or their 'adequate' realization in the next stage of history, in the coming of the new order, their 'transforming' power or their realizability in an individual's life. Mannheim himself mentions the difficulties of determining what is true utopia and what is mere ideology.[92]

The fundamental critical point which von Schelting makes is that Mannheim's value-criteria of ideas are altogether beyond logic. They are material criteria, applicable only after the event—'to be found, if at all, primarily in the functions or efficacy of the thought-process in reality, in action, in practice'.[93] However, this is not the end of the matter: the problem of assimilating 'particular' views into a comparative framework is disposed of by Mannheim as the result of the synthesizing efforts of the 'free-floating intelligentsia'. The synthetic products of the intelligentsia form the most divergent kinds of human thought: social philosophies, party programmes, political ideas, ethical norms and mental concepts; in this 'the confusion created by Mannheim is permanent'.[94]

If one made a more general comparison between Mannheim's social-contextual theory of knowledge and Pareto's and Weber's sociological analyses of sentiments, tradition and values, in order to determine his contribution to sociological knowledge, one might find, first, that the fundamental points of Pareto and Weber on the nature of social reality are inevitable elements of sociological discussion. Second, the notion of ideology and utopia as a social dialectic is at the centre of sociological explanation. Third, an attempt to determine the significance of such ideas in the formation of social reality depends not on illustrative insights that a descriptive discussion, such as Mannheim's, provides, but on the possibility and validity of their sociological analysis. The ultimate reference to the ubiquity of the 'social context' in no way contributes to one's understanding of their role in the formation of social reality. For instance, if one compares the Mannheimian concept of ideology with Pareto's concept of derivation, one finds that it is impossible to determine, as von Schelting shows, what is theoretically an ideology. If it is possible to describe an ideology in Mannheimian terms, it refers to the premise of the social context as the total determinant of all action. So, without a specific formulation—on the relationship of social context and ideology, i.e. which aspects in the general social context relate to the defining element of ideology—even an analytical description of actual, historical ideologies is impossible. This descriptive form is in fact the limit of Mannheim's empirical applicability of the whole of sociology of knowledge. The question of validity is a question of the formal *universal* relationship between one category and another; therefore, a comprehensive substantive notion like the social context needs to be defined in formal terms before it can be related to the variability of empirical elements like ideology, derivation, sentiments, beliefs or ideas or the contents of an individual's thought even when it is related to a collective belief. In Mannheim there is no analytic attempt to define the social context; in other words, there is no methodology for analysing the manifest reality of ideologies and utopias. In Pareto, on the other hand, derivations are not explained as self-contained entities of autonomous form and substance, as reflecting miniatures of another amalgam of form and substance, the social reality or the social context, but through *their formal connections of reasoning* to a more constant substantive entity, the residue or the sentiment. The sentiment is the actuality, the residue its concept. Pareto's theory does not attempt to *reify* the conceptual-analytic elements which make up a residue into the describable contents of actual sentiments, precisely because the analytic elements would then lose their formal connections. The purpose of an explanation is to justify the describable connections of reality in a general form, so that such real connections can be understood in theoretical, predictive relationships with real connections in other contexts. Therefore, an explanation must make correct empirical references: its truth depends on it. The form of an explanation is thus important not for itself, but for the clarity of the empirical relationships it envisages. It is on this point that much of sociological thought fails, and it is this point itself which makes the generalized conceptual explanation of sociological theory possible.

Mannheim's conception of ideology is not only comparable to Pareto's derivation but to his whole theory of sentimental action, because Mannheim's ideology is not just an argument—or a specific active belief, which derivation is as well—but the whole of the sentimental consciousness, distinguished from utopia only by whether an argument or action is *considered* successful by the subjectivity of the observer/participant, i.e. in a *value-judgment*. The conception of utopia, therefore, does not make a differential point, but simply describes an aspect of the total ideological consciousness—which is, evidently, the same as the sentimental consciousness. Pareto's analysis of sentimental action clearly shows the way in which ideologies—both as arguments or as associations of ideas, acts and things—can be explained. It further shows—which Mannheim, because of his conception of a total undifferentiated social context, is unable to provide—the variety of analysable contents of the sociology of knowledge, ideas, thoughts, beliefs, literature and art-styles in a framework of action which relates them both to the sentimental areas of consciousness as a whole and to the rational and value-rational differentially. The sociological explanation of this essentially creative aspect of social reality is an answer of the question: why are such creative phenomena neither products of private individual talents (and thus only re-experienceable by others) nor given circumstances (like natural reality) which condition individual lives, and *yet* are, in certain contexts, both private experience and given circumstance? This is the paradox of social reality which needs to be explained. A descriptive analysis, like Mannheim's sociology, on the basis of one or the other aspect of social reality is bound to fail on the question of its generalizability and criterion of truth: i.e. if it is true of one aspect, is it true of the other?

Mannheim's value-criterion of truth cannot, thus, be linked by a descriptive form with the notion of an inherent realizability of the meaning of history either through an existential objectivity of the social class or a formal objectivity of the 'free-floating intelligentsia', if it seems impossible to maintain any proposition free of social-existential determinism—even if the 'inherent' meaning of history is seen entirely in its empirical manifestation, i.e. in events and actions. This is not only because values are subjectively valid and must, therefore, always refer to the individuals concerned or that the 'meaning' of history is a metaphysical assumption, therefore impossible to determine objectively, and again valid only as the subjective belief of an individual; but also because a descriptive form can only account for specific and individual facts *in relation* to a given premise; it cannot explain the relations between the specified facts—however general it may be in phraseology—without assuming the validity of the premise. In Mannheim's theory, the validity of 'the social context' is assumed and relations between the elements of his descriptive analysis are asserted without establishing a definition of the premise, i.e. the social context, on the basis of the value-criterion of truth.

Although there is obvious recognition of the basic principle of values as the meaningful context of truth in social reality, it is not made a formal principle of description as it is in Weber's value-relevance. In fact, Mannheim takes it as being the same as value-judgment and attempts to build a scientific and objective sociology through a 'critical' awareness of it. But a critical awareness of value-judgments as the stuff of social reality was seen by Weber to be a methodological principle of value-relevance, not a generalized version of the individual value-judgment, related to a collectivity of individuals. Mannheim's edifice of misunderstanding is valuable in so far as it proves conclusively that objectivity can never be a function of shared values or common consent or of the existentiality of values themselves.

6 Parsons's 'theoretical' sociology and the solution of the problem of order in society

Parsons's unacknowledged debt to Mannheim's arguments on 'systematization' and the value-criterion of truth becomes clear when we consider some of his well-known criticisms of Weber and his efforts to improve upon Weber's theoretical structure of methodology and definitional concepts. The debt lies not in his theory as such, but in the immediate acceptance and presentation of certain significant assumptions, both epistemological and sociological, which were argued and asserted at length by Mannheim and cannot be understood without his arguments. One can say that Parsons's efforts in constructing a 'theoretical' sociology is a refinement of Mannheimian notions rather than either an 'improvement' on Weber and Pareto—even Durkheim—or an eclectic selection of the best elements in the past 'theories of society'.[1]

The fundamental element of Mannheim's notion of systematization is that 'every concept implies, as its tacit presuppositions which for the most part do not become the object of conscious reflection, certain connections, certain configurations reaching beyond the seemingly isolated concept.'[2] Further—Mannheim points out—conscious reflection on these presuppositions becomes necessary only when a doubt arises on the meaning of a concept and the whole context is brought to bear upon it, as its meaning is 'rooted in its whole context'. In the formation of a new concept there are, according to Mannheim, three conditions: (i) the 'indeterminate' matter of the concept; (ii) concepts already known; and (iii) 'the systematization as a whole as [sic] the general patterns of the entire context'. These conditions lead to all concepts being 'closely correlated with

132

others'—in other words, 'any one concept implies others as having been already posited.' This 'mutual interdependence of concepts' makes a 'continuum' or a 'chain sequence' and 'seems to suggest an infinite progression'. It can be shown, in Mannheim's opinion, that even unsystematic concepts like proper names involve a systematization.[3] Incidentally, the history of philosophy—which, for Mannheim, would include sociology—is best presented as a history of problems where the permanence of problems 'does constitute a kind of supra-temporal unity'. But philosophy is also in the 'theoretical' sphere to which the assumption of systematization applies 'as a guiding principle'.[4]

Thinking in general can be regarded—Mannheim adds—'as an endeavour to find the logical place of a concept in the total framework of the mental spheres'.[5] Pure systematizations are those series of concepts, if their internal connections are traced back far enough, which 'will eventually lead to fundamental concepts or correlations of concepts in which the series in question originated'.[6]

Parsons's contribution to sociological theory arises primarily from two sources. First, a 'critical estimate of Weber's total significance to the social sciences' necessary for his own ideas on sociological analysis—as Weber gave more explicit attention to methodological problems than Pareto or Durkheim. Second, his own development of some of the limits of Weber's methodological 'self-interpretation' to their full logical possibilities—which are neglected in von Schelting's commentary.[7] The two main points of his 'critical' development are: (i) Weber's rigidly developed methodological relations between the natural and social sciences;[8] and (ii) his insufficient emphasis on 'the fact that what is experienced is itself determined, in part, by what scientific knowledge we have and, above all, by the general conceptual schemes that have been developed'.[9] Both these critical points are related, in fact and by Parsons, to the primary methodological principle of value-relevance —but in different ways.[10] The second point, in Parsons's thought, however, makes a methodological interest in values a step removed from a similar interest in theoretical systems, because 'in so far as there is an instrumental interest in the social field, the general conceptual products of this interest will tend to become integrated in the same systems as those issuing from the value aspect.'[11] Value-relevance, for Parsons, 'helps to explain the element of relativism, in

133

scientific methodology, but it is applicable to both groups of science, not to one alone'.[12]

Before one analysed the methodological question of value-relevance in its Parsonian interpretation, it would be important to know what Parsons's notions of a theoretical structure or a conceptual framework and their relation to empirical analysis and explanation entail.

As we can see by comparing Mannheim's notions on systematization, mentioned above, with Parsons's notions of a conceptual framework or a 'theoretical structure', there is a very striking similarity between their assumptions on the 'functional' interrelatedness of concepts as well as on the scientific-theoretical structures developing an objectivity or validity within the subjectivity of original value-choices. On a substantive level, both Mannheim's and Parsons's versions of a systematic sociology form a series of concentric circles of biology, psychology and culture around the social context or the social system. This substantive-definitional theory depends on their suggested solutions to the methodological questions of the relationship between the natural and social sciences and of value-relevance, as they are vital for any possible answer.

Let us, therefore, examine Parsons's view on theory in his article 'The role of theory in social research',[13] which is the only discussion by him on this question—as distinct from repetitious statement. In this article, he states his fundamental doctrines: (a) that no empirical science 'can be developed to a high point without reference to generalized conceptual schemes, to theory'; (b) that one must go beyond 'bald, discrete facts' and 'maintain the existence of relations of interdependence, causal relations'; and (c) that 'such an imputation of causal relationship cannot be proved without reference to generalized theoretical categories'. This assertion, Parsons says further, is 'logically dependent on these categories whether they are explicit or implicit'. Even though 'the inevitability of theory in science naturally cannot be proved on this occasion', he thinks that Weber may be said 'to have proved it' by 'definitively' refuting 'the claims of the German Historical schools that it is possible to have valid empirical knowledge of causal relationships with no logical implication of reference to generalized theoretical categories'.[14] He adds further that 'if generalized theory is essential to science, it does not follow that anything and everything which goes by

134

that name is of equal value'. The failure of sociological theory to achieve this high standard has been due to a lack of adequate distinction between 'the various conceptual elements which either go to make up, or have become associated with, what are generally called theoretical structures in science, particularly in social science'.[15]

According to Parsons, three classes of elements should be distinguished: (1) *Philosophical*, i.e. so far as the scientific content of an intellectual tradition is clearly interwoven with 'elements of a different character', and these elements 'are conceptually formulated'. (2) The type of conceptual element involved in bodies of theory which may be called '*broad empirical generalization*'. 'Such "theories" embody a generalized judgment about the behaviour of, or causes in, a hugely complicated class of empirical phenomena.' (3) Those elements of scientific theory which Parsons would like to call '*generalized analyticrl theory*', i.e. 'a body of logically inter-related generalized concepts (logical universals) the specific facts corresponding to which (particulars) constitute statements describing empirical phenomena'. The use of this concept in empirical research, according to Parsons, 'inherently tends to establish logical relations' between descriptive statements and their particular contents—which he calls their 'values'—so that 'they come to constitute logically interdependent systems'; corresponding phenomena to which they apply can be seen as empirical systems, 'the elements of which are in mutual interdependence'.[16] Further, the 'facts relevant to any system of analytical theory are *never* all the facts knowable about the phenomenon in question, and only part of these are values of the variables'. 'A variable is a logical universal or combination of them', and 'values' are the corresponding particular facts—which can only be obtained by empirical observation.[17] The problem of these undefined and inexplicable 'logical universals' and their relationship with particular facts of empirical observation is immediately 'solved' by him in a characteristic statement:[18]

But it is the essence of the ordering function of theory that any old fact, however true, will not do, but only those which 'fit' the categories of the system. What facts it is important to know are relative to the logical structure of the theory. This is not to be understood to mean that theory should dictate factual

135

findings, but only the definition of the categories into which the findings are to be fitted.

Before, however, examining what in Parsons's arguments could possibly clarify this circular relationship—of facts selected according to a definition and the definition justifying the selection—one should realize that the Parsonian notion of variables and their so-called 'values' is evidently not the same as Weber's notion of ideal types and their inherent values—even in this pseudo-scientific neutral phraseology. It is an over-simplification—or rather a neutralization —of the concept of ideal types. The 'value' which illustrates a variable cannot be derived from the meaning which its inherent value gives to an ideal type and determines the logical relevance of facts to the ideal type. This notion of analytical theory, variables and their values, therefore, cannot be understood by relating them to Weber's arguments on definitional concepts, methodology and empirical analysis but *by relating them to* Mannheim's assertions on systematization as 'the first ordering of the "elements of experience" (in the most general sense)', already 'containing germ of the possible solutions to problems with which the reflecting subject is going to be confronted'.[19] Mannheim's argument on 'The make-up of history and the idea of a system' is particularly relevant to Parsons—apart from the Mannheimian notions of 'logically interdependent' and corresponding 'empirical' systems already incorporated—as Mannheim deals with a similar question on the relationship between the definitional theory and empirical analysis: 'what does typology contribute to the history?'[20] The argument is basically the same—if one can penetrate the mystifying language—as Parsons seems to use for the inevitability of theory in science. So is Mannheim's answer to the question, 'What is required of a structural analysis of epistemology?'[21] Mannheim's definition of structural analysis of a theoreticial discipline as a logical investigation—'primary dealing with the systematization of the discipline in question and seeking to interpret all other components of the discipline in terms of the systematization'[22]—is the only meaning one can give to Parsons's notion of analytical theory. For, Mannheim says further, 'a structural analysis thus defined must ultimately aim at a typology to show up the affinities and interrelations among the individual systems of epistemology (not in their historical interplay but as consequent upon their structure).'[23]

136

Parsons sees four main functions of 'analytical theory': (i) it provides 'selective criteria as to which (elements) are important and which can be neglected'; (ii) it provides 'a basis for coherent organiza- tion of the factual material thus selected without which a study is unintelligible'; (iii) it provides 'a crucially important guide to the direction of fruitful research', by revealing 'the *gaps* in our existing knowledge and their importance'; (iv) it provides 'a cross-fertilization of related fields of utmost importance' through 'the mutual logical implications of different analytical systems for each other'.[24]

In these functions, one can easily see that the first two belong to sociological description and the last two to sociological theory *based on empirical causal analysis*. Parsons recognizes all the elements of sociological analysis, but one cannot help noticing that he fails to distinguish the steps by which sociological theory can be constructed, for in his distinction of 'the various conceptual elements of theoretical structures in science'[25] one finds a confusion of analysis. One recog- nizes the philosophical and the 'broad empirical generalization' as two distinct categories; but in the third category of elements, which he calls 'generalized analytical theory'—and which is the most crucial for the relationship between theory and empirical research—he makes no distinction at all between the theory or generalization based on empirical analysis, i.e. arrived at through induction, and the theory based on deductions from *a priori* assumptions. Inductive theory is in fact absent from Parsons's formulation altogether; the 'broad empirical generalization' does not by itself become analytical theory for the simple reason that its definitional aspect remains unjustified as a conceptual scheme. Its status, in so far as it is not an empirical generalization and becomes a definitional theory, is the same as the deductive or the Parsonian 'analytical' theory, which should justify the last two functions proposed by Parsons. Therefore, both 'broad empirical generalization' and deduction from *a priori* assumptions become an arbitrary descriptive theory based on a subjective judgment of facts by the theorist; or a set of concepts which must be illustrated by examples and never be tested by empirical analysis. The kind of deductive sociological theory which would make Parsons's views on the role of theory in sociological research objectively valid as well as logically consistent must be inferred from broad empirical generalizations and not from *a priori* assumptions, as such inferences can be validated on both empirical and logical grounds by the

K

137

justification of the generalization as a valid premise through further analysis; while the *a priori* assumption cannot be, as it derives its justification from the subjective judgment of the theorist. The kind of reasoning seen in this article permeates the whole of Parsons's work. It has become glaringly obvious in his recent misreading of Weber—because one is momentarily free from the entangled web of his 'theoretical' language which hides the banality of his reasoning elsewhere—as a 'social evolutionist'.[26] Indeed, his combination of Durkheimian theory of sociological description—i.e. recording and classification of the structure and function of a 'social organism' (which he prefers to re-name 'social system')—with Weberian definitional concepts, as the basis of his own theory of social action, could not have been possible without this kind of *unanalytic* reasoning.

In order to understand Parsons's criticisms of what he calls 'the Rickert-Weber-von Schelting position',[27] one has to go back to his earliest essay in sociological theory, 'The place of ultimate values in sociological theory'.[28] In this essay many things which are obscure in Parsons's later writings show up clearly, and enable one to judge his contribution to sociological theory quite decisively.

First of all, there is clear evidence of his failure to distinguish between definitional and empirical concepts. In this essay he formulates his now famous theory of voluntaristic action, which became the basis of his thesis of convergence of theoretical structure in *The Structure of Social Action*, and which justifies the use of the action frame of reference rather than that of behaviourism in his later work. In spite of this notion of 'voluntaristic' action, we find—as a second revelation—his actual frame of reference in all his writings to be essentially behaviouristic, in spite of his deliberate introduction of ultimate values, subjective and objective points of view, etc.[29] However, at present we are concerned only with Parsons's general failure to distinguish definitional from empirical concepts.[30]

The aim of Parsons's theory of voluntaristic action, which is presented in the 'ultimate value' essay, is to distinguish between the subjective and the objective points of view. He defines the subjective point of view as that 'of a person thought of as acting himself'; and the objective point of view as that of an outside observer. These, he says, should be kept clearly distinct and adds that 'only on this basis is there any hope of arriving at a satisfactory solution of their relations to each other'.[31]

'End' and 'value' are, according to Parsons, subjective categories. 'The subjective analysis of action', in his view, involves the schema of the means-end relationship; and it is the most 'favourable' starting point of such an analysis.[32] The idea of means-end relationship, one may notice, is borrowed specifically from Weber's methodology, but in its application he takes a direction completely different from Weber. For empirical analysis on the basis of a general methodological principle like the schema of means-end relationship, he finds it—unlike Weber—a legitimate exercise *generally* to categorize and define ends and means to be found in real situations.

An 'end' is defined by Parsons 'as the subjective anticipation of a desirable future state of affairs towards the realization of which the action of the individual may be thought of as directed'.[33] Ends, he says, are a factor in action; they are thus an 'analytical category'. He adds: *'If the means-end relationship, involving this sense of the term "ends" is employed in this analysis, it is clear and should be pointed out at the outset that the whole analysis involves a metaphysical position of a "voluntaristic" character'*[34] (my italics). The norm of this schema is rational action. In this norm 'neither the knowledge of the relation of means and end on which action is based nor the application of that knowledge comes automatically'; *'both are the result of effort, of the exercise of will'*[35] (my italics). 'The concept of action'—Parsons goes on to say—'has no meaning apart from "real" ends and a rational norm of means-end relationship'; it dissolves into mere behaviour; neither has any meaning without 'obstacles to be overcome by effort in the realization of the norm'.[36]

However, these concepts, in his view, are not empirical generalizations but 'ideal types'.[37] In fact they are neither empirical generalizations nor ideal types, but a set of hypothetical or, rather, speculative *substantive* definitions: they cannot be ideal types in the empirical sense, because they refer to no specific context; nor can they be ideal types in the definitional sense, because the primary principle of definitional ideal types, or 'pure' types, is that they treat the four categories of rationality as being fully realized in the corresponding sets of definitions of actions, i.e. they have a premise of logical consistency with the particular category of rational action. If Parsons has rejected the categories for his theory, it does seem rather strange that he should use the phrase 'Max Weber's term, "ideal types" ', and thus imply its Weberian justification.

Further, hypothetical definitions have to be empirically validated to become empirical definitions, and the ideal type is a methodological means for achieving this validation. Parsons's system of hypothetical definitions—either in the tentative form of this essay or in the elaborate façade of his later 'theoretical' contributions—is an unnecessary and, in fact, useless restriction on the concept of ideal-type. A hypothetical definition may become a definitional ideal type, if it is also possible to construct an empirical ideal type for the causal analysis of an actual situation which would allow one to arrive at a scientifically valid generalization. But, to assert that a definition which one presents of a *possible* situation is, by virtue of one's presentation, an ideal type, shows a complete incomprehension of the processes of causal analysis, let alone of Weber's methodology. Even though the whole of the exercise involved in the 'ultimate value' essay is derived from Weber's principle of means-end relationship as the basis of causal analysis, it is glaringly obvious how little Weber has, in fact, to do with it. The definition becomes straight away a generalization, even though it is called an ideal type. We shall soon have occasion to see how this is.

Therefore, to continue with Parsons's theorizing. 'Deviations from the rational norm', he says, 'will be explicable in one or more of three sets of terms: ignorance of intrinsic relationships, lack of effort, or presence of obstacles beyond the power of the actor to remove.'[38] After detailing 'the principal types of elements of the means-end relationship', he goes into 'their inter-relationships in systems of action'.[39] At one end are those elements 'which are ultimate means or conditions of action, but not, from any point of view, ends'. At the other end is the 'factor of ultimate ends, which are, looked at in intrinsic terms, ends in themselves and not means to further ends'.[40] 'The standard of rationality applicable to the intermediate sector of the intrinsic means-end chain is that of efficiency'—which is, for Parsons, 'a matter of intrinsic adaptation of means quite apart from other considerations'.[41]

But efficiency is quite obviously a substantive definition of rationality because it would depend on the situation and its context: it cannot define the form of the situation as rational, irrational or non-rational, however 'intrinsic' it may be to the situation, because the judgment of efficiency can only be made on the basis of the extrinsically determinable form of its logicality and on comparable experience of other situations. Unless, of course, one envisages that situations are rational beyond experience or logic, if they are 'intrinsically' efficient.

The ultimate ends are, however, what Parsons is mainly concerned with in this essay. Therefore, let us now consider his discussion of 'ultimate ends'. He says, 'in so far as individuals share a *common* system of ultimate ends, this system would, among other things, (i) *define what they all held their relations ought to be*; (ii) *and would lay down norms determining these relations and limits on the use of others as means, on the acquisition of power in general.*'[42]

Then Parsons adds what is the briefest possible solution to the problem of order in society—which is, according to his own often repeated statement, the beginning of his massive sociological-theoretical investigations and formulations: 'In so far then as action is determined by ultimate ends, the existence of a system of such ends common to the members of the community seems to be the only alternative to a state of chaos—a necessary factor in social stability.'[43]

The 'safest procedure', according to him, for sociologists would be to take the diversity of value-systems as a starting point, to determine 'what are the ultimate value-systems relevant to understanding action in a given society at a given time'. Then it would be 'quite legitimate to attempt to discover relationships between such systems—to classify them according to types, to establish genetic relationships'. But, we are once again cautioned, 'all this should be done with the greatest of care to avoid the common fallacy of reading arbitrarily into the facts a tendency to the ultimate realization of the investigator's own particular values.'[44]

This admonition strikes an illogical note if one considers that the aim is to realize the metaphysical value of voluntarism. However, if one is concerned with the more general question of relationships between different value-systems and their classification into types, to establish 'genetic relationships' one can as legitimately ask of Parsons: in the first place, how does classification into types lead to genetic relationships; and, in the second place, if one takes the principle determining the types of action to be voluntarism, how does voluntarism become the 'genitor' of these types of action? Parsons obviously thinks—like Mannheim—that by announcing his metaphysical position or value-premise—in this essay, as voluntarism—he will

141

have answered the question. If, however, one takes it that he is assuming Weber's argument on values as the starting point of action, then, again Weber is not relevant to him. For, even though a metaphysical position or a non-scientific assumption—whether of the participant or of the participant/investigator—is made explicit, it does not validate or invalidate a theory on scientific grounds. The validity of the theory, in such cases, depends on how the value-position or assumption has been related as a theoretical premise to the empirical elements of the theory. If the assumption is irrelevant—as strongly suggested by Parsons's admonition to the sociologist to be objective in his empirical investigation—to the theory as a whole, then one can ignore it, and judge the theory on its empirical merits.

Let us see why Parsons's metaphysical position of 'voluntarism' is in fact irrelevant to his theory of voluntary action and its relation to ultimate values.

First, although Parsons's aim in contributing to sociological theory is to *solve* the Hobbesian problem of order, the metaphysical position of voluntarism is not related to it in any empirical sense except as a morally chosen means to a moral-philosophical problem. It is surely obvious that one cannot solve a moral or philosophical problem by saying it is the only alternative to its opposite state and claiming it as a scientific solution. The problem of social order is not a scientific problem, but an experiential one; and voluntary action can only be considered as a means of subjective experience to achieve this extra-scientific aim. This kind of subjective commitment—it should be obvious to anyone acquainted with Weber's work—is quite different from one's commitment to the principle of value-relevance. Therefore, to make his theory value-relevant to—rather than value-determined by—the philosophy of voluntarism, Parsons would have to show on what principle he has selected the various empirical ends and means—in however definitional or abstract a form—to justify the *a priori* assumption of voluntarism. The only justification which he gives is that 'in so far as action is determined by ultimate ends, the existence of a system of such ends common to the members of the community seems to be the only alternative to a state of chaos.'[45] This assertion is not a justification of the various categories of voluntary action *in terms of the voluntary or rational action as the principle of life*; because such a justification would mean

142

a demonstration of the whole range of action to be more or less rational, i.e. deliberate in means and in desired end—according to his own definition. Parsons in making the categories of means and ends, in fact, only assumes—he does not demonstrate—that such is the case. This means that there is in reality no connection between the metaphysical principle he professes and the empirical means and ends which he categorizes. He can, therefore, quite easily construct such a classification of voluntary actions without in any way involving a metaphysical position: it will be equally arbitrary.

Second, because voluntary actions are empirical data, it is quite legitimate to analyse them either as autonomous units or parts of a larger unit; but to make a metaphysical position explicit in relation to them must mean that one's aim is to justify it on the basis of valid evidence. So, although Parsons seems to make the empirical part of his analysis 'value-free' by making his metaphysical assumption clear, he in fact makes it only too clear that it is quite unnecessary— not only by the 'dogmatic' procedure but also by the 'hypothetical' procedure.

Since it has proved unnecessary, therefore irrelevant, we can now judge the theory itself on its empirical merits. To take an example, religious action, according to Parsons, 'forms along with action in immediate pursuit of ultimate empirical ends and with institutions, a third aspect of the incidence of ultimate ends on social life'. He adds that these three phenomena are not to be taken as three 'factors', but 'rather as three modes of expression, in different relations to action, of the same fundamental factor—the ultimate common value-system'.[46] Religious ritual—which forms 'the most difficult question for this paper'—'although falling outside the realm of applicability of "scientific" norms of rationality in the full sense, is still . . . subject to analysis *in terms of what are, in a sense* rational norms'[47] (my italics). This sentence is a prize example of academic compromise,[48] which seems to have become an increasingly popular means in contemporary sociology of reconciling facts which do not seem quite reconcilable in an apparently comprehensive theoretical scheme.

Parsons has confined sociological analysis in this essay to the determination of the ultimate value-system relevant to understanding action; and the discovery of relationships between them—i.e. to classify them into types—for establishing genetic relationships.

But it becomes quite clear that his beginning, from the relevance to the value 'of ultimate ends as a necessary factor in social stability', and classification of such ends, are only preliminary steps towards objective generalization *on the relevance of ultimate value systems to the understanding of action in a given society at a given time*—to paraphrase his own statement. In the two divisions of his essay, 'Of the means' and 'Of the ends', Parsons has taken the analytical concepts of means-end relationship and comparison with rational action from Weber's methodology not to analyse actual relationships but to build an elaborate framework for 'proving' hypotheses on the assumption that a 'common system of ultimate ends' is a necessary factor in social stability. In Weber we do not find that there is such a dogmatic relationship between a metaphysical value and sociological analysis, let alone a 'genetic' link between a 'metaphysical' position held or introduced by the investigator and sociological knowledge. In fact, the missing link in Parsons's 'theoretical' sociology is the empirical causal analysis of the hypothesized relationship between ultimate values or ends and action; for without it, the conclusions arrived at on 'genetic' relationship would remain value-judgments or dogmatic assertions.

The basic difference between Weber's approach and Parsons's should be clear now: while Weber would formulate a logical structural relationship between means and ends of social action which held for all specific and individual actions and situations, Parsons would give us specific means and ends and would also specify their relationships. While the sociological rationality of action in Weber's theory would be determined by the value inherent in the action itself, Parsons would define the rationality in terms of a 'metaphysical' position which did not have even a logically, let alone experientially, inevitable relationship to the particular means and ends which he formulates, but which *seems* to him to be the only alternative to an undesirable state of affairs.

Further, while Weber would leave the question open, that is, whether the existence of a system of ultimate ends or values is a necessary factor in social stability, Parsons would proceed by first assuming it to be a necessary factor. Moreover, his question 'what are the ultimate value systems relevant to the understanding of action?' becomes a question of simple enumeration, when he has already taken ultimate ends, institutions and religion (including its

144

ritual element) to be but three modes of expression in relation to action.

One is hard put to discover any way—except itemized enumeration of pre-defined 'empirical' entities like ends, systems, values, norms and action—in which Parsonian theory would allow sociological analysis. If such enumeration, or construction of such ideal types as we find in this essay, or a system of abstract ideal types or 'typologies' as he suggests in his Introduction to Weber's *Theory of Social and Economic Organization*,[49] were the only ways in which sociology could develop, then we can easily understand why Parsonian ideas have contributed little, except banalities in solemnly high-flying jargon, to the understanding or explanation of social reality.

His notion of rationality—which as a concept is at the centre of sociological analysis—is, as we have seen, a question of 'effort' or 'will' because he wished to emphasize the voluntariness of action and link it to rationality; but, again, one can immediately see that 'with the best will in the world' one does not achieve the most rational action, and whatever degree of rationality and irrationality one does achieve is determined by the context of the given end and means and not by one's effort or will. The synonymity which Parsons asserts between 'rational' and 'willed' action is only understandable in relation to Mannheim's notion of substantial rationality as an intelligent act of thought[50] and the three theses he presents in his 'Rational and Irrational Elements in Contemporary Society': (i) 'the contemporary social order must collapse if rational social control and the individual's mastery over his impulses do not keep step with technological development'; (ii) 'the unfolding of reason, the ordering of impulses and the form taken by morality, are by no means an accident': 'it depends on the problems set by the existing order of society'; and (iii) societies which existed in earlier epochs could afford a certain disproportion in the distribution of rationality and moral power, because they were themselves based on precisely this social disproportion between rational and moral elements. These three Mannheimian theses present the preoccupations of Parsons with voluntarism and the problem of social order in much simpler form, and with the same inter-connections of 'scientific knowledge' as 'normative' action, intelligent act of thought or deliberately chosen means and ends, and social stability or the solution to the problem of social order.

145

The question of rationality in sociological analysis is linked, as we have seen, with the question of values in many different ways: science and reality, objectivity and subjectivity, sociological knowledge as norm of action, intelligent or voluntary action and 'irrational' impulses, social stability and change, social order and chaos.

It all centres on the problem of how evaluations, value-orientations, beliefs and non-empirical ideas can be related to rationality and logic. It has not entirely been a question of how the structure of rational knowledge can be used to understand or explain the value-related sphere of human existence with Mannheim and Parsons, as it was with Weber and Pareto. With Mannheim and Parsons the question has become: how is rationality a norm of social reality?—not epistemologically or empirically, but existentially. Both of them answered it in remarkably similar ways. For Mannheim rationality is a sign of social progress and can be recognized on the basis of intelligent, existential awareness of values, which play an important part in the formation of the social 'context'. For Parsons, rationality is the social part of human evolution, and it can be recognized by a theoretical awareness of the deliberate, voluntary choice of means and ends, which human beings make in terms of their shared values. In both Mannheim and Parsons the theoretical discourse on the social inter-relationships must be in terms of values—but only ultimately. Because, the theoretical structure becomes the immediate concern of the discussion and it dictates a systematic order of thought to the concepts and ideas that may be formulated. Without this theoretical discussion intervening between values and action, there can be no objective recognition or knowledge of real forces or factors, leading to rational action. Thus, theoretical knowledge becomes for both of them the basis of rational *action*. In Mannheim, theoretical knowledge is a manifestation of the social forces themselves, but it clarifies the eternal problems of existence. In Parsons, theoretical knowledge derives from the values of the society in which it occurs, but it becomes 'normative' as pure rational action.

These existential interpretations do not, in spite of their plausibility on a superficial level, answer the questions of valid explanation of value-related aspects of social reality—which, incidentally, include scientific knowledge as a social belief. The fundamental solution to the problem of explanation remains that of the Weberian principle of value relevance—whatever description it may take in different theories.

In his review[51] of von Schelting's *Max Webers Wissenschaftslehre*, Parsons makes certain criticisms of the Weberian view of sociological analysis, which remain fundamental to all his own 'theoretical' endeavours. They reveal a fundamental misunderstanding of value-related explanation in sociology—faithful to the original confusion of existence and understanding, which has had a retarding effect on the whole of sociological knowledge.

He writes that the net result of Weber's methodological work has been to go a long way towards bridging the division between the logic of the natural and the historical-social sciences with his 'insistence not only on the necessary role of general theoretical conceptualization, but on the abstractness of this theory in the case of both groups of sciences'. Otherwise, the 'obvious concrete differences between their subject-matters tend to force the methodologist into maintaining an untenable logical distinction between the sciences'.[52]

His criticism of Weber and von Schelting is that 'they have not completed the process'. It is applicable, in his view, on two main points: (i) 'Weber, following Rickert, tried to maintain an untenable distinction between the relative roles of generalizing and individualizing concepts in the natural and the social sciences respectively'; (ii) 'both Weber and [von] Schelting failed to see that the "elements" and "general laws" of the schema of proof are not homogeneous categories, but that under each two different types of concepts are included.'[53]

The Rickert-Weber position, according to Parsons, is that the natural sciences aim at forming systems of general theoretical concepts; in the social sciences such concepts 'serve only as means to the understanding of unique historical individuals'. To Parsons, it seems that the 'bifurcation' is in 'the direction of the scientist's interest': 'One group of sciences, such as theoretical physics and theoretical economics, is primarily concerned with building theoretical systems, while the other, like geology and history, is concerned with understanding unique historical individuals.' 'In the one case', according to Parsons's understanding, 'general concepts constitute an end in themselves; in the other as means.' This distinction as 'the two bases of classification of the empirical sciences', which do not

147

coincide but cut across each other—lies 'at a deeper methodological level' (he does not state why) than that between the natural and the social sciences; Rickert-Weber-von Schelting thus make 'an unwarranted assimilation of the two distinctions to each other'.

There are a number of misleading arguments inherent in this criticism. First, a factual one: the Rickert-Weber-von Schelting distinction is on the basis of absence or presence of value, or subjective meaning and individuality in a particular scientific subject-matter, as the key to its explanation or understanding. It is not, and cannot be, based—as Parsons implies—on either the traditional distinction of subject-matters or the Parsonian notion of 'scientist's interest' in theorizing or describing. It may coincide with the traditional categories of subjects—in spite of Parsons's assimilation of theoretical physics and theoretical economics into one category and of geology and history into the other—because the character of natural reality is not determined by human valuation or meaning, nor has its explanation any significance if made in terms of the unique characteristics of specific phenomena; while the character of social reality is determined particularly by these factors. The 'direction of the scientist's interest', for example, in theoretical economics does not make economic activity itself devoid of human valuation or individual choice, but simply makes valuation or choice a remote rather than an immediate factor. In so far as any sphere (whether intrinsically value-related or not) is value-relevant, it has to be understood in social scientific terms, i.e. in which general concepts serve as means to individual explanation; and vice versa.* Geology and history, therefore, cannot, because they are both descriptive, be put in the same category. Description does not necessarily relate to value or meaning or to the individuality of the subject-matter: it can be general, analytical and unrelated to human values or meanings, as all *natural* scientific descriptions are. History is social scientific, precisely because it must take these factors of value and meaning,

* For example, if a cult of worship arose on the basis of the geological knowledge of the earth's crust, it obviously cannot be understood geologically. Although a value has attached itself to a scientific knowledge, the substance of the scientific knowledge itself cannot, in any empirical sense, be connected to the value. It becomes an object of the value, and thus makes the scientific substance value-relevant, even though it remains 'scientific' in the strictest sense. This is a simple enough point of Rickert's theory of value. It is strange that Parsons should have chosen to ignore it.

148

uniqueness and individuality into account; geology, if it deals with the chronology and structure of one unique or individual phenomenon, the earth, does not take into account any of the multitude of human values and meanings which the earth is subject to.

Therefore, Parsons's distinction based on a deliberate use of the ambiguity in the term 'direction of the scientist's interest' is entirely fallacious. In this context it simply means that the analytical part of different sciences—or different analytical sciences themselves—are in one category because they are conceptual and abstract—or 'theoretical', and not because they seek general *relations* of phenomena; and the descriptive parts or descriptive sciences are in the other because they are descriptive and factual, and not because they seek the *specific* relations of phenomena. In either of the Parsonian categories, 'theoretical' or 'individual', the fundamental difference in the characters of natural and social reality is not accounted for. Analysis leads, inevitably, to the explanation of *relations*, whether it deals with conceptual hypotheses or specific descriptions; therefore, the categories of 'theoretical' or 'individual-descriptive' cannot even superficially form a methodological division of sciences. The unity of all science, which presumably is what Parsons has in mind, is not created by the scientist's psyche or culture, but by the structure of rational analysis.

Parsons's second criticism—that the 'elements and general laws' of the schema of proof 'are not homogeneous but include two different types of concepts'—is directly related to this confused distinction of the theoretical and the descriptive, and easily disposed of. He gives the example of the generalizing ideal type, and says that it is ambiguous in the sense that it may either mean a 'hypothetical "objectively possible" fictional entity', i.e. a unit; or it may mean 'part of the historical individual'.[54] He adds that Weber's theoretical work 'tended to bifurcate in these two directions, with the former tendency predominating in his explicit formulations'. But he feels that 'even with these corrections, the substantive theoretical propositions of science, both natural and social, are subject to the relativity inherent in their relevance to value.' At this point Parsons clearly identifies his 'direction of the scientist's interest' with Weber's value-relevance,[55] and relates both to his division of sciences into the 'theoretical' and the descriptive. But when Rickert, Weber or von Schelting use the concept of value-relevance as the distinguishing principle between natural and social scientific description and explanation, they are referring generally to human evaluations and their social consequences; and not to the fact of whether a particular science, in a restricted context (like theoretical economics or sociology), seeks general uniformities *or* description and classification of the constituents of a particular phenomenon. Parsons's inability to accept the concept as it is presented in their common formulation is because he attributes an 'analytical' role to descriptive or substantive concepts like 'the historical individual' or 'the ideal type'. He does not separate the methodological role of their formal characteristics—derived from the fundamental 'analytical' concept (or principle) of value-relevance—from their contents. He thus confuses the role of general 'analytical', i.e. methodological, with the role of general 'descriptive', i.e. substantive, concepts in both natural and social sciences, as well as definitional and empirical concepts.[56] The two kinds of general concepts are both abstract in their form, but their aims and their roles are different: the methodological concept defines the form of the analysis, while the descriptive concept defines the form of the contents.

Therefore, when general substantive concepts—which, in effect, is what Parsons is concerned with—are considered not an end in themselves but means to the understanding of unique *historical* individuals (not *natural* individuals, like the earth), it is because the determination of uniformities of historical or social behaviour still leaves the real phenomenon under investigation empirically unexplained; the empirical reality of historical-social facts is their meaning in terms of the values they refer to, not their common classifiable characteristics. Thus, what is in the nature of a general law in natural sciences—that is, when it corresponds to a uniformity of social behaviour in the social sciences—is only *an element* in a meaningful but unique historical individual. An historical individual is, in itself, a combination of elements, in which some elements are common to other such constructions and some are unique to it. Where, then, is the contradiction, which Parsons sees, between an ideal type as a 'hypothetical objectively possible fictional entity'—a definition—and a part of an historical individual or its 'general property'—and an empirical element?

In reality, Parsons's exegesis of Weber is based on a very simple traditional relationship of the theoretical and the descriptive: the 'theoretical' provides 'a basis for coherent organization of the factual material',[57] and therefore governs the descriptive. The first 'function' —according to his own formulation[58]—of providing the selective criteria, is, in his actual discussion, inherent in 'the scientist's interest': a term which can mean both the objective aims and purposes of science, general and particular, and the subjective choice of the scientist. This he equates to the Weberian principle of value-relevance in a way which leaves little doubt about its primary influence: Karl Mannheim's theory of values.

How can a discussion of values in general methodological terms, which we find in Rickert, Weber and von Schelting,* become embedded in the psychological orientation of the scientist,[59] except through a confusion of the compositeness of existential reality and individual subjective view *with* the logical distinctions of rational explanation, which are, nevertheless, perfectly separable in a practical, systematic analysis.[60]

Parsons's concern with the dichotomy of the 'theoretical' and the 'descriptive' has, as we have seen, led him to confuse the formal and the substantive aspects of sociological analysis generally; and within the substantive aspect, (i) the deductive and inductive generalizations, (ii) the definitional and empirical concepts, and, finally (iii) analysis and description.

It is, therefore, not surprising that he should choose, for his eclectic, convergent 'theoretical structure', Mannheimian epistemology and Durkheimian methodology—and not Weberian.† Although he devoted most of his exegetical effort to Weber's work, the opposition between the two perspectives, of science *as* social existence and science *of* social existence, is too fundamental to be reconciled by a refinement of the first, which Parsons seems to have attempted.

* His work is, by Parsons's own acknowledgment, *the principal secondary source* of his exposition of Weber's methodology in *The Structure of Social Action*. Especially noteworthy in this connection is von Schelting's critique of Mannheim's value-criterion of truth, which *totally* contradicts this interpretation of value-relevance, if his text on Weber does not seem to do for Parsons.

† It would be impossible for anyone to understand Pareto's methodological framework without a clear idea of the distinctions of rational explanation, and without eliminating from his consciousness the folk-tale that scientific statements are the only statements which are existentially true. Mannheimian sociological epistemology is very similar to Durkheim's sociologism in any case.

Durkheim's methodology, of structural-functionalism, and his general orientation, evolutionary perspective, are, therefore, entirely suited to the Parsonian notion of 'theoretical' sociology.[61] For Durkheim's sociology, as a whole, can only be called general-descriptive, because his empirical work is concerned with either classifying or correlating social facts with pre-defined assumptions of concepts, and his methodology, with determining the structure and functions of institutionalized social facts. The concepts that Parsons borrowed from Weber and Pareto are not analytical, but descriptive: for example, definitional ideal types from Weber[62] and 'social system' and 'equilibrium' from Pareto; ultimate value-systems are, of course, from Durkheim.

7 Merton and Bendix: generalizations of limited range and comparative study of societies

Weber's sociological theory is a norm of comparison for others' theories because of its comprehensiveness, logical structure and, above all, its empirical reference.* It is not because of the originality of ideas in their pure form. His ideas, in this sense, were not original. The originality of Weber's sociology lies in his use of these ideas, in their practical applicability; and in the insight they provide us into the mysteries of social reality.

Robert Merton's essay 'Unanticipated consequences of purposive action'[1] appears to give us a theoretical framework of analysis of the *indirection* of social action—which is, incidentally, the whole reason for sociological analysis—in the 'middle-range' (to use Merton's famous phrase) of generalization.[2] But we have, instead, a rambling exercise in arranging the possibilities of 'unanticipated consequences of purposive action'. For example: 'Unforeseen consequences should not be identified with consequences which are necessarily undesirable from the standpoint of the actor'. Or, 'Concretely, however, the consequences result from the interplay of the action and the objective situation, the conditions of action'.[3]

Merton is primarily concerned, we find, with the 'sum-total results of action under certain conditions': that is to say, consequences to the actor, and consequences to other persons mediated through (1) the social structure, (2) the culture and (3) the civilization.[4]

He does not assume 'that in fact social action always involves clear-cut, explicit purpose'. Nor must, he says, it be 'inferred that

* It is immaterial, from this point of view, whether the theorist is 'indebted' to Weber or not.

L   153 purposive action implies "rationality" of human action', that is, people always use the objectively most adequate means for achieving their ends.[5] In fact, part of Merton's 'analysis is devoted to the determination of those elements which account for concrete deviations from rationality of action'.[6] According to him, these elements or factors in action can be (a) unorganized or (b) formally organized; and he names these elements as (i) 'stochastic' or conjectural association (and 'not, as in many areas of the physical sciences, functional associations'), (ii) ignorance, (iii) error, which includes reification, (iv) 'the imperious immediacy of interests' (i.e. 'where the actor's paramount concern with the foreseen immediate consequences excludes the consideration of further or other consequences of the same act'), and (v) basic values (which differ from the factor of immediacy of interests 'in a highly significant theoretical sense').[7]

As an example Merton takes Weber's Protestant ethic thesis. He says: 'after the acute analysis by Max Weber, it goes without saying that action motivated by interest is not antithetical to an exhaustive investigation of the conditions and means of successful action.'[8] Weber's thesis is, in Merton's view, a 'classical' analysis of the factor of basic values. Merton adds that 'Weber has properly generalized this case, saying that active asceticism paradoxically leads to its own decline through the accumulation of wealth and possessions entailed by decreasing consumption and intense productive activity.' From this Merton himself generalizes and says: 'Here is the essential paradox of social action—the "realization of values" may lead to their renunciation.'[9]

Merton is really concerned, we discover at this point in his essay, with circumstances 'peculiar to human conduct, which stand in the way of successful social prediction and planning',[10] i.e. 'in the major elements involved in one fundamental social process'.[11]

This essay, clearly, cannot be a theoretical basis for any kind of sociological analysis—whether of 'renunciation of values as an unanticipated consequence' or of 'social planning as a fundamental social process'—because, in spite of the limits Merton has imposed on his theoretical concern, the factors which he has enumerated are not analytical concepts. That is, they do not enable us to explain the causes of unanticipated consequences by analysis of any empirical material. They in fact impose an explanation, which must, like Parsons's theory, be illustrated by the facts gathered. For a descriptive theory of unanticipated consequences, which Merton presents in this essay, becomes in an analytical translation equivalent to the selective principle. While the Weberian selective principle, value-relevance, does not impose an explanation but only gives a form to the organization of facts or 'empirical data', Merton's essay presents a theory with an inbuilt principle of both selection and explanation.

The empirical problem set in this essay is not to discover 'the circumstances peculiar to human conduct which stand in the way of successful prediction and planning', but to collect—and presumably to classify—examples of such circumstances as are conditioned by the five 'factors' Merton has enumerated. This early view of socio-logical analysis in Merton's work remains completely consistent with his later attempts to wed sociological theory and research through 'middle-range theories'. The form of his eclecticism in this essay—which is similar to Parsons's—as well, remains a persisting character-istic of his work as a whole. The subject-matter of this essay, derived from his reading of Weber and Pareto,* is an interesting example of his theorizing, for it also reflects the influence of Parsons's notions on theory and social research much more clearly than one might expect from his rejection of 'grand theory'. The influence lies in Merton's personal selectivity in ideas and their interpretation and in his dis-regard of the main point of Weber's and Pareto's contributions to sociology: the exact analytic relationship between definitional concepts in their substantive theories—which Parsons and Merton have been interested in—and analytical concepts in their method-ologies, without which no empirical analysis would have been possible.

Weber's thesis on the Protestant ethic and the spirit of capitalism is not concerned with demonstrating the proposition that 'the "realization" of values may lead to their renunciation'; but with the hypothesis that the rationalization of life which was a consequence of the Protestant ethic, as an empirically unique phenomenon (i.e. an historical individual), may have been causally significant in the creation of the spirit of capitalism (which was another empirically unique phenomenon or historical individual). Even if we regard the study as being concerned, in general terms, with the 'realization' of values—and not with a consequence of certain ideal interests created

* Also Mannheim. Merton has been a great deal more explicit in his interest in Mannheimian ideas than Parsons.

155

by the world-view of Protestantism which governed men's conduct in a particular period of history—the 'renunciation' of values is hardly central either to the hypothesis or the empirical analysis. The unanticipated consequence of purposive action, in the Weber thesis, is, therefore, obviously not the renunciation of Protestant values, but the spirit of capitalism and the industrial bourgeois capitalism. Neither Luther's nor Calvin's interpretation of Christian values can conceivably be regarded as having been made with a concern for the then unknown future of capitalism.[12] Weber's theory of 'active asceticism'—to use Merton's phrase—is, therefore, a more practicable sociological theory, or a general substantive proposition, than Merton's.

The elements of Merton's theory which are derived from Pareto can be similarly shown to have value for him only as illustrations for his conjectures. Pareto's analytical concepts, like Weber's, have practical applicability. They would enable one both to test his theory of residues as well as to distinguish the sentiments of an actual society, as the theory of residues is not an axiomatic statement for which it has been mistaken.[13]

In a later essay of his, 'Sociological theory',[14] Merton points out 'the need for a closer connection between theory and empirical research'. But the implications are the same as the essay we have just discussed. The 'conventions' for sociological research which he suggests are: (1) 'formalized derivation' and (2) 'codification'. These are, in effect, deduction and induction. His 'sole interest' at this point is to translate these logical procedures into terms which seem to him appropriate to 'current sociological theory and research'. According to him, the conclusions of a research may have a 'statement of the findings on initial hypotheses' and also 'indicate the order of observations needed to test its further implications'.[15] One result, in his view, 'of such formalization' is 'the control over the introduction of undisciplined and diffuse interpretations'.[16] 'Codification'—which Merton borrowed from Lazarsfeld[17]—is the systematization of 'available empirical generalizations which are in apparently different spheres of behaviour', in order to construct 'provisional hypotheses' for extending theory, 'subject to further empirical inquiry'.[18] In this formula, 'theory' obviously means an abstraction from certain empirical conclusions which have limited validity—in other words, arbitrary generalization. It negates, then,

156

his apparent aim of relating theory with empirical analysis: such a theory is merely a generalized description of 'unrelated, undisciplined and diffuse interpretations'—which Merton himself condemns.

There is, as he says at the beginning of the essay, 'a clear and decisive difference between *knowing how to test* a battery of hypotheses and knowing the theory from which to derive hypotheses to be tested'.[19]

Reinhard Bendix in his 'Concepts and generalizations in comparative sociological studies'[20] has the same theoretical concern as Merton: 'to develop concepts and generalizations at a level between what is true of all societies and what is true of one society at one point in time and space'.[21] Bendix's essay is a practical contribution to sociological analysis. Although Bendix has avoided an application of Weber's complete methodology in his work since his earlier puzzlement with the concept of value-relevance in Weber's sociology,[22] his selectiveness is not of the same kind as Merton's or Parsons's. He has attempted to use Weber's means of analysis both for the clarification of theoretical concepts and for empirical studies. His long essay 'Tradition and modernity reconsidered'[23] is a good example of Bendix's use of the historical ideal type both as a theory and a concept of comparative description.

In his view, the contributions of the 'comparative approach' are at least three:[24] (i) Comparisons between 'related phenomena in different societies are made possible by referring them to some sociological universal' or a 'problematic of social condition'. Comparative sociological studies 'take a single issue that is to be found in many (conceivably in all) societies and seek to illuminate it by showing how different societies have dealt with the same issue'. An example of this, in Bendix's view, is Weber's study of 'the secular causes and consequences of religious doctrines', in which he 'identified one such issue'. (ii) 'Many sociological concepts are composite terms formulating a limited body of the evidence', and their use 'without regard to this limitation can be prevented by comparative studies'. (iii) 'Social structures have a space-and-time dimension', and 'to formulate concepts appropriate to such structures it is necessary to allow for the variations which are compatible with—even characteristic of—each type of structure.' The enumeration of a cluster of interrelated attributes is not sufficient for this purpose. 'Where analysis emphasizes the chronology and individual sequence' it is historical; 'where it emphasizes the pattern' it is sociological. Comparative sociological studies are particularly appropriate for explaining such patterns 'because they tend to increase the "visibility" of one structure by contrasting it with another'. In Bendix's view, such exposure of concepts and generalizations to wide evidence is 'likely to impart a salutary degree of nominalism to the terms we use'. In this essay he attempts 'to hold a balance between grand theory and the descriptive accounts of area studies', which is what Merton had suggested, but with much less success.

However, Bendix's limited use of Weber's theoretical structure and his indecision about the difference between history and sociology can be explained by his essay 'Max Weber's interpretation of conduct and history' mentioned earlier. It will also be of some use to see whether a balance between the so-called 'grand theories' and descriptive studies does relate the two extremes or whether it is just a precarious attempt to hold on to both through a set of 'comparative' concepts and generalizations, without a proper analytical framework. It raises the question, for instance, of the irreconcilable variety of inherent values in different societies with which we are constantly confronted in comparative studies. Although Bendix has ignored this problem, his limited and tentative contribution to the descriptive aspects of sociological theory does not suffer too much from it; but it does leave the validity of such studies in doubt. What are they attempting to do? If this is not clear, then, one can hardly judge whether they succeed or not. It may seem that if such researches deal with facts correctly and present a detailed account of whatever they are concerned with, it is pedantic to ask for more. But the judgment of whether they deal with facts correctly or not is inevitably related to the following questions: On what basis have the facts been collected? How would they provide a valid explanation? Finally, how can one determine their significance? All these questions were answered by Weber in his methodology, and tested in his empirical comparisons. If one avoids these questions by saying that they will be answered to a great extent by 'scientific' comparative studies, it is to leave their significance as much in doubt as both those who construct grand theories (or extended axiomatic definitions) and those who write descriptive studies (or scholarly catalogues of incidental minutiae).

In his essay 'Max Weber's interpretation of conduct and history', which is, perhaps, his earliest attempt to come to terms with Weber, the impossibility of combining a psychological orientation of value-relevance—which the Parsonian phrase 'the scientist's interest' in all its variations means—with the objectivity of a scientific causal explanation becomes obvious. Bendix refers to a sentence in Weber's *Aufsätze zur Wissenschaftslehre* (p. 261) which, correctly translated, is as follows: 'It is not the statement or determination of historical "causes" of the given "object" of explanation which is subjective . . . but the *delimitation* of the historical object itself, for here *relations of value* are decisive—whose interpretation is subject to historical change.'[25] Bendix's translation is: 'It is not the statement of historical "causes"—given the "object" to be explained—which is subjective; it is rather the *delineation* of the historical "object" itself, which is subjective, since in this case *values* are decisive, which are subject to historical change" (my italics).[26]

The noticeable fact in Bendix's translation is that he translates the word *Abgrenzung* (delimitation) as delineation; and *Wertbeziehungen* (value-relations) simply as values. He then adds: 'which are subject to change'; when Weber clearly says: 'whose interpretation' (*Auffassung*) is subject to historical change.

Following his translation, Bendix comments: 'It is futile to argue about the interests which prompt the historian to select one problem rather than another, because these interests are based on value-orientations which cannot be "changed" by discussion.'[27] We see in this comment that Bendix has made the same error as Parsons, in making value-relevant interpretation a form of value judgment. It seems inexplicable in the case of someone who quotes from an original source, but the real explanation seems to be that Bendix has accepted Parsons's exposition of Weber's ideas without question and has translated the passage according to Parsons rather than Weber. His comment on Weber's 'methodological difficulties'[28] shows why this is not an unreasonable assumption. For, Bendix says—in agreement with Parsons—that 'despite his considerable caution', Weber did not entirely escape the difficulties of his own methodology. According to him, Weber 'insists again and again that the Protestant ethic was only one of many factors making for the development of modern capitalism'; 'Yet his own work on the comparative sociology of religion was undertaken in order to show that this one factor was the decisive one, since its absence in other civilizations is, in the main, responsible for the failure to develop

159

modern capitalism.' Apart from showing a Parsonian confusion of existential truth and logic of explanation, this misunderstanding represents one of the commonest forms of criticism in sociological thought. The point is not that Weber was methodologically contradicting himself, but that: first, in reality (as Weber said), there must be many factors which develop into an historical event, like modern capitalism, but to understand their significance one has to analyse them one at a time, as there is no way of legitimately showing the workings of several factors at once. Therefore, if Weber's sociology of religion shows the causal significance of the Protestant ethic in the formation of modern capitalism through the determination of *its absence* in other civilizations, one cannot attribute a causal significance to the Protestant ethic *for the failure of 'other civilizations'* to develop an event which was part of a civilization which is historically distinct from them—unless, of course, one believes in the suprahistoricity of the Western civilization (which Weber did not, but Parsons seems to do in his recent contribution, *Societies: Evolutionary and Comparative Perspectives*) or, in its contemporary variation, 'systemic' sameness of all human societies.

However, since Bendix is unable to reconcile the 'inconsistency' in Weber which he has created himself by his mis-translation, it is understandable that he has put aside the aspect of the logical distinctions of description and explanation and the principles relating them— the principle of value-relevance being the fundamental one—and concentrated exclusively on painstakingly applying the historical ideal type in all the areas of research he has undertaken.*

In spite of these rather serious limitations on sociological analysis, which Bendix has imposed upon himself under Parsons's influence, his essay deserves discussion because of the issues involved in his analysis of the relationship of sociology and history.

Depending upon the Parsonian notion of value-relevance, Bendix says that the selection of the research problem is 'determined by the values of the historian'.

These values vary with changes in the historical situation and the problems to which they give rise. New historical perspectives

* Even in his book *Max Weber: An Intellectual Portrait* he deliberately avoids any discussion of Weber's methodological ideas—which is a pity, because his exposition of Weber's substantive work is an accurate and valuable contribution to the understanding of Weber's sociology.

are, therefore, constantly arising. While our interests make it possible for us to select what is historically significant for us, it is to be noted that these interests or values function only as selective criteria. Such selection is always necessary, since all earlier events have contributed to the genesis of all later events. It depends, therefore, on the preferences of the historian.[29]

Bendix then draws the inference, on behalf of Weber, 'that different historians would have to arrive at identical results, *if* they select the same research problem'; and adds, on his own behalf, that 'Weber's insistence on the merely selective function of values in historical research is not without difficulty': 'in selecting a subject-matter for analysis, we single out those events *we* regard as significant.'[30] At this point, it is interesting to see how Bendix transforms *the inevitable subjectivity of the selection of a research problem into the scientific objectivity of value-relevant selection of facts which we find in Weber's theory.*

The subjective choice of a problem, in his view, is cumulative in the sense that 'the selection of other scholars'—past and present— 'tends to influence our own choice'. This means that the investigator's own personal values do not *really* allow him to choose his field of interest and investigation. Further, the 'social' pressure from the predecessors and contemporaries of a scholar, according to Bendix, 'in effect contributes, inadvertently perhaps, to the *causal significance* [Bendix's italics] of those factors which have been selected for study'. He gives an example: if one selects 'the element of "calculability" in capitalism for analysis', 'it means that unwittingly we have given it a certain "eminence" in the hierarchy of all possible causes. *This need not detract from the validity of the final results at which the investigation arrives*'[31] (my italics). This sentence is the familiar refrain of all such arguments; but the virtue of Bendix lies in turning such common beliefs into *the doubts of a believer.*

First of all, the point which he is making here—that the explanation is already contained in the hypothesis—raises certain interesting doubts on the theory of existentiality of knowledge. If, as he implies, the whole process is so biased from the start, if everything that is objective and scientific depends on the chance or accident of one's predecessors' and contemporaries' good sense in choosing their research problems and somehow hitting upon the right explanation, the question that arises is: How would we ever know that the result they or we achieved was the right or the correct one? And, is not the pursuit of knowledge a time-wasting ritual? One cannot help thinking that those who persevere in such muddled scholarship are to be congratulated for their reverence to the deity of knowledge and learning rather than on their ability to accomplish anything.

Bendix then goes on to say: 'But, apart from these difficulties, *which are always surmountable to a degree*'—(how, one may ask?)—there are some problems 'which still remain': (1) 'whether the causal analysis of the historian lends itself to scientific generalization'; and (2) 'whether the historical analysis presupposes some form of generalized knowledge'. In parentheses, Bendix comments that, with regard to the first problem, Weber denied it and, with regard to the second, he 'asserted that the causal analysis of unique events requires a prior knowledge of the regularities of human conduct'.[32]

In Bendix's view, 'the rationale of these views' can best be known through an analysis of Weber's ideas on the relation between history and sociology.[33] He adds in a footnote at this point that whatever he concludes from these theoretical and methodological points should not 'invalidate Weber's historical research'. Further, as he thinks that there are a number of incompatibilities between Weber's research and theory, he confines himself in this essay 'to a discussion of some basic postulates' of his sociological theory.[34]

According to Bendix, 'Weber's two major interests are causal historical analysis and comparative sociological casuistry.' Casuistry is a term which, he says, Weber himself used, meaning 'a system of ideal types, which encompasses all regularities of human social conduct', derived from comparative world history.[35] The inference that Bendix draws is that history, then, 'seeks to explain the unique', and sociology, 'to establish a complete "inventory" of human behaviour in order to provide us with a knowledge of the range of recurrent types of individual conduct'.[36] In other words, history explains facts and sociology provides the theory of history.

Bendix, then, mentions 'Weber's procedure in selecting his field of interest', inevitably taking the Protestant ethic thesis—as it fits his 'description of the relation between history and sociology'—as the 'substitution of rational and empirical for sacred and magical modes of thought', or, as Weber referred to it at times, as 'the disenchantment of the world'. In Bendix's view, Weber 'never speaks of "rationalization" as the "content" of Western European historical development', but (i) 'as the object of his own specific value (or interest) orientation', and (ii) as 'the over-all designation of an ascetic mode of conduct, which uniquely distinguishes the "way of life" of western Europeans from the "way of life" prevailing in any other civilization'.* The second proposition is based on 'a universal historical comparison', according to Bendix. Further, 'it is this unique aspect of *our* civilization which calls for an explanation' (my italics). One can have little doubt that in spite of his having sensed the objectivity of Weber's work (which comes through in his analysis), Bendix is firm about relating it, in deference 'to other scholars' perhaps, to the subjective interest which Weber had in studying Western rationalism.

Following this line of thought, Bendix—naturally enough— finds that 'Weber the historian seems to come into conflict with Weber the sociologist.' 'The historian selects his subject matter on the basis of his interests, without claiming for it on that ground any causal historical significance. But the sociologist claims that he is able to discover the "unique" aspects of a historical configuration and that this "uniqueness" indicates its historical significance.' This means for Bendix *what should be a uniquely confusing proposition*: 'that the historian selects the object of his inquiry on the basis of his value-orientation, while the sociologist can ascertain that which is to be explained by the historian by nonevaluative methods.'[37]

Bendix finally makes a point of relating this 'irreconcilable' duality of history and sociology to the 'ideological implications' of Weber's methodology:[38] 'The past consists of an infinity of events which, in conjunction, inevitably lead to the present.' But since the future is predetermined and since the struggle of individuals cannot change the 'course of events', therefore the future of society cannot be affected by the spontaneous aspirations of men. It is the tragedy of human life that we must continue our efforts in the service of ideals, while we know that these efforts—among an infinity of factors—affect the events but cannot change their predetermined course.

* This curious comment derives its confusion, as one can clearly see, from Bendix's *firm* designation of 'interest' as a scholar in a problem as the *value*-orientation of a study. Otherwise, how is what Bendix thinks Weber never said (but should have?—one wonders constantly with Bendix's analyses) different from the second proposition?

163

Although Bendix would relate this metaphysical description of social reality, which he derives from Weber's inferences on the nature of historical and social reality—and calls it Weber's 'orientation'—to Kaiser's Germany and Weber's liberal-nationalism in order to explain Weber's ideological context, it is rather obvious that it has little to do with the truth of Weber's sociological analyses. Yet again, Bendix's merit in turning others' dogmatic assertions to reasonable doubts becomes evident, and shows up their confusions. This time it is the dogma of Mannheimian social-contextual analysis which reveals its muddle.

In his conclusion, Bendix says that the ideal type is not just 'a "standard" against which the "deviations" of historical events are "measured" ', but 'a strange mixture of ethical principles, cultural pessimism, and the hope for a precarious chance of human freedom'.[39]

This essay is interesting to us because it is an illustration both of the fundamental importance of the concept of value-relevance in Weber's methodology and of how the misunderstanding of a basic methodological principle can lead one to misrepresent the whole theoretical system. Also, it illustrates the fallacy of the notion that a philosophy of history determines sociological knowledge; or of the implication that sociological analysis can be deduced from an axiomatic theory—like Parsons's 'framework of all human action conceived as a system'[40]—which shows 'the regularities of human conduct'.

8 Dahrendorf: conflict as a reorientation of sociological analysis or a substitute 'grand' theory

All the confusing tendencies in contemporary sociology discussed so far are displayed in a large measure in Ralf Dahrendorf's attempts to contribute to sociological theory. Apart from Bendix's style of implicit doubt, Dahrendorf shares many of his ideas and interpretations. One can easily apply the criticisms made against one to the other without much loss of relevance.

In the preface to his book *Class and Class Conflict in Industrial Society* he makes a statement of intent. He says that it is desirable to 'try to free sociology of the double fetters of ideographic historical and a meta-empirical philosophical orientation and weld it into an exact science—with precisely formulated postulates, theoretical models and testable laws'. 'Ideally', he says, 'all this should be done mathematically.'[1] Later, he says that, with R. K. Merton, he regards 'theories of middle-range' to be the immediate aim of sociological research. He explains the phrase slightly differently from Merton: theories of the middle-range are those generalizations 'which are inspired by or oriented towards concrete observations'.[2]

In his more recent book, *Essays in the Theory of Society*, he talks about values and social science—in the first chapter—and remarks that Weber's definition of value-judgment is useful; and agrees with Weber that value-judgments cannot be derived from scientific insights. But later,[3] he adds that scientific inquiry begins, 'at least in temporal terms', with the choice of a subject, and it is at this point we find the first encounter between value-judgments and social science. He spends some time debating whether value-judgments inherent in the choice of a subject should be eliminated or not, and

165

their place at this point in a sociological inquiry; a debate similar to Bendix's anxious discussion of the subjectivity of the problems one may choose to study historically or sociologically. Dahrendorf calls this twilight area 'the antechamber of science', because the investigator is still free from the rules or procedure that will later govern his research.[4]

However, his discussion of value-judgment leads him to formulate what he calls 'two guiding values'. They are—in his own words— 'both important and defensible in objective terms'. The values themselves are: (1) that sociologists should not be deterred by social taboos from investigating certain 'objectionable' subjects;[5] and (2) their research should promote 'people's understanding of their own society'. These two principles are rather beside the point if they are considered to be contributions to sociological theory or to the discussion of values relevant to the subject-matter of sociology, as opposed to the sociologists' morality. However, this preoccupation with a moral code for sociologists has been a worry for Dahrendorf as long as he has considered himself a sociologist. He named this preoccupation in his essay, 'Out of utopia: towards a reorientation of sociological analysis',[6] 'problem-consciousness'. In this essay, he advocates a sociological science that is 'inspired by the moral fibre of its forefather's'.[7] This 'problem-consciousness' is, in fact, the subjective impulse of the scientist to choose a particular field of study. Since it has nothing whatever to do with the actual content of his study, how, one may ask, is it going to affect the knowledge he might gain or impart to the world, through his researches. Dahrendorf does not, however, consider this a question at all. Yet, it is impossible to see how an impulse to do good can, by itself, affect the value of the knowledge gained by scientific investigation. However, it points to the futility and absurdity of this kind of discussion as a preliminary to announcing the results of one's sociological-theoretical—or empirical—investigation. If the investigation is scientific, it will promote the moral position of the investigator by his having contributed to knowledge which is a moral achievement in itself more than by emphasizing his 'moral consciousness' without making any attempt to be scientific in his actual investigation. However, Dahrendorf pursues his 'problem-consciousness' theory further and says that *'a scientific discipline that is problem-conscious at every stage of development is very unlikely to find itself in the prison of utopian thought or to separate theory and research.*[8] But Dahrendorf's suggestion for 'a re-orientation of sociological analysis' through a 'commendable rediscovery of empirical problems of investigation'[9] has neither the practical—though limiting—applicability of Bendix's ideas nor is it in any way a less 'utopian' formulation than Parsons's 'social system' which he criticizes.

Dahrendorf would start with 'a fact or a set of facts that is puzzling the investigator', inviting the question 'Why?', a question which—in his own words—'has always inspired that noble human activity in which we are engaged—science'.[10] He sees, however, 'little point in restating methodological platitudes', but his formula is: *'Problems require explanation; explanations require assumptions or models and hypotheses derived from such models; hypotheses, which are always, by implication, predictions as well as explanatory propositions, require testing by further facts; testing often generates new problems'* (my italics).[11] This methodology of 'problem-consciousness' is taken further by Dahrendorf, and is linked to what he believes is a 'not so trivial methodological point—that we realize the proper function of empirical testing': 'as Popper has demonstrated'—in Dahrendorf's view—'in many of his works since 1935 [the year of publication of *Logik der Forschung*], there can be no verification in science; empirical tests serve to falsify accepted theories, and every refutation of a theory is a triumph of scientific research. Testing that is designed to confirm hypotheses neither advances our knowledge nor generates new problems.'[12]

But, at the very beginning of *Logik der Forschung*, we find a sentence which may be translated as follows:[13]

> The task of the scientist is to present propositions or systems of propositions and to test (we should note: *not* 'to falsify') them systematically; in empirical sciences they are, specifically, hypotheses, theoretical systems, presented and tested, according to empirical data, through observation and experiment.

In the section on the deductive testing of theories, Popper writes that the method of critical testing, the selection of theories—in his view—is always as follows:

> From the preliminary ungrounded anticipation of the notion, hypothesis or theoretical system are drawn inferences—upon which one determines the logical relations (e.g. equivalence,

167

derivability, compatibility and contradiction) that exist between them.

There are four ways in which the test can be applied (i) the logical comparison of inferences with one another, through which the system's inner consistency is to be investigated; (ii) an investigation of the logical form of the theory with the object of determining whether it has the character of an empirical-scientific theory, that is, it is not tautological; (iii) comparison with other theories, to determine, among other things, whether the theory which is being tested is confirmed in the comparison to be a scientific improvement; and finally, (iv) through empirical application of the inferences drawn.

The last test should determine whether the new conclusions which the theory maintains can be confirmed in practice, perhaps in scientific experiments or technical application. Even here the process of testing is deductive: from the system (with the use of the propositions already accepted) empirical—possibly easily testable or usable—inferences ('Prognoses') are deduced, and those which are not derivable from known systems, or are contradictory, can be separated from them. On these inferences experiments, etc., together with practical application, are decisive. If the result is positive, then the odd or singular results are accepted, *verified*, so the system under investigation is for the time being confirmed or corroborated and we have no reason to reject it. In case the result is negative, the inferences are falsified; so that the falsification applies to the system from which they are derived, as well.

The positive result can only support the system temporarily; it can always be rejected later by negative results. But so long as a system comes through an incisive and strict deductive test and is not surpassed by a progressive development in science, we say that it is confirmed. Elements of inductive logic do not at all come into the process sketched here; we can never conclude from the validity of individual propositions the validity of theories.[14]

From the brief evidence of this translation of certain relevant passages in Popper's *Theory of Knowledge in Modern Natural Science*, one can easily judge that there are two aspects to it. First, with which one assumes Dahrendorf is concerned, the description of the process of scientific critical or empirical testing; and, second, the philosophical question of 'demarcation', with which Popper is primarily concerned, between empirical science and metaphysics.[15] Dahrendorf, obviously, does not see any distinction between the two aspects: he would use the description of the process to refute any objections to the philosophical conclusions that Popper might make on the question of induction or philosophical 'verifiability' versus deductive testing or philosophical 'falsifiability'; as he has made a rarified interpretation of 'falsifiability' to say that 'empirical tests serve to falsify accepted theories'. The criterion of falsifiability in Popper is a criterion of demarcation between empirical and metaphysical theories— i.e. on their respective uses of evidence and assumptions and their logical connections. It does not infuse a metaphysical 'spirit of progress' into scientific theories as Dahrendorf seems to believe.[16] Dahrendorf's blithe interpretation of Popper's theory of critical testing is an obvious example of the confused use of philosophical concepts in empirical discussions which has come to be designated 'philosophy of social science' in contemporary sociological discussions, which takes as its point of departure any fashionable philosophical notion and attempts to lay down the laws of the substantive discipline with which that notion might be connected in any way, without any doubts arising on the feasibility of a programme which is based either entirely on the 'pure' thoughts of the *a priori* thinker or, at best, on an *ad hoc* acquaintance with certain theories in the subject.[17]

Dahrendorf's notion of problem-consciousness, as we have seen, is a variant of Parsons's notion of the scientist's interest, with the same confusion of the subjective impulse 'to solve a problem' with the objective principle of value-relevance. This confusion is fundamental to Dahrendorf's theories of conflict,[18] role-interests[19] and *homo sociologicus*.[20] It has dictated not only the moral choice which Dahrendorf has made—on behalf of sociology—in favour, first of the Marxist theory of conflict[21] and later of individual freedom,[22] but also the way in which his theories lack objective validity. It is hardly possible, with such a background, to accept his theoretical essays as contributions 'towards a reorientation of sociological analysis'.

For instance, he criticizes Parsons for having a utopian model, characterized by 'immobility', 'isolation in time and space', 'absence of conflict and disruptive processes'.[23] He is not concerned, he adds, with Parsons's 'excellent and important philosophical analysis of *The Structure of Social Action*', nor with 'his numerous perceptive contributions to the understanding of empirical phenomena.'[24] This is a strange discrimination, as Parsons has been quite consistent in developing his particular view of sociology—as his 'solution to the problem of order'—from his earliest essay, 'The place of ultimate values in sociological theory'. The notion of 'social system' is a logical development from Parsons's fundamental assumptions, both substantive and formal, on the nature of social reality and its analysis.

Dahrendorf also rejects the cure of the 'malady of utopianism' through the prescriptions of T. H. Marshall's 'sociological stepping stones in the middle distance'[25] and R. K. Merton's 'theories of the middle-range', because both are based on a 'wrong diagnosis': 'that by simply reducing the level of generality we can solve all problems'.[26]

But, in Dahrendorf's—as in Merton's and Marshall's—view 'no theory can be divorced from empirical research', and vice versa;[27] and his 'problem-consciousness'—which we have already discussed—'is not merely a means of avoiding ideological biases, but an indispensable condition of progress in any discipline of human inquiry'.[28] It also led to his suggestion of 'an alternative model' which he calls the 'conflict model of society':[29] 'the great creative force that carries along change in the model' is social conflict.[30] According to him, conflict is not 'always violent and uncontrolled': 'there is probably a continuum from civil war to parliamentary debate, from strikes and lockouts to joint consultation.'[31]

The three notions which are his alternative to Parsons's 'utopian' notion of the social system are: change, conflict and constraint—'not by universal agreement but by coercion of some by others'.[32] His assumption is that conflict is ubiquitous because constraint is 'ubiquitous wherever human beings set up social organizations'.[33] But he would not 'fall victim to the mistake of many structural-functional theorists and advance for the conflict-model a claim to comprehensive and exclusive applicability'. 'We need'—in Dahrendorf's view—'for the explanation of sociological problems both the equilibrium and the conflict models of society.'[34] He adds in a footnote: 'In philosophical terms, however, it is hard to see what other models of society there could be which are not of either the equilibrium or the conflict type.'[35]

Apart from the contradiction in claiming ubiquity for 'conflict' first and then making it complementary to 'equilibrium', Dahrendorf's belief that this imposition of 'an alternative model of society' *as a means of sociological analysis* is an improvement on Parsons— especially if sociologists through their 'problem-consciousness' concentrate on problems of conflict, which, incidentally, means any social interaction in Dahrendorf's formulation—is understandable, if absurd. It is understandable in view of Dahrendorf's utter vagueness about the relationship between theory and empirical analysis: for him, first, exact concepts mean the ideal of mathematical formulas; second, hypothesis means explanation; third, a statement of an opposite notion to an 'accepted' theory means that it is 'falsified' empirically; fourth, this opposite notion becomes not exactly a deterministic assumption but 'a model of society', which— since Dahrendorf has already postulated that hypotheses are explanations—'explains'. Since it explains, then it goes without saying that 'a reorientation of sociological analysis' had already been demonstrated.

The question that might have been asked is: how should this 'model of society' be related to the facts of a society? If, for example, one hypothesized a correlation between two social facts in terms of either Parsons's or Dahrendorf's substantive assumptions for their models, or even a composite model, the explanation that will almost certainly have to be made is that these facts are an example—of 'social equilibrium', of 'conflict', or of 'equilibrium-conflict' respectively. But these principles have already been assumed, and, therefore, known: so what new explanation or insight can be gained through exemplification or illustrative empirical 'analysis'?

If, however, we take Weber's methodology to be implicit, since Dahrendorf is, presumably, concerned with the process of social change—through his model of conflict—then the confusion of problem-consciousness (or, Parsonian scientist's interest) on the principle of value-relevance and the *a priori* assumption of conflict (or equilibrium) precludes the construction of any objectively valid ideal types whose causal relationships could be investigated.

If, on the other hand, we ignore Dahrendorf's implied rejection of the structural-functional methodology, in view of his acceptance of the equilibrium-model as complementary, and consider it applicable to his model, we find that the best an empirical test can do, is to classify the examples of consensus and conflict, and perhaps statistically measure their ratio in different societies. The question which will remain unanswered is which facts, exactly, are being measured? In simple terms, therefore, Dahrendorf's theory—like Parsons's, which it claims to 'falsify'—is true by definition and not by experience.

Dahrendorf's significance, from our point of view, lies in showing, first, that a forceful essay-style cannot compensate for an overwhelming vagueness and confusion about the principles of empirical knowledge; second, philosophical notions do not, if used without a sense of relevance, clarify empirical problems; and third, sociological analysis is not a question of supplanting one kind of generalized substantive–descriptive notion with another; fourth, the facts of existence are neither created by the sociologist's consciousness when he is studying them nor understood by him as an exercise in moral concern.

9 Conclusion

We have considered the recent trends in sociological thinking through an analysis of the ideas on theory and empirical research of a number of writers. They, apart from their own influence on contemporary sociology, also provide a representative variety of interpretations on the recurring themes of sociological thought and practice in their solutions. Therefore, the purpose of the analysis is served if the reader can see the importance of the several points made throughout the book in judging any other theories he may be interested in.

The main aim of the analysis has been to show how certain questions which have eluded philosophical and theoretical solutions are part of social reality—and what their sociological explanations could be. Weber's and Pareto's works show the achievements of sociological analysis in this traditionally 'inexplicable' area of human existence. Their analysis and understanding of the complexities of social reality also show the intellectual poverty of recent sociological endeavours: the jargonizing of the trite in theories and the journalistic anecdotism of commentaries have both lost for the subject its main assets of methodological principles, exact concepts and empirical generalizations, and substituted for them certain 'axiomatic' feelings[1] which have led to an absurd collection of 'schools' of sociology, and of theorists and essayists whose main function is to introduce a 'new' sociology with the publication of each of their 'contributions'. Since such a 'revolution' of thought means that no one need discipline himself to study the classics of the subject systematically and analytically, and to make sense of them, before embarking upon an 'original' solution to the 'eternal' problems of sociological analysis, it can only make sociology a haven for poor dilletantism.

However, one's understanding of such a rich, complex aspect of life as the social reality, a world in which one's consciousness is formed, may not be restricted—let alone dominated—by such theories, hypotheses and conjectures as we have had in recent decades, for more than a generation or so. The possibilities of knowledge and understanding which earlier sociological writings offer us have become much more urgent now than they were in the post-war era of the 'fifties and 'sixties. Our consciousness of the world is no longer satisfied with the comforts of dogmatic beliefs on the form of social reality; but, since no social change is inherently demarcated, we find the legacy of the recent past in sociological writings with us as a burden. This burden cannot be discarded unless we undertake a fundamentally new appraisal of the whole of the sociological material which can be described as theory and methodology.

What possibilities, then, are opened for us by this systematic appraisal of sociology? First, that the principles of sociological knowledge have already been definitively analysed: we cannot justifiably modify them or do without them if we wish to understand the social aspect of human existence, both in the individual and the collective sense. These principles define the form of social reality, the role of sentiments and values in the creativity of human intelligence, in the endurance of beliefs, ideas, skills and knowledge, both as positive and negative factors, in the formation of historical and social reality as a whole; and in the individual consciousness of it, as well as individual participation in specific contexts.

Through this definition of the form, one can begin to understand the interrelationships of content: for the content of social reality is what we are more deeply concerned about. Yet the form and content are not intrinsically separate: they are recognizable only in analysis. For the understanding of the content of social reality, one needs to know the limits of experience, for, in simple terms, social reality is all that is experienced in life. Experience is understandable only through rational analysis; even sympathy can only be fully communicated if it is explained. It is this point which makes the concept of sociological rationality one of the most fundamental bases of knowledge. It is through sociological rationality that one can consistently translate the variety and complexity of all human social experience—upon which the individual's experience of life, however subjectively intense, depends for its meaning—into a generally understandable language, i.e. with an objective meaning of experience as such.

One can readily discern in this form the significance of sociological analysis as an aspect of one's exploration of life's meaning in experiential terms. It is impossible to know the ultimate meaning of life itself—as it is of experience—but one can understand the *significance* of the meanings which human beings have attributed to life in the past and attribute now. It is this significance which contains the sociological explanation of the 'metaphysics' which seems to permeate the consciousness of human beings as the 'source' of their activity. One can, thus, see that to include the 'metaphysics' of life in a sociological explanation is not to go beyond experienceable reality. One does not 'explain'—because one cannot—the source of the metaphysics itself. Those who seek its explanation in the psychological or biological aspects of life are, in fact, extending their analysis beyond what is logically or empirically justifiable. Metaphysics cannot be said to owe its existence to the psychological or biological constitution of human beings, only that it *may be* affected by these factors.

Sociology can only be defined in these general, ultimate experiential terms—it cannot take the details, the facts of one or another historical or social segment of reality as its microcosmic definition. The meanings of social facts are not recognizable in such a discrete, isolated form; which means that social facts themselves are not identifiable in isolation. Sociological analysis is restricted by this isolating approach because of its failure to recognize the form of social reality. The interrelatedness of social facts, through meaning, to values and sentiments, and ultimately to the whole creative aspect of human life, makes sociology only partially a descriptive pursuit: without the analysis of the interrelations, no definition of the categories of facts—which a descriptive approach is concerned with —becomes possible. It is for this reason that sociology can neither make any deterministic assumptions or *a priori* theories, nor classify observable 'facts' into various 'fundamental' categories. It achieves only *inferential* knowledge, which is dependent upon the simultaneous use of deductive analysis and inductive generalization. One without the other leads to the kind of sterility which one finds in much of recent sociology.

Substantively, sociological analysis has even more fundamental insights to offer into the nature of social reality: for example, into the sources of world problems or the relationships *between* the beliefs and assumptions of dominant societies, past and present, *and* the results of their dominance; as well as, into the problems of individuals in society or the problems of equality and inequality, harmony and conflict, acceptance and rejection of élitism in different spheres of life, and the changing relationship of the majority with the minorities.

All these problems have been over-documented, described and speculated upon: but what knowledge have we gained from it all? Only what the *apparent* instrument of dominance of one society over another is, and, what 'elements' of the social system impinge upon an individual.

We do not know, for example, what makes a particular society successful in its attempts to dominate others—especially when one finds that the apparent unassailability of that society—which one believed in—seems to be easily penetrable by, again, *apparently* 'powerless' activities. Similarly, if the social system appears for a long period of time to be more than all the individuals in it and seems to work to a relentless logic of its own, it becomes vulnerable to the activities of even one individual which become acceptable to just a small minority of people. It would seem from such observable, superficial evidence that the institutions, systems, stylized relationships of individuals to one another and to groups and collectivities—even societies as a whole—are based on a socially accepted belief in their reality and in their power to realize certain experiences. So the analysis of such entities as institutions or systems and other manifest complexities of social organization must eventually lead to an analysis of the relationship of human beliefs and activities.

It is at this point that sociological knowledge as understanding of the realities of existence and its individual form, experience, begins to be realized. This stage of analysis and understanding is reached only in Weber and Pareto; in contemporary sociology they have remained matters of philosophical, subjective or dogmatic speculation, as they were before Weber and Pareto. If one takes the case of modernization, for example—which contains both the aspect of world problem and of individual problem together—in sociological analysis, one finds that sociologists have considered several approaches, from the modernizing role of imported films, education, economic development, political change to revolution, but have been unable to see the *significance* of the resistance to the *alienness* (and, therefore, subjective meaninglessness) of these isolated factors, which one can find in the relationship of the subjective beliefs to the manifest forms and interrelations of the society in which these factors may be introduced or spontaneously arise. Instead, the sociologists of modernization assumed that these factors must be causally significant; and, when this assumption failed, they turned to *literal* similarities or dissimilarities in the rituals, institutions, religions, social or philosophical doctrines or codes of ethics—the supposed combination of Durkheim and Weber—which, still did not bring the explanation within their grasp. For the key to sociological problems always lies in the question, *why does not the 'logically possible' course of events happen?*

Thus, the significance of the resistance must lie—it should have been obvious—in what Weber calls 'the ethical orientation', and Pareto, 'the logic of sentiment', of the people; and not in their 'traditionality' or ignorance of the 'modernizing' forces and their benefits. This would have been obvious if the matter had been analysed, and not conjectured upon without a systematic study of the *sociological* theories of values and sentiments. The puzzle of the strange 'resistance' and the alienated character of 'traditionality', for those whose 'modernity' has become their traditional way of life, would have been explicable if Pareto's theory of residues had been applied to the circumstances of modernization. It would also have made the sociologists—and 'modernists'—critically aware of their own assumptions on the perfections of the 'modern' world.

One can, thus, see how the sociology of knowledge is *necessarily* complementary to knowledge itself. Without a critical awareness of one's own assumptions, what one gains is a reinforced 'sentimentality'. This is the most profound lesson of Pareto's sociological work; it is also the reason why sociologists have not appreciated the importance of his analysis. The banality and smugness of contemporary sociology lies in its uncritical approbation of 'scholarship'— that is, in its admiration of the manner, in its respect for the pomposity, and its awe of the rituals, of scholarship—rather than the

177

self-awareness and the insight into the mysteries of existence that give scholarship its meaning.

The centrality of sociological knowledge, and of the scholarship and imaginative perception of reality which went into its making, at the present time, depends upon the only unexplored aspect of existence that remains: its social context.

The exploration of this social context is what sociological analysis is about: this exploration is not the gathering of social facts, nor the conjectures of a limited individual intellect, but a *conceptual analysis* of the intricate fabric of beliefs, ideas and artifacts which one might call the social world. For conceptual analysis defines knowledge itself. The objectivity of sociological knowledge transcends the simple object-orientation of 'scientific' description. Sociologically, the 'scientific' description of the world is only one of many existential forms of belief-statements. The recent mistake of sociology and philosophy has been to equate the substance of this description to the 'knowledge' of the world. The knowledge of the world derives from the application of the form of rational experience to the 'irrational', or the unexplored, experience; and sociology has, through its definition of rationality in terms of its social meanings, made it a more comprehensive knowledge.

This concept of the sociologically rational explanation has the most profound possibility of relating the subjectivity of human experience to the objectivity of knowledge, which no other concept in any branch of intellectual analysis has succeeded in doing. The inferential character of sociological explanation which brings together thought and reality in a logical relationship (as we have seen in the discussion of Weber and Pareto)—and which makes Mannheim's notion of a sociology of knowledge, in spite of its glaring weaknesses, so fascinating—is of the utmost importance in the solution of this problem. For this problem is the problem of the whole of social reality: the interaction of thought and reality, of the mind and society, of values and action, of belief and knowledge, of sentiment and experience.

If one were to deny the validity of the inferential generalizations of sociological theory, social reality would remain an 'eternal' mystery, for there is no perceptible aspect to it—not even as nature is to divinity.

The inferences of sociology, therefore, must depend on the validity

178

of the form of rational experience. It is this reason which makes the relationship of theory and analysis the most fundamental question of validity in sociology. All sociologists have to raise it because the factual research that they may undertake in avoidance loses its meaning and significance very soon. If it is an attempt to make sociology respectably 'philosophical', it fails as miserably as the attempt to make it factual and 'scientific'.

The relationship of theory and analysis in sociology is, therefore, an *intrinsic* problem and its solution depends on the nature of the phenomenon, social reality, itself.

It is an explicit relationship because, as it should be evident by now, social reality is constituted by the interaction of thought and activity. The conceptual elements of thought which relate to activity are not, therefore, recoverable by pure ratiocination. They have to be distinguished by what Weber means in his terms 're-experience' and intellectual 'understanding': the question is of the relevance or the exact applicability of one or the other form of understanding. Pareto's method of analysis from the interpretation or the 'theory' to sentiments seems to minimize the role of 're-experience' but the judgment of the relationship between the element of experience and the element of sentiment in the theories one would analyse depends on the range of re-experienceability as well as intellectual understanding that one can have. In fact, the judgment of objective truth when it is said to be based on experience means precisely this; and the extension of this judgment with the progress in knowledge, as a point consistent with this definition of objectivity, depends on the definiteness of both re-experience and intellectual understanding.

In practical terms, therefore, this means that a theory—either when it is a set of *a priori* general statements (or what we have called 'definitional concepts') based on logical deductions from a *hypothetical* premise; or when it is a set of empirical general statements (or what we have called 'empirical' concepts) based on inductive generalizations or inferences on the possible connections of empirically true but specific statements—is not a purely logical proposition. It depends in both its distinctive forms on the analysis of the phenomenon on which it makes a statement. In the first case— that is, in its definitional state—it is a *hypothetical* arrangement of logical possibilities *without* a knowledge of the details of its object of definition; in the second case—that is, in its empirical state—it is a *logical* arrangement of empirical possibilities *with* a knowledge of the details of its object of definition.

One can easily see why the term 'theory' must be used for both: for the valid definition of an object which is also its explanation, the two aspects of analysis must coincide. The point of coincidence is where the justification of *a priori* definitional concepts and the justification of the generalized inferences from empirically specific statements meet. For definitional concepts derived from *a priori* assumptions—or what are called hypotheses—remain extensions of pure thought or subjective distinctions till one can prove their exact reference to reality or experience; and inductive generalizations— or empirical concepts—remain arbitrary extensions of specific facts, without a conceptual or theoretical justification. In other words, given the form of rational explanation, it is as impossible to develop a 'theoretical' sociology without an empirical knowledge of the individuality of social facts, as it is to develop general statements from such empirical knowledge without a conceptual analysis of possible interrelations of these individual characteristics. Both the empirical justification of *a priori* assumptions—from which definitional concepts are derived—and the conceptual analysis of empirically individualized knowledge—or inductive inferences—must depend on certain methodological principles and concepts. It is at this stage that *one needs a valid definition of social reality*: and to reach this valid definition one needs sociological analysis. If sociological theory, i.e. the body of these methodological principles, exact definitional concepts and empirical generalizations, has seemed to remain confused and undeveloped in its fundamental distinctions of the elements which constitute it, it is because the search for these elements was misdirected into the natural scientific sphere, where the methodological principles rest in the assumption of rational determinism of both the explanation and the object of explanation—even though the metaphysical belief in the rationality of the object, the natural world, is actually irrelevant to the rationality of the explanation. Since methodological principles of the natural sciences are really dependent on a dogma of the substantive rationality of the explanation, rather than its structure, the hypothetical definitions and the empirical generalizations must necessarily coincide. It is this coincidence that gives rise to the proposition of pure and applied sides of the same science. In sociology the counter-partition of 'pure' (theoretical) sociology and 'applied' (empirical) sociology is impossible, for the purity of sociological concepts is not the purity of *a priori* or dogmatic reasoning, but of accurate reference; and the application of these concepts to reality is analytical and explanatory. Any 'practical' application is, at best, a matter of value-choice, i.e. a part of social reality or the material of analysis, explanation and understanding; at worst, it is an imposition, a value-judgment or an exercise in social engineering.

The only conclusion one can draw from this integrity of sociological knowledge is that its value for a society will depend upon the value it places on knowledge as such. There is an intrinsic contradiction in social evaluations: if knowledge is power, then it can mean both the exploration of all unknown aspects of life *and* the statement of the obvious in service of the sentiments and values that may prevail at a given time in a society, through promotion of social and political policies. Sociology is particularly vulnerable to this ambiguity, as we can see in its fluctuating achievements and failures in the last hundred years of its recognition as an independent concern of knowledge and intellectual inquiry.

The statement of the obvious can be infinitely more subtle than the promotion of policies through the public objectivity of population-samples and statistically average behaviour: it can take on the 'virtues' of everyday life and its private relationships—of 'inter-subjectivity'.[2]

This subtility which appears to be different from behaviourism is the conception of a 'basic attitude' which—in Schutz's words— 'accepts naively the social world with all the alter egos and institutions in it as a meaningful universe, meaningful namely for the observer whose only scientific task consists in describing and explaining his and his co-observers' experiences of it' (p. 5).

This description—in terms of 'what does this social world mean for me the observer?'—requires answers to two 'quite different questions': 'What does this social world mean for the observed actor within this world and what did he mean by acting within it?'. According to Schutz, it is the study of the 'process of idealizing and formalizing as such, the genesis of the meaning which social phenomena have for us as well as for the actors, the mechanism of the activity by which human beings understand one another and themselves' (p. 7).

181

The basic methodological postulate for 'social science', Schutz envisages, must be of the following order:

Choose the scheme of reference adequate to the problem you are interested in, consider its limits and possibilities, make its terms compatible and consistent with one another, and having once accepted it, stick to it. If, on the other hand, the ramifications of your problem lead you . . . to the acceptance of other schemes of reference and interpretation, do not forget that . . . all terms in the formerly used scheme necessarily undergo a shift of meaning (p. 8).

This, Schutz adds, 'is harder than it seems', for most of the fallacies in the social sciences can be reduced to a mergence of subjective and objective points of view. 'But for a theory of action the subjective point of view must be retained in its fullest strength'; otherwise it loses its basis, i.e. its 'reference to the social world of everyday life and experience'—which is 'the only but sufficient guarantee that the world of social reality will not be replaced by a fictional non-existing world constructed by the scientific world' (p.8).

Although the aim of Schutz's 'phenomenological' sociology is a modest one, to describe 'everyday life and experience' from a subjective point of view, the question whether it is the 'world of social reality' or a new 'fictional non-existent world' constructed by the scientific observer, is not even debatable: it is an assertion which is meaningful from his own point of view, based on *his* observation of the actions and interpretations of 'the actor in the social world'; and not a representation of the world of social reality from the actor's point of view. Unless the scientist and 'the actor in the social world' merge in every circumstance, the description is as much a 'fictional' one as the publicly objective declarations of the behaviour-ist; but, of course, the behaviourist is looking at the behaviour without its motive: the phenomenologist attributes it a meaning, in terms of 'in-order-to' or 'because' motives. . . .

This meaning comes from the assumption that 'the world is experienced by the self as being inhabited by other Selves, as being a world for others and of others', although this 'intersubjective reality' is neither homogeneous nor simple.[3] So the task of attribut-ing meaning is to describe 'the origin of the differentiated structures of social reality as well as to reveal the principles underlying its unity and coherence' (p. 20). In Schutz's view this 'careful description of the processes which enable one man to understand another's thoughts and actions is a prerequisite for the methodology of the empirical social sciences'. For, 'the question of how a *scientific* interpretation of human action is possible can be resolved only if an adequate answer is first given to the question how man, in the natural attitude of daily life and common sense, can understand another's action at all' (p. 21). Further, 'the construction of the categories and models of the social sciences is founded on the pre-scientific common sense experience of social reality' (p. 21). 'The world of daily life is not', according to Schutz, 'a private world': it depends on 'degrees of intimacy and anonymity.' The immediacy of one's fellow-men 'shades into the larger world of contemporaries', since one can impute to contemporaries 'typical motives with a high degree of likelihood' (p. 22).

There are, of course, 'regions of social reality which are neither actually nor potentially accessible to direct experience': 'the world of predecessors' and 'the world of successors' (p. 23).

The direct experience is a shared experience (p. 28), but direct observation also can be taken as an expression that indicates 'the other's conscious processes' (p. 33). Words, signs, gestures and movements 'can be interpreted by the observer as standing in a subjective configuration of meaning for the individual observed': for 'the world which is within reach of the observer is congruent with the world within reach of the observed person' (p. 34).

But since the observer cannot know the motives of the observed individual, Schutz suggests three ways to proceed: (1) 'he may remember from his own past experience a course of action similar to the one observed and recall its motive'; (2) if this is not possible, 'he may yet find in his general stock of knowledge typifications of the observed individual from which he may derive a typification of the observed individual's typical motives'; (3) 'if the observer possesses no knowledge at all about the observed individual, or insufficient knowledge about the type of individual involved, he must fall back upon an inference from "effect to cause" ' (p. 35). But any of these three ways of understanding motives are not, Schutz warns us, likely to be correct in the same way (p. 36).

On the problem of historical knowledge, Schutz's solution is that it too 'can be derived from communicative acts of fellow-men or contemporaries in which they report their own past experiences (e.g. childhood reminiscences of my father) and their past experiences of fellow-men and contemporaries (e.g. my teacher telling me about a Civil War veteran he knew)'; and through 'documents and "monuments" in the broadest sense' (pp. 58–9). The science of history has 'the momentous task of deciding which events, actions and communicative acts to select for the interpretation and reconstruction of "history" from the total social reality of the past'; but 'all historical events *can* be reduced to genuine experiences of other men, experiences which occurred in the duration of individual conscious life and referred to fellow-men and contemporaries' (p. 61). Therefore, in Schutz's view, an historical interpretation 'can be a history of "objective facts" as well as a history of conduct, meaningful to the individual historical subject' (p. 62).

Finally, 'the world of successors', the future, is totally indeterminate and indeterminable and one cannot—in Schutz's opinion—'apprehend this domain of social reality by any method, not even by typification' (p. 62).

In this résumé—in Schutz's own formulations as far as possible—we find a gentle introduction to sociological problems, a conversational and private interpretation of life's relationships, of the past with the present and its partial extension into the future. There is no difficulty in intuiting the kind of relationships which Schutz envisages, but the question is: how far can one *infer* from this intersubjective statement of whatever one's individual experience may extend to about the nature of social reality? It would seem too insignificant for Schutz to answer.

Schutz, however, also considers the problem of rationality.[4] For him, the different meanings of rationality in the study of the 'social world' 'represent only very inadequately the underlying conceptual scheme' (p. 64). To 'isolate the question of rationality' one has to, in his view, inquire more extensively into 'the different attitudes towards the social world adopted, on the one hand, by the actor within this world, and, on the other hand, by the scientific observer of it.'[5] An individual's analysis reveals that he is the centre of his own social world; but for the observer, the social world is the object of his detached, equanimous contemplation, 'essentially solitary' (p. 81). There is a shift in the point of view which, as a consequence for the scientist, 'replaces human beings he observes as actors on the social stage by puppets created by himself and manipulated by himself'. ('Puppets' correspond in Schutz's view to Weber's ideal types— without any irony that this description of the observed individual may suggest (p. 81).)

The scientist observes 'events caused by human activity', establishes 'a type of such proceedings' and then 'co-ordinates with these typical actors as their performers'. Finally, he constructs 'personal ideal types which he imagines as having consciousness'—but without human frailties. The personal ideal type or the puppet is never 'a subject or centre of spontaneous activity'.[6]

'What counts'—in Schutz's 'conceptual scheme'—is the point of view from which the scientist envisages the social world; and the central point of view is the 'scientific problem under examination'. It has 'exactly the same significance for the scientific activity as the practical interests have for activities in everyday work'. It is, in Schutz's view, the way in which the relevance 'of possible propositions' and 'a scheme of reference for construction of all ideal types which may be utilized as relevant' are created.[7]

This is Schutz's 'principle of relevance';[8] but there are also two postulations that go with it: (i) of 'subjective' interpretation and (ii) of 'adequacy'. The first, to explain the type of individual mind and the result of its activity within an 'understandable' relation; the second, to construct 'each term used in a scientific system referring to human action' in a way that 'a human act performed within the life-world by an individual actor' would be understandable for the actor as well as his fellow-men in its typical form.

This is Schutz's conception of 'pure theory' in sociology. A social scientist does not need more than 'these clarified methods, governed by the postulate mentioned', which 'give him the assurance that he will never lose contact with the world of daily life'. 'Methodology is not the preceptor or the tutor of the scientist. It is always his pupil...'

If 'social science' involves nothing more than what Schutz's 'pure' —and gentle—theory describes, then, one must agree, it does not need methodology either as a preceptor or even as a pupil. The phenomenology of everyday life is as obvious and comforting as the interchange of sympathy among friends. As a theory it eliminates *all* 'intrinsic difficulties hidden in the foundation of this scientific edifice' —which is more than Schutz asks of methodology![9]

N

185

Notes

Chapter 1 Problems of sociological analysis

1 *Philosophical Investigations*, tr. G. E. M. Anscombe, para. 97.
2 *Notebooks* 1914–16, tr. G. E. M. Anscombe, p. 53.
3 *Tractatus Logico-Philosophicus*, tr. D. F. Pears and B. F. McGuinness, para. 1.
4 It is immaterial how much he personally valued metaphysics, as K. T. Fann insists in *Wittgenstein's Conception of Philosophy*.
5 *Notebooks* 1914–16, p. 82
6 Para. 11.
7 *Philosophical Investigations*, para. 489.
8 Cf. Dilthey's analysis of the forms of understanding in Patrick Gardiner (ed.), *Theories of History*.

Chapter 2 Weber's ideas on the analysis of rationality and its effects on modern society

1 Von Schelting, op. cit., p. 182; cf. Weber's essay, 'Objectivity in Social Science' in *The Methodology of the Social Sciences*.
2 Cf. Weber, *Gesammelte Aufsätze zur Wissenschaftslehre*, pp. 64, 221.
3 *Gesammelte Aufsätze zur Wissenschaftslehre*, p. 67.
4 Ibid., p. 403
5 Cf. H. Rickert (tr. G. Reisman), *Science and History*, p. 35. Rickert's formulation of the principles of historical knowledge gives a complementary discussion of Weber's methodological ideas, as Weber follows Rickert in essential points.
6 The principle of the historian Eduard Meyer which Weber criticizes in 'Critical Studies in the Logic of the Cultural Sciences', *The Methodology of the Social Sciences*.
7 Cf. von Schelting, op. cit., p. 257.

8 Cf. Weber, 'Antikritisches Schlusswort 1910', reprinted in E. Baumgarten, *Max Weber, Werk und Person*, p. 173.
9 Cf. von Schelting, op. cit., p. 285.
10 Cf. von Schelting, op. cit., p. 290.
11 Cf. W. Sombart, *The Quintessence of Capitalism.*
12 Cf. Weber, *Gesammelte Aufsätze zur Religionsoziologie*, I, p. 201.
13 Ibid., p. 41 n. 1, p. 530 n. 1.
14 Cf. von Schelting, op. cit., p. 296.
15 These factors are extracted from Weber's discussion by von Schelting, with individual references given, op. cit., p. 297.
16 Weber, *Religionsoziologie* I, pp. 534–5; cf. von Schelting, op. cit., p. 299.
17 Weber, *Religionsoziologie* I, p. 535 ('. . . doch auch Kraft der ihren Eigengesetzlichkeiten zuzurechnenden Wirkungen an jenen Hemmungen stark mitbeteiligt gewesen sind').
18 Von Schelting, op. cit., p. 300.
19 Cf. von Schelting, op. cit., pp. 306–7.
20 Ibid., p. 308.
21 Cf. B. Pfister, *Entwicklung zum Idealtypus*, p. 143.
22 Cf. H. Oppenheimer, *Die Logik der soziologischen Begriffsbildung*, p. 13. He was the first, according to von Schelting (op. cit., p. 356 n. 2), to point this out, but he seems to have overlooked the role of understandable causal explanation in Weber's work.
23 Cf. my discussion of Weber's methodology with John Rex's contribution in *Max Weber and Modern Sociology.*
24 Von Schelting, op. cit., p. 362: 'ein Teil dieser Forschung den durch seine methodologische Reflexion erfassten formalen Rahmen "sprengte".'
25 Weber, *G.A.z. Wissenschaftslehre*, p. 190, n. 1.
26 Cf. von Schelting, op. cit., p. 358.
27 Von Schelting, op. cit., p. 360.
28 Von Schelting, op. cit., p. 361 et seq.
29 Von Schelting, op. cit., pp. 374ff.
30 Von Schelting, op. cit., p. 377.
31 Von Schelting, op. cit., p. 377; cf. Weber, *G.A.z. Religionsoziologie* I, pp. 81, 82, n. 1, 86, 135, 144, 192, 259, 112n.
32 Von Schelting, op. cit., p. 378.
33 Von Schelting, op. cit., p. 379.
34 Cf. Part III chapters 1 and 2 of my thesis 'Hindu Reformist Ethics and the Weber Thesis . . .', in which it has been possible to construct such an ideal type of Luther's as well as Calvin's doctrine-ethic systems for a comparison with similarly constructed ideal type of four independent historical Reformist movements.

Chapter 3 Pareto's analysis of sentiments and tradition in society

1 Cf. V. Pareto, *The Mind and Society*, para. 2062 and n. and para. 2066.

2 Ibid., para. 2329: 'The problem of interdependence of waves'.
3 Ibid.
4 Cf. paras 2329 and 616ff.
5 Ibid., para. 2339.
6 The discussion of the intrinsic aspect of the 'oscillation' is to be found first in paras 616f. then in para. 1678 and concluded in para. 2340.
7 Cf. para. 2341.
8 Cf. para. 2343.
9 Cf. para. 2410.
10 Cf. para. 2083.
11 Cf. paras 2204–7
12 Para. 2354.
13 Para. 2357.
14 Cf. paras 2384–6.
15 Cf. paras 2140ff.
16 Cf. para. 2143.
17 Cf. Weber's concept of value-relevance.
18 Cf. *The Mind and Society*, para. 2145.
19 Cf. para. 2146.
20 Ibid.
21 Cf. para. 2147.
22 Ibid., example 1 incl. notes 1–10.
23 Para. 2111.
24 Para. 2111 n. 1.
25 Para. 2115.
26 Para. 2120.
27 Cf. Weber's use of collectivities as 'historical individuals'.
28 Cf. para. 2134.
29 Cf. para. 2153.
30 Cf. para. 2154.
31 Cf. paras 2155ff.
32 This is because, in Pareto's view, 'human mind requires the ideal and the real in varying doses' (para. 2159).
33 Cf. para. 2160. Pareto equates this assumption or conviction of such writers to: 'derivations determine the form of society'. This statement has important consequences for any comparison between Pareto's and Weber's theories of action and social reality. See below, p. 107.
34 Cf. para. 2161.
35 Cf. para. 2162.
36 Para. 2163.
37 Cf. Pareto's discussion of the histories of the French Revolution, especially para. 2168.
38 Para. 2163.
39 Para. 2169.
40 Cf. para. 2169. This and following sentences are generalized from Pareto's discussion of various examples.
41 Para. 2169.

42 Para. 2170.
43 Cf. para. 2175.
44 Para. 2176
45 Cf. para. 2176 incl. n. 1.
46 Para. 2178.
47 Cf. paras 2178–9.
48 Para. 2253.
49 Para. 2254.
50 Para. 2254.
51 *Mind and Society*, chapter 1, para. 2.
52 Para. 4.
53 Para. 6. One can add that it still is, and the reason for this persistence may become clearer as we look a little more deeply into Pareto's discussion.
54 Para. 7
55 Pareto's technical term is 'narration'. See para. 7, ed's n. 1.
56 Para. 7.
57 Ibid.
58 Cf. paras 9–11.
59 Para. 16.
60 Para. 29; cf. para. 97.
61 Para. 13: the non-logical nexus is characterized, for Pareto, by 'logical sophistries, or specious reasonings calculated to deceive'.
62 Para. 13.
63 Para. 14.
64 Para. 14.
65 Para. 15.
66 Para. 32   .
67 Para. 33. These two kinds of critical comments are all too common in sociological writings, even though they appear commonplace.
68 Para. 22.
69 Para. 24.
70 Para. 43.
71 Para. 46; cf. para. 69.
72 Cf. para. 69.
73 Para. 50.
74 Cf. paras 48–9.
75 Paras 54–5; cf. para. 63.
76 Para. 56.
77 Cf. para. 57.
78 Para. 59.
79 Para. 60.
80 Para. 65.
81 Para. 66.
82 Para. 74.
83 As an example of such a mechanical explanation in a neutral language, see A. L. Stinchcombe, *Constructing Social Theories*.

190

84 Cf. Weber's concept of the ideal type.
85 Para. 146.
86 Para. 149. This is entirely consistent with his postulate of standard of logico-experimental truth lying in experience and observation, rather than in logic, rationality or in any substantive notions of reality as is frequently implied, if not stated, by philosophers, scientists, sociologists, etc.
87 Para. 150.
88 Para. 183.
89 Para. 184.
90 Cf. para. 216.
91 Cf. para. 219 and paras 155ff.
92 Para. 219.
93 Para. 219; cf. para. 14. This is provided by Pareto in his theory of derivations.
94 Para. 220.
95 Para. 221.
96 Para. 223.
97 Ibid.
98 Para. 225.
99 Para. 226.
100 Cf. para. 227.
101 Para. 228.
102 See paras 229–31 for Pareto's discussion of the changeover from kingship to magistracy in Greek and Latin cities.
103 Para. 232.
104 Para. 236 incl. n. 1 for a detailed analysis of the term by Pareto in justification of his definition.
105 Para. 238.
106 Para. 239.
107 Ibid.
108 Para. 241.
109 Ibid.
110 Para. 242.
111 Para. 244.
112 *Mind and Society*, vol. III.
113 Para. 253.
114 Ibid.
115 Paras 283 ff.
116 Cf. para. 284.
117 Cf. para. 285.
118 Cf. para. 287.
119 Cf. para. 290.
120 Para. 291.
121 Cf. paras 293–4.
122 Cf. para. 1399.
123 Cf. para. 1397.

124 Para. 1400.
125 Cf. para. 1400 for Pareto's discussion of the first stages in the elaboration of derivations.
126 Cf. para. 1400. These are class IV derivations. The first three classes are: (I) simple assertions; (II) appealing to the authority of socially accepted maxims; (III) abstract interpretations of sentiments (i.e. systems of metaphysics, theologies, etc.).
127 Cf. para. 1402.
128 Para. 1403.
129 Paras 1410–12.
130 Para. 1412.
131 Ibid.
132 Cf. paras 1413–14.
133 Para. 1415.
134 For a description of 'the logic of sentiments', see para. 480.
135 Para. 1416.
136 Cf. para. 1416.
137 Para. 1418. For the classification and discussion, through examples, of various kinds of derivation, see paras 1419ff.
138 Cf. para. 1431. The sentiment of authority is defined in para. 1157. Sentiments as such are discussed below, pp. 92ff, since they are not observable elements, in Pareto's theory, but are inferred from the analysis of logical and non-logical theories and derivations. This is the only way in which Pareto's theory of sociological analysis can be properly constructed.
139 Cf. para. 1435.
140 Para. 1443.
141 Cf. para. 1447.
142 Para. 1449.
143 Para. 1466.
144 Cf. para. 1469.
145 Para. 1475.
146 Para. 1476.
147 Paras 1477–8.
148 Cf. para. 1479.
149 Cf. para. 1481.
150 Para. 1485; the analysis of Bentham's philosophy follows in paras 1486–92.
151 Cf. para. 1489; incl. n. 3, in which he mentions that these conceptions will be reduced to exact definitions in due course—i.e. Vol. IV, chapter 12, 'The general form of society'.
152 Cf. para. 1492.
153 Cf. para. 1544. Also my comments on Wittgenstein's philosophy, above, chapter 1.
154 Para. 1546.
155 Cf. para. 1545.
156 Para. 1547.

157 Cf. para. 1548 incl. n. 1.
158 Cf. paras 1549–51.
159 Cf. para. 1552.
160 Cf. para. 1555.
161 Cf. paras 1614–66.
162 Cf. paras 1667 ff.
163 Cf. paras 1668–9.
164 Para. 1675.
165 Cf. para. 1678.
166 Para. 1682.
167 Para. 1683.
168 Cf. paras 803 and 848.
169 Para. 861.
170 Cf. para. 861.
171 Cf. para. 864.
172 Cf. paras 876–7.
173 Cf. para. 889.
174 Para. 891.
175 Cf. para. 896.
176 Cf. paras 1089–112.
177 Cf. paras 1113–206.
178 Cf. paras 1208–9.
179 Cf. paras 1240ff.
180 For reasons, see para. 852.
181 Cf. para. 1324.
182 Para. 1396.

Chapter 4 Comparative analysis of Weber and Pareto

1 The substance of this section (pp. 98–104 of the present chapter) was originally published as part of my editorial comment, 'Some ideas on sociological analysis', in *Sociological Analysis: A Discussion Journal of Research and Ideas*, Department of Sociological Studies, University of Sheffield, vol. 1, no. 1, October 1970.
2 A. von Schelting, op. cit., p. 44.
3 Cf. A. von Schelting, op. cit. pp.; 8ff.
4 Cf. above, pp. 18. Von Schelting's distinction between the theoretical value and theoretical premise should now become clearer.
5 In the sense Weber uses it. Cf. 'From a sociological point of view an "ethical" standard is one to which men attribute a certain type of value and which, by virtue of this belief, they treat as a valid norm governing their action', *Theory of Social and Economic Organization*, p. 129.

Chapter 5 Mannheim and social conditioning of knowledge

1 Based on lectures given at the London School of Economics 1934–5 and published posthumously.

2 Ibid., p. 1.
3 Ibid., p. 2.
4 Ibid., pp. 2–3.
5 Cf. ibid., p. 3 and p. 1.
6 Ibid., p. 131.
7 Cf. ibid., p. 133.
8 Ibid., p. 133.
9 Ibid., p. 143. This part of the book is based on his lectures on 'Social Structure'.
10 Ibid., p. 146.
11 Published subsequently in *Essays on Sociology and Social Psychology*, chapter 5.
12 Ibid., p. 195.
13 Ibid., p. 203.
14 Ibid., p. 204.
15 Ibid.
16 Cf. ibid., pp. 204–6.
17 Ibid., p. 206.
18 Cf. ibid., pp. 206–7.
19 Ibid., p. 207.
20 Ibid., p. 208; cf. Pareto's discussion of residues of combination and group persistence.
21 Cf. ibid., pp. 211–13.
22 Ibid., pp. 213–14.
23 Cf. ibid., pp. 214–17.
24 Ibid., p. 219.
25 Ibid., p. 220.
26 Cf. ibid., p. 220.
27 Cf. ibid., p. 221.
28 Cf. ibid., pp. 222–3.
29 K. Mannheim, *Ideology and Utopia*, p. 1.
30 Ibid., p. 4.
31 Ibid., p. 2.
32 Ibid., p. 4.
33 Ibid., p. 5.
34 Cf. ibid., pp. 10–11.
35 Cf. ibid., pp. 12–30.
36 Ibid., p. 12; cf. below, pp. 122ff for a discussion of his *Structural Analysis of Epistemology* to which he refers at this point.
37 Cf. *Ideology and Utopia*, pp. 12–14.
38 Cf. ibid., pp. 14ff.
39 Ibid., p. 28.
40 Ibid., p. 30.
41 Cf. ibid., p. 30.
42 Ibid., p. 36.
43 Cf. ibid., p. 36.
44 Cf. ibid., p. 40.

45 Ibid., p. 42.
46 Cf. ibid., p. 42.
47 Cf. ibid., p. 45.
48 Cf. ibid., pp. 45–6.
49 Cf. ibid., p. 47.
50 'The structural analysis of epistemology', see below, pp. 122 ff.
51 In *Max Weber's Wissenschaftslehre*, the chapter on methodology and the sociology of knowledge, pp. 65ff. For a summary of his critique of *Ideology and Utopia*, see his review article in *American Sociological Review*, August 1936.
52 Cf. e.g. 'it is, of course, true that in the social sciences, as elsewhere, the ultimate criterion of truth or falsity is to be found in the investigation of the object, and the sociology of knowledge is no substitute for this', *Ideology and Utopia*, p. 4.
53 Republished in his *Man and Society in an Age of Reconstruction*, as Part I; see especially pp. 52–3.
54 Cf. ibid., pp. 53–4.
55 Ibid., p. 55.
56 Ibid., p. 56.
57 Cf. ibid., p. 58.
58 Ibid.
59 Cf. ibid., pp. 56–8.
60 Ibid., p. 52.
61 First published as 'Die Strukturanalyse der Erkenntnistheorie' in *Kant-Studien*, Suppl. vol. no. 57, Berlin, 1922. The English translation was published in his *Essays on Sociology and Social Psychology*.
62 *Ideology and Utopia*, p. 12; cf. above, p. 118.
63 Mannheim, *Essays on Sociology and Social Psychology*, p. 15.
64 Ibid., p. 15.
65 Ibid., p. 22.
66 Ibid., p. 23.
67 Cf. ibid., p. 25.
68 Cf. ibid., pp. 22–3.
69 Cf. ibid., p. 43.
70 Cf. ibid., pp. 47–8.
71 *Ideology and Utopia*, pp. 262–3.
72 Ibid., p. 263.
73 Cf. ibid., p. 263.
74 Cf. ibid., p. 264.
75 Cf. ibid.
76 Cf. ibid., p. 266.
77 Cf. ibid., pp. 267–8.
78 Cf. ibid., p. 270.
79 Cf. ibid., p. 271.
80 Cf. ibid., p. 272.
81 Cf. ibid., p. 273.
82 Ibid., pp. 275–6.

83 Cf. ibid., p. 276.
84 Ibid.
85 Ibid., p. 277.
86 Cf. ibid., p. 277.
87 Ibid.
88 Cf. ibid., pp. 277–8
89 Cf. ibid., p. 278.
90 *American Sociological Review*, vol. 1, no. 4, August 1936, pp. 664–74.
91 Von Schelting uses the word 'untheoretical'; see ibid., p. 667.
92 Cf. Mannheim, *Ideology and Utopia*, pp. 183–4.
93 *American Sociological Review*, August 1936, pp. 671–2.
94 Ibid., p. 673.

Chapter 6 Parsons's 'theoretical' sociology and the solution of the problem of order in society

1 Cf. the encyclopaedic selection of social theories under this title, edited by Parsons *et al.*, claimed as a background to 'the modern sociological theory'.
2 Mannheim, *Essays on Sociology and Social Psychology*, p. 18.
3 Cf. ibid., pp. 18–19.
4 Cf. ibid., pp. 20–1.
5 Ibid., p. 22.
6 Cf. ibid., p. 23.
7 Cf. Parsons, *The Structure of Social Action*, p. 579 inc. n. 1. Parsons, nevertheless, acknowledges his 'great indebtedness' to von Schelting's work.
8 Ibid., pp. 594ff.
9 Cf. ibid., p. 597. This is due to a lack of appreciation by Weber, in Parsons's view, of an inherent tendency for the theoretical structures of all science in whatever field to become logically closed systems. This view is a clear Mannheimian axiom, as is the technique for achieving theoretical objectivity—by removing value-premise to a point outside the specific interest-part of Mannheim's 'sociology of knowledge'.
10 See below, p. 146.
11 Ibid., p. 597.
12 Ibid.
13 *American Sociological Review*, vol. 3, no. 1, February 1938.
14 Cf. ibid., pp. 14–15.
15 Ibid., pp. 15–16.
16 Cf. ibid., pp. 16–18.
17 Cf. ibid., p. 19.
18 Ibid.
19 Cf. Mannheim, *Essays on Sociology and Social Psychology*, pp. 24–5.
20 Cf. ibid., pp. 36–9.
21 Ibid., pp. 41–8.

22 Ibid., p. 41.
23 Ibid., p. 43.
24 Parsons, 'The role of theory in social research', op. cit., p. 20.
25 Cf. ibid., p. 16; and above, p. 135.
26 Weber's *Socoilogy of Religion* (tr. E. Fischoff), London, 1965, p. xxvii; cf. below, p. 152, my comments on his 'evolutionary perspective' itself.
27 Cf. Parsons's review article on von Schelting's book, *Max Weber's Wissenschaftslehre*, in *American Sociological Review*, vol. 1, no. 4, August 1936, p. 678.
28 *International Journal of Ethics* (now *Ethics*), vol. 45, no. 3, April 1935, pp. 282–316. The importance of this essay for understanding the genesis and development of Parsons's theory was realized by J. Finley Scott in his article 'The changing foundations of the Parsonian action scheme', *American Sociological Review*, vol. 28, no. 5, October 1963. But he fails to see that the question posed by Max Black—which is his starting point—'how are the basic categories of Parsons's theory obtained?'—can be answered not by describing the changes in the vocabulary of Parsons but by examining the basic formulations or concepts *and the reasoning behind them.*
29 In this, Finley Scott's article, op. cit., is a very useful guide.
30 Cf. above, p. 137.
31 'The place of ultimate values', *Ethics*, April 1935, p. 283.
32 Ibid., p. 284.
33 Ibid.
34 Ibid., p. 285.
35 Cf. ibid., pp. 286–7.
36 Ibid., p. 287.
37 Cf. ibid., p. 287.
38 Ibid., pp. 288–9.
39 Ibid., p. 293.
40 Ibid.
41 Ibid., p. 294.
42 Ibid., p. 295.
43 Ibid.; cf. 'General interpretation of action' in *Theories of Society* (ed. Parsons *et al.*), p. 96, and *The Structure of Social Action* (p. 89) for at least two references to the aim of his life's work in sociological theory: the solution of the Hobbesian problem of order.
44 Ibid., p. 297.
45 Ibid., p. 295; cf. above, p. 141.
46 Ibid., p. 305.
47 Ibid.
48 Another is: 'This paper has attempted in very brief compass to cover an enormous amount of ground', ibid., p. 312.
49 Cf. 'Further development from Weber's starting point would, logically, lead to a generalized scheme of the structure of social relationships and groups which is logically an indispensable immediate background

197

for a typological classification of the possibilities of variation within each basic category' (pp. 28–9).

50 Cf. *Man and Society in an Age of Social Reconstruction*, p. 53.

51 *American Sociological Review*, vol. 1, no. 4, August 1936, pp. 657–81. These criticisms are also found in Parsons's *The Structure of Social Action*, but they are in a more convenient form here.

52 Ibid., p. 678.

53 Cf. ibid., pp. 678–9.

54 Ibid., p. 679. This seems to be the only way one can construe the point, both on the basis of the grammatical structure of the sentence and on the meaning of Weber's theory. The relevant passage in Parsons's text is rather odd:

> It may mean either a hypothetical 'objectively possible' fictional entity, a 'unit' or 'part' of a historical individual . . . If this is the 'element', then the law is a generalization about the behaviour of this hypothetical entity under assumed conditions.
>
> On the other hand, the element may be a 'general property' of historical individuals, such as 'economic rationality' . . . Then a 'law' is a uniform mode of relationship between the specific 'values' of two such elements or properties. Both are abstract, general concepts, but the logical distinction between them is vital.

55 This interpretation of value-relevance has had far-reaching consequence for contemporary sociology (see next few chapters). It is remarkably similar to Mannheim's (cf. my chapter on methodology in *Max Weber and Modern Sociology*).

56 Discussed above, pp. 138 ff.

57 See his article 'The role of theory in social research', discussed above, pp. 134–8.

58 See above, p. 137.

59 Cf. I 'In the first place, the principle of value-relevance combined with that of the relativity of value-systems introduces an element of relativity into the social sciences which raises in an acute form the question of their claim to objectivity. Even though a value-element enters into the selection of the material of science, once this material is given it is possible to come to objectively valid conclusions about the causes and consequences of given phenomena free of value-judgments and hence binding on anyone who wishes to attain truth, regardless of what other subjective values he may hold', Talcott Parsons, *The Structure of Social Action*, p. 594.

II 'The first source of difficulty seems to lie in Weber's attempt to draw too rigid a distinction between the *subjective* directions of interest of the scientist in each of the two groups of sciences', ibid., p. 595.

III 'The motives for interest in problems, which is inherently value-relative, and the grounds of the validity of judgments, which in the nature of the case cannot be relative in the same sense', Parsons, 'An approach to the sociology of knowledge', *Sociological Theory and Modern Society*, p. 140.

IV Parsons, *The Structure of Social Action*, p. 593, refers to Weber, *Aufsätze zur Wissenschaftslehre*, p. 178, to say that 'relevance to value' 'constitutes the selective principle for the empirical material of the social sciences'. Weber says in the relevent passage on p. 178 (in the essay 'Die Objektivität sozialwissenschaftlicher und sozial-politischer Erkenntnis'): 'in jedem Fall nur ein Teil der individuellen Wirklichkeit für uns Interesse und Bedeutung hat, weil nur er in Beziehung steht zu den Kulturwertideen, mit welchen wir an die Wirklichkeit herantreten.' (In every case only a part of the individual reality has interest and meaning for us, because only that has relevance to the *cultural* values with which we approach reality.)

One should note that there is no mention of a *subjective* interest of the scientist 'which is relevant to his approach to reality'.

60 Cf. my thesis 'Hindu reformist ethics and the Weber thesis . . .'.

61 Cf. my 'Sociology of caste and sect: analysis or description?' *Sociological Analysis: A Discussion Journal*, vol. 1 no. 1, pp. 51–60 and my thesis, chapter 1, for a detailed discussion of structural functionalism and evolutionary and comparative perspectives.

62 The means-end relationship has in Parsons's theory become 'of means' and 'of ends'.

Chapter 7   Merton and Bendix: generalizations of limited range and comparative study of societies

1 *American Sociological Review*, vol. 1, no. 6, December 1936, pp. 894–903.

2 We find an impressive list, by the way, of Merton's predecessors, i.e. who have treated this problem in the long history of social thought, as his authority for treating it once again, ibid., p. 894, n. 1.

3 Ibid., p. 895.

4 Ibid. The concepts are borrowed by Merton from Alfred Weber's *Kultursoziologie*.

5 Ibid., p. 896, referring, of course, to Weber: *Wirtschaft und Gesellschaft*, Tübingen, 1925, pp. 3ff.

6 Ibid., p. 896.

7 Cf. ibid., pp. 896–903 incl. notes. 'Stochastic' associations, according to Merton, 'are not inherent in social knowledge but derive from our lack of experimental control', ibid., p. 896.

8 Ibid., p. 902.

9 Ibid., p. 903.

10 Ibid. One wonders whether this preoccupation is directly derived from Mannheim or from Weber!

11 Ibid., p. 904.

12 For an ideal typical selection, in the Weberian sense, of their interpretation of Christian doctrines and ethics, see my thesis, Conclusion (Part III chapter 1).

13 A recent example of this mistaken view is S. E. Finer's 'Assessment and critique', *Pareto: Sociological Writings* (ed. Finer), pp. 72–87. Finer bases his criticisms primarily on M. Ginsberg's chapter on Pareto in his book *Reason and Unreason in Society*.

14 *American Journal of Sociology*, vol. 50, no. 6, May 1945, pp. 462–73.

15 Ibid., p. 472.

16 Ibid., p. 473.

17 Cf. his reference, ibid., p. 473 n. 31.

18 Ibid., p. 473.

19 Ibid., p. 463.

20 *American Sociological Review*, vol. 28, no. 4, August 1963, pp. 532–539.

21 Ibid., p. 532.

22 'Max Weber's interpretation of conduct and history', *American Journal of Sociology*, vol. 51, July 1945–May 1946, discussed below, p. 158.

23 *Comparative Studies in Society and History*, vol. 9, no. 3, April 1967.

24 Cf. 'Concepts and generalizations . . .', *American Sociological Review*, August 1963 pp. 535–8.

25 This sentence is translated correctly in Finch & Shils translation of Weber's *Methodology of Social Sciences*, p. 159, though slightly differently phrased. Cf.

'Subjektiv' in einem bestimmen, hier nicht nochmals zu erörternden Sinn ist nicht die Feststellung der historischen 'Ursachen' bei gegebenem Erklärungs-'Objekt', sondern die *Abgrenzung* der historischen 'Objektes', des 'Individuum' selbst, denn hier entscheiden Wertbeziehungen, deren '*Auffassung*' dem historischen Wandel unterworfen ist' (my italics).

26 *A.J.S.* vol. 51, p. 521.

27 Ibid., p. 521.

28 See ibid., p. 523, n. 22.

29 'Weber's interpretation of conduct and history', *A.J.S.* vol. 51, p. 521.

30 Ibid.

31 Ibid.

32 Ibid.

33 Cf. ibid., pp. 521ff.: sections III and IV: 'Sociology and history' and 'Weber's interpretation of history'.

34 Ibid., n. 18.

35 Ibid., pp. 521–2, incl. n. 19.

36 Ibid., p. 522.

37 Cf. ibid., p. 523.

38 Cf. ibid., p. 525.

39 Ibid., pp. 525–6.

NOTES TO PAGES 164-169

40 See, for example, Parsons's *Sociological Theory and Modern Society*, chapter 5, 'Some preliminaries', p. 140.

Chapter 8 Dahrendorf: conflict as a reorientation of sociological analysis or a substitute 'grand' theory

1 Cf. below, p. 167 ff., my discussion of his notion of falsifiability.
2 Dahrendorf: *Class and Class Conflict in Industrial Society*, Preface.
3 *Essays in the Theory of Society*, chapter 1, section III, p. 6.
4 Ibid., p. 7.
5 Ibid., p. 8.
6 *American Journal of Sociology*, vol. 64, September 1958, reprinted in *Essays in the Theory of Society*.
7 Ibid., p. 124.
8 Ibid.
9 Cf. ibid., p. 123.
10 Ibid.
11 Ibid., p. 124.
12 Ibid., p. 124n.
13 Cf. Karl R. Popper, *Logik der Forschung zur Erkenntnistheorie der Modernen Naturwissenschaft*, p. 1: 'Die Tätigkeit des wissenschaftlichen Forschers besteht darin, Sätze oder Systeme von Sätzen aufzustellen und systematisch zu überprüfen; in den empirischen Wissenschaften sind es insbesondere Hypothesen, Theoriensysteme, die aufgestellt und an der Erfahrung durch Beobachtung und Experiment überprüft werden.'
14 Cf. ibid., pp. 5–7 (Die deduktive Überprüfung der Theorien).
15 Cf. Popper, *Logic of Scientific Discovery*, pp. 34 ff. This book is an extended translation of the *Logik der Forschung* by Popper himself. (Cf. ibid., p. 6, Translator's Note.)
16 This test, applied to Dahrendorf, shows his own theory of conflict to be an extra-empirical one—unfalsifiable, neither provable nor disprovable, see below, p. 171.
17 Cf. above, chapter 1.
18 Cf. 'Out of utopia', *A.J.S.*, p. 120 incl. n.10.
19 See, for example, his *Conflict after Class, New Perspective on the Theory of Social and Political Conflict*, pp. 16–17.
20 Cf. *Homo Sociologicus*, p. 16. This is a theory about the 'sociological man' who stands between the individual and the society and is the carrier of the socially pre-formed role. The individual thus is his social role, and sociology is concerned with the 'discovery of the structure of the social roles'.
21 Cf. *Conflict after Class*, p. 16.
22 Cf. *Homo Sociologicus*, p. 74: 'Soll die Soziologie nicht zum Instrument der Unfreiheit und Unmenschlichkeit werden, so ist mehrvorn Soziologen verlangt. Das Bewusstsein des ganzen Menschen und

seines Anspruches auf Freiheit muss als Hintergrund jeden Satz, den er spricht oder schreibt, bestimmen . . .'

(. . . it is demanded of the sociologist that every sentence that he writes or speaks should have the claim of all men to freedom as its background).

23 'Out of utopia', *A.J.S.*, p. 118.
24 Ibid., p. 122.
25 Cf. Dahrendorf's theory of conflict with Marshall's notion of social phenomena being divided into non-system, pro-system and anti-system, in his *Society at Crossroads and Other Essays*, p. 28 and p. 31.
26 'Out of utopia', *A.J.S.*, p. 123 n.14.
27 Ibid., p. 123.
28 Ibid., p. 124.
29 Ibid., p. 126.
30 Ibid.
31 Ibid.
32 Ibid., p. 127.
33 Ibid., p. 126.
34 Ibid.
35 Ibid., p. 127 n. 19.

Chapter 9 Conclusion

1 Cf. *Max Weber and Modern Sociology*, chapter 4.
2 Cf. Alfred Schutz's proposal of an alternative to behaviourism, in his 'The social world and the theory of social action', *Collected Papers*, vol. II (Studies in Social Theory), especially pp. 4–5:

> The fathers of behaviourism had no other purpose than that of describing and explaining real human acts within a real human world. But the fallacy of this theory consists in the substitution of a fictional world for social reality by promulgating methodological principles as appropriate for the social sciences which, though proved true in other fields, prove a failure in the realm of intersubjectivity.

3 Ibid., p. 20, 'Dimensions of the Social World'.
4 Ibid., pp. 64ff., 'The Problem of Rationality in the Social World'.
5 Ibid., p. 64. He approves of Parsons's definition of 'rational action' in *The Structure of Social Action* (p. 58) but finds that this theoretical formulation needs to be 'contrasted' with 'other levels of our experience of the social world' (cf. ibid., pp. 64–5).
6 Cf. ibid., pp. 81–3.
7 Cf. ibid., p. 83.
8 Ibid., p. 84.
9 Cf. ibid., p. 88.

Bibliography

BAUMGARTEN, E., *Max Weber, Werk und Person*, Tübingen, 1964.

BENDIX, R., 'Concepts and generalizations in comparative sociological studies', *American Sociological Review*, vol. 28, no. 4, August 1936.

BENDIX, R., 'Tradition and modernity reconsidered', *Comparative Studies in Society and History*, vol. 5, no. 3, April 1967.

BENDIX, R., 'Max Weber's interpretation of conduct and history', *American Journal of Sociology*, vol. 51, July 1954–May 1946.

BENDIX, R., *Max Weber: An Intellectual Portrait*, Anchor Books, New York, 1962.

DAHRENDORF, R., *Essays in the Theory of Society*, Routledge & Kegan Paul, London, 1968.

DAHRENDORF, R., *Class and Class Conflict in Industrial Society*, Stanford, 1959/London, 1963.

DAHRENDORF, R., 'Out of utopia: toward a reorientation of sociological analysis' *American Journal of Sociology* (reprinted in *Essays in the Theory of Society*), vol. 64, September 1958.

DAHRENDORF, R., *Conflict After Class, New Perspective on the Theory of Social and Political Conflict* (Noel Buxton Lecture, University of Essex), Longman, London, 1967.

DAHRENDORF, R., *Homo Sociologicus*, Cologne and Opladen, 1965.

FANN, K. T., *Wittgenstein's Conception of Philosophy*, Blackwell, Oxford, 1969.

FINER, S. E. (ed.), *Pareto: Sociological Writings*, Pall Mall Press, London, 1966.

GARDINER, P., *Theories of History*, Allen & Unwin, London, 1960.

MANNHEIM, K., *Man and Society in an Age of Reconstruction*, Kegan Paul, London, 1940.

MANNHEIM, K., *Ideology and Utopia* (tr. L. Wirth and E. Shils), Routledge & Kegan Paul, London (3rd impression), 1946.

MANNHEIM, K., *Essays on Sociology and Social Psychology* (ed. P. Kecskemeti), Routledge & Kegan Paul, London, 1953 (3rd impression, 1966).

203

MANNHEIM, K., *Systematic Sociology* (eds J. S. Eros and W. A. C. Stewart), Routledge & Kegan Paul, London, 1957.

MARSHALL, T. H., *Society at Crossroads and Other Essays*, Heinemann, London, 1963.

MERTON, R., 'Sociological theory', *American Journal of Sociology*, vol. 50, no. 6, May 1945.

MERTON, R., 'Unanticipated consequences of purposive action', *American Sociological Review*, vol. 1, no. 6, December 1936.

OPPENHEIMER, H., *Die Logik der soziologischen Begriffsbildung*, Tübingen, 1925.

PARETO, V., *The Mind and Society* (tr. by A. Bongiorno and A. Livingston), Cape, London, 1935.

PARSONS, T., *Sociological Theory and Modern Society*, Collier-Macmillan, New York and London, 1967.

PARSONS, T., 'The place of ultimate values in sociological theory', *International Journal of Ethics* (now *Ethics*), vol. 45, no. 3, April 1935.

PARSONS, T., Review Article on A. von Schelting's *Max Webers Wissenschaftslehre*, *American Sociological Review*, vol. 1, no. 4, Augus 1936.

PARSONS, T., 'The role of theory in social research', *American Sociological Review*, vol. 3, no. 1, February 1938.

PARSONS, T., *The Structure of Social Action*, Free Press (paper edn), New York; Allen & Unwin, London, 1968.

PARSONS, T., *Societies: Evolutionary and Comparative Perspectives*, Prentice-Hall, Englewood Cliffs, 1966.

PARSONS, T., et al., *Theories of Society*, Free Press, New York, 1961; Collier-Macmillan, London, 1965.

PFISTER, B., *Entwicklung zum Idealtypus*, Tübingen, 1928.

POPPER, K. R., *Logik der Forschung zur Erkenntnistheorie der Modernen Naturwissenschaft*, Vienna, 1935.

POPPER, K. R., *Logic of Scientific Discovery*, Hutchinson, London (rev. edn), 1968.

RICKERT, H., *Science and History* (tr. G. Reisman), Van Nostrand, Princeton, 1962.

SAHAY, A., *Max Weber and Modern Sociology* (ed.), Routledge & Kegan Paul, London, 1971.

SAHAY, A., 'Hindu reformist ethics and the Weber thesis: an application of Max Weber's methodology', London University Ph.D. thesis.

SAHAY, A., 'Some ideas on sociological analysis', *Sociological Analysis: A Discussion Journal of Research and Ideas*. Department of Sociological Studies, University of Sheffield, vol. 1, no. 1, October 1970.

SAHAY, A., 'Sociology of caste and sect: analysis or description?', ibid.

SCHELTING, A. VON, *Max Webers Wissenschaftslehre*, Tübingen, 1934.

SCHUTZ, A., *Collected Papers*, The Hague, 1964.

SCOTT, J. FINLEY, 'The changing foundations of the Parsonian action scheme', *American Sociological Review*, vol, 28, no. 5, October 1963.

SOMBART, W., *The Quintessence of Capitalism*, Unwin, London, 1915.

STINCHCOMBE, A. L., *Constructing Social Theories*, Harcourt Brace & World, New York, 1968.

WEBER, M., *The Theory of Social and Economic Organization*, Free Press, New York (paper edn), 1964.

WEBER, M., *Gesammelte Aufsätze zur Wissenschaftslehre*, Tübingen, 1922.

WEBER, M., *The Methodology of the Social Sciences* (tr. & ed. by E. A. Shils and H. A. Finch), Free Press, New York, 1949 (5th printing 1969).

WEBER, M., *Gesammelte Aufsätze zur Religionssoziologie*, vol. I, Tübingen, 1920 (reprinted 1963).

WITTGENSTEIN, L., *Tractatus Logico-Philosophicus* (tr. by D. F. Pears and B. F. McGuinness), Routledge & Kegan Paul, London, 1961.

WITTGENSTEIN, L., *Notebooks 1914–16* (tr. G. E. M. Anscombe), Blackwell, Oxford, 1961.

WITTGENSTEIN, L., *Philosophical Investigations* (tr. G. E. M. Anscombe), Blackwell, Oxford, 1953.

Index

Abgrenzung, 159
Abstraction, personified, 91
Action, 25; determinants of social, 15; free, 21; human, 66, 154; logical, 98; rational, 21, 104, 139, 142, 146; rationality of, 154; responsible, 98; sentimental, 98, 107n
Actiones legis, 78
Actions, voluntary, 143
Actor, consequences to the, 153
Actor-observers, 22
Actors, 22
Advance, technological, 31
Affectual-rationality, 46n
Analysis, aim of, 173; analogical, 30, 33, 37, 45; *a priori*, 4, 8; causal, 25, 26, 33, 43, 99, 101, 162; comparative, 98; concept in, 44; conceptual, 178; empirical, 10–11, 15, 46, 50; empirical causal, 137, 144; epistemological, 123; experimental, 15, 32; linguistic, 3; means-end, 106; Pareto's, 53, 130; problems of sociological, 1; scientific, 6, 7, 9, 72; social-scientific, 7, 12, 98; valid, 18; Weber's sociological, 98
Approach, scientific, 66
A priori, theoretical, 37
Argument, 'derivational', 53
Arguments, relational, 43
Association, conjectural, 154
Assumptions, *a priori*, 30n, 57
Auffassung, 159

Augur, 78
Authority-derivation, 87

Bastiat, F., 57
Behaviour, human, 22
Behaviourism, doctrines, 97
Belief, 1, 11; collective, 129; derivational, 53; dogmatic, 107
Berufsarbeit, 35
Betrieb, 35

Capitalism, industrial, 31; modern, 31, 160; political, 32, 34, 35; spirit of, 27, 155; study of, 17; Western, 30
Casuistry, 162
Categories, general, 12, 15, 31; Parsonian, 149; substantive, 11
Causality, 45
Change, cyclical, 81
Civilization, Chinese, 33n
Class, governing, 64; subject, 59, 64
Classes, the ruling, 59
'Codification', 156
Combination-residues, 65
Comte, Auguste, 82
Concept, inferential, 92
Concepts, definitional, 45, 105, 180; empirical, 138; general, 20, 22, 31, 45, 47, 147; historical, 23; interdependence of, 133; logical structure of, 20; social scientific, 19; Weber's methodological, 38
Conceptualization, general theoretical, 147

207

Conclusions, hypothetico-deductive, 72
Conditions, adequacy of, 41
Conduct, human, 61; logical, 51, 92, 103; non-logical, 51, 82, 85, 92, 103; sentimental, 103; value-determined rational, 103
Conflict, social, 170
Conformity, intellectual, 64
Conscience, 61
Consequences, historical, 43; normative, 41, 43; social, 107
Construction, hypothetico-deductive, 28
Constructions, hypothetical, 30

Darwinism, social, 56
Definition, meaningful, 12; processes of, 11
Definitions, abstract, 30n, 45; *a priori*, 15; empirical, 140
Derivation, formalized, 156
Derivations, 19, 51, 53, 57, 88; character, 57; sentimental, 109; specific, 62n; theory, 82; verbal, 90
'Derivative', 105
Description, analytical, 43; historical, 17; scientific, 6, 178; valid, 50
Descriptions, ideal-typical, 25; sociological, 15; value-relevant, 24
Destiny, human, 24
Determinants, 120; social, 85
Determinism, rational, 6, 7, 12, 20
Development, future, 16; historical, 17; past, 16
Differences, individual perceptual, 47
Doctrine, 2
Doctrines, 42; methodological, 29; theory of, 54
Dynamics, social, 112

Element, conceptual, 133

'Élites', circulation of, 49
Empiricism, practical, 63
'End', 139
End-rationality, 46n
Entities, aesthetic, 108; empirical, 145
Epistemology, 117, 124; Mann-heimian, 151
Equilibrium, 49; concept, 50
Erklärung, 115
Ethic, Protestant, 27, 34, 35, 155; economic, 27
Ethics, 42; religious, 107
Events, historical, 21
Existence, 123
Experience, 9; interdependence of, 118; social, 14, 100
Experienceability, 46, 46n
Explanation, 8; *a priori* theoretical, 6; causal, 24, 26, 44, 101; empirical, 6; meaningful, 25, 101, 105; principle of, 20; rational, 47; 178; scientific, 47, 52; value-related, 147
Explanations, deductive, 6; empirical, 29; ideal typical, 30n; logical, 88

Fact, social, 53
Factor, causal, 30, 34; historical, 32, 34
Facts, experimental, 68; historical-social, 150
Falsifiability, 169
Fann, K. T., 187 n4
Forces, social, 65
Form, ideal-typical, 101; logical, 77
Frame-group, 112
Function, notion of, 128

Generalization, *a priori*, 16; empirical, 42, 137; inferential, 15; sociological, 28
Generalizations, empirical, 6, 11, 45, 50; hypothetical, 45
Generalizations of Limited Range, 153

Gesinnungsethik, 104

History, individuality, 20; 'irrationality', 20; philosophies, 81; problem, 62; scientific, 60
Hypotheses, *a priori*, 14; intuitive, 28

Ideal type, 26, 45, 150; acausal, 37, 44; causal, 42, 45; general, 36; historical causal, 36; individualizing, 101n; meaningful, 41, 42
Ideal types, 101, 126, 136, 139; definitional, 139; empirical, 140; personal, 185
Idealities, description, 44
Ideas, ethical, 44; non-empirical, 146
'Ideology', concept, 118
Identity, objective, 24
Implications, logical, 66
Impulses, non-logical, 59 volitional, 117
Imputation, 126; causal, 26, 45, 150
Individual, historical, 43, 44, 149, 150
Individuality, concept, 19; description, 45; value-relevant, 26
Inferences, general, 45; linguistic, 2
Intelligentsia, free-floating, 117, 128
Interdependences, 49
Interest, direction of scientists', 149
Interests, 95; immediacy of, 154
Interpretation, causal, 38; logical, 75
Interpretations, existential, 146
Interrelation, causal, 36
Intuitions, *a priori*, 45
Investigations, Philosophical, 4
Irrationality, 20; concept, 20; meaning, 21

Judgments, ethical, 61; moral, 61; rational, 101

Knowledge, *a priori*, 6; axiom of, 109; empirical, 46; historical, 22, 38; natural-scientific, 4, 7, 13, 21; objective, 17, 98; philosophical duality of, 39; principle of rational, 9; principle of sociological, 11, 174; rational, 118; rational concept, 36; scientific, 7n, 18, 47, 49, 145, 148n; social conditioning of, 1n, 112; social-scientific, 18, 20, 47, 100; sociological, 39, 49, 99, 105, 147, 176; sociology of, 1n, 108, 112, 115, 124, 126; subject, 19; theory, 123, 125; understandable, 43, 44
Kreislauf, 114

Language, *a priori* structure, 4; derivational, 85n; form and content, 5; logic, 3; neutral, 74, 85n; structure, 2; theory, 3
Law, rational, 31
Laws, causal, 20; elements and general, 149
Lazarsfeld, 156;
Legitimacy, moral, 58
Logic, 18; unity, 122; use, 2

Matter, experimental, 70; non-experimental, 70
Maxims, practical, 43   [43
Meaning, 11, 25; adequacy of, 41,
Meaningfulness, 45; antithesis of, 44
Metaphysics, Hegelian, 71; realized, 7
Methodology, 18; Durkheimian, 151; individualizing, 20; objectivist, 20; social scientific, 7; structural-functional, 171; Weber's, 17, 44, 98
Meyer, Eduard, 187n 6
'Middle-range', 153
Mill, John Stuart, 85
Mobility, social, 96
Modernization, 176
Morality, sociologist's, 166
Motivation, human, 43; psychological, 43

Motive, ideal, 41
Motives, pure ideal, 43
Movements, historical-social, 17; Reformist, 188n 34; social, 51

Nexus, logical, 70, 103; non-logical, 70, 103
Nominalism, 73
Noology, 124
Norm, ideal-typical, 44
Norms, 62; social, 65
Notion, *a priori*, 13
Notions, philosophical, 3

Objectivity, 1, 25; empirical, 22
Order, *a priori*, 2
Orientation, ideological, 30
'Oscillations', 51; social, 51

Pacifism, 59
Paganism, 55
Perception, 11
Phenomena, non-understandable, 40; social, 45, 52, 60, 84
Phenomenology, 97
Phenomenon, historical, 20, 22; natural, 6, 20
Philosophy, Bentham's, 89; Comtean, 67
Planning, social, 154
Pluralism, methodical, 122
Position, Rickert-Weber, 147
Postulates, deterministic, 101; quasi-axiomatic, 122
Prediction, scientific, 16
Premise, theoretical, 18, 106
Principle, *a priori*, 102; methodological, 12, 21, 29, 50
Principles, metaphysical, 6; rational, 7; substantive, 102
Problem, data of, 56
Problem-consciousness, 166, 169
Process, fundamental social, 154; historical, 20
Processes, historical-causal, 42; social, 116

Profit-motive, 32
Proposition, scientific, 4
Protestantism, ascetic, 33
Proudhon, P. J., 57

Rationalism, Western, 33n
Rationality, 69, 120; analysis of, 17; acausal meaningful, 42; causal, 42, 46; functional, 120; ideal, 47; objective, 45; premise of, 21; problem of, 184; sociological, 46, 109, 174; subjective, 17, 98; traditional, 46
Realism, 73
Reality, 91; conceptual, 3, 6, 22; empirical, 28, 150; existential, 151; historical, 20, 100; individuality of, 21; logico-experimental, 91; manifestation, 47; psychological, 44, 45; social, 2, 11, 12, 14, 17, 20, 22, 46, 56, 57, 60, 70, 93, 102, 106, 128, 164, 174; social-historical, 45, 100; understandable actual, 40
Reason, 55
Reasoning, form, 53
Reasonings, derivational, 83, 88, 91; logico-experimental, 56; sentimental, 57
Re-experience, 45; inner, 40
Relationalism, 124
Relations, causal, 134; explanation of, 149
Relationship, causal, 22, 31, 44, 134; empirical, 66; means-end, 20, 21, 47, 104, 109, 139 ,144
Relevance, Schutz's principle, 185
Religio, 79
Religion, sociology of, 79n
Renaissance, 55
Research, social-scientific, 101
Residues, 49, 54, 89; classes, 52; concept, 66, 93; nature, 93; Pareto's theory, 56, 92
Rhetorica, Aristotle's, 90
Rickert, H., 187n 5

Science, generalization, 15; natural, 3
Scott, J. Finley, 197n 28
Seinverbundenheit, 127
Selection, valid, 23
Self-rationalization, 121
Sentiments, 96; general, 52; humanitarian, 64; logic, 86
Sex-residues, 95
Significance, causal historical, 163
Sinnadäquanz, 41
Situation, value-generating, 113
Social processes, results, 1
Social science, philosophy of, 169
Socialism, 59
Sociality, sentiments of, 62
Societies, abstract, 55; comparative study, 153
Society, modern ,17; tradition in, 49; use of force in, 62
Sociology, comparative, 112; definition of, 66; historical, 112; Mannheim's, 126; Max Weber's, 17, 21, 153; Parsons's theoretical, 132, 144; Schutz's phenomenological, 182; structural, 114
Sombart, W., 188n 11
Spencer, Herbert, 82, 83
Spirit, conservative, 79
Stability, social, 144
Structural-functionalism, 152
Structure, modern economic, 31; industrial-economic, 31; logical, 19, 26
Studies, comparative sociological, 157
Study, inductive, 13
Subjectivity, metaphysical, 20
Successors, the world of, 183
Superstition, 55
Syllogism, 89
System, economic, 27; social, 49, 50, 110n
Systematization, 122, 132, 136; epistemological, 123

Taboos, social, 166

Tests, logical, 6
Theologies, history of, 84
Theories, *a priori*, 73; intuitionist, 19; logico-experimental, 72, 86; middle-range, 155, 165; non-logical, 86, 91; objectivist, 19
Theory, analytical, 137; *a priori* systematic, 12; deductive, 137; generalized analytical, 135, 137; 'grand', 155; Pareto's, 130; sociological, 12; substitute 'grand', 165; 'truth-function', 2; workable, 19
Thesis, Protestant ethic, 31
Thought, *a priori*, 15, 30; categorical, 46; phenomenology of, 124; scientific, 106
Thought-patterns, values of, 18
Traditionalism, 31
Traditions, 87
Truth, empirical, 119; experimental, 53; logico-experimental, 69, 72; normatively valid, 120; objective valid, 119; substantive, 105

Unconscious, the collective, 118
Understanding, causal, 46
Universal, sociological, 157
Unreality, the ideally-understandable, 40
Utility, 49; individual, 59; maximum, 59; problem of, 60; social, 51, 53, 58, 61, 91, 104; theory of, 55; variation in, 59
'Utopia', concept of, 118, 128

Validation, analytical, 13
Validity, 1, 123; criteria, 18; empirical, 29, 45, 106; judgment of, 102; meaningful subjective, 25; objective, 15, 99, 127; principles, 28n; question of, 129
Value, theoretical, 18
Value-actions, 107
Value-criterion, Mannheim's, 131
Value-ends, transcendental, 35

Value-facts, 81
Value-ideas, 23, 24, 43
Value-interpretations, 104
Value-judgment, 24, 130, 144
Value-orientations, 146, 159
Value-position, 23
Value-premise, 106, 141
Value-rationality, 46n
Value-relevance, 23, 25n, 37, 100, 134, 142, 148n, 151n, 155; Weber's, 149
Value-system, ultimate, 143
Value-systems, 141
Values, 96, 136; basic, 154; clarification of, 43; substantive, 53; supra-historical, 23
Verantwortungsethik, 104

Verifiability, 169
Verstehen, 115
View, objectivist, 20
von Jhering, R., 78
von Schelting, A., 18n, 37, 98, 119, 126

Weltanschauungen, 117
Wertbeziehungen, 159
Wertrationalität, 103
Wirksamkeit, 23
Wittgenstein, Ludwig, 2
World, nature of, 2
'World-views', 108, 117, 120

Zweckrationalität, 103

International Library of Sociology

Edited by
John Rex
University of Warwick

Founded by
Karl Mannheim

as The International Library of Sociology
and Social Reconstruction

*This Catalogue also contains other Social Science
series published by Routledge*

Routledge & Kegan Paul London and Boston

68-74 Carter Lane London EC4V 5EL
9 Park Street Boston Mass 02108

Contents

General Sociology 3
Foreign Classics of Sociology 3
Social Structure 3
Sociology and Politics 4
Foreign Affairs 5
Criminology 5
Social Psychology 5
Sociology of the Family 6
Social Services 6
Sociology of Education 7
Sociology of Culture 8
Sociology of Religion 8
Sociology of Art and Literature 9
Sociology of Knowledge 9
Urban Sociology 9
Rural Sociology 10
Sociology of Industry and Distribution 10
Anthropology 11
Documentary 11
Sociology and Philosophy 12

Other Routledge Social Science Series
International Library of Social Policy 12
Primary Socialization, Language and Education 12
Reports of the Institute of Community Studies 13
Medicine, Illness and Society 13

Routledge Social Science Journals 14

● *Books so marked are available in paperback*
All books are in Metric Demy 8vo format (216 × 138mm approx.)

GENERAL SOCIOLOGY

Belshaw, Cyril. The Conditions of Social Performance. *An Exploratory Theory. 144 pp.*

Brown, Robert. Explanation in Social Science. *208 pp.*

Cain, Maureen E. Society and the Policeman's Role. *About 300 pp.*

Gibson, Quentin. The Logic of Social Enquiry. *240 pp.*

Homans, George C. Sentiments and Activities: *Essays in Social Science. 336 pp.*

Isajiw, Wsevold W. Causation and Functionalism in Sociology. *165 pp.*

Johnson, Harry M. Sociology: *a Systematic Introduction. Foreword by Robert K. Merton. 710 pp.*

Mannheim, Karl. Essays on Sociology and Social Psychology. *Edited by Paul Keckskemeti. With Editorial Note by Adolph Lowe. 344 pp.*

Systematic Sociology: *An Introduction to the Study of Society. Edited by J. S. Erös and Professor W. A. C. Stewart. 220 pp.*

Martindale, Don. The Nature and Types of Sociological Theory. *292 pp.*

● **Maus, Heinz.** A Short History of Sociology. *234 pp.*

Mey, Harald. Field-Theory. *A Study of its Application in the Social Sciences. 352 pp.*

Myrdal, Gunnar. Value in Social Theory: *A Collection of Essays on Methodology. Edited by Paul Streeten. 332 pp.*

Ogburn, William F., and **Nimkoff, Meyer F.** A Handbook of Sociology. *Preface by Karl Mannheim. 656 pp. 46 figures. 35 tables.*

Parsons, Talcott, and **Smelser, Neil J.** Economy and Society: *A Study in the Integration of Economic and Social Theory. 362 pp.*

● **Rex, John.** Key Problems of Sociological Theory. *220 pp.*

Stark, Werner. The Fundamental Forms of Social Thought. *280 pp.*

FOREIGN CLASSICS OF SOCIOLOGY

● **Durkheim, Emile.** Suicide. *A Study in Sociology. Edited and with an Introduction by George Simpson. 404 pp.*

Professional Ethics and Civic Morals. *Translated by Cornelia Brookfield. 288 pp.*

● **Gerth, H. H.,** and **Mills, C. Wright.** From Max Weber: *Essays in Sociology. 502 pp.*

Tönnies, Ferdinand. Community and Association. *(Gemeinschaft und Gesellschaft.) Translated and Supplemented by Charles P. Loomis. Foreword by Pitirim A. Sorokin. 334 pp.*

SOCIAL STRUCTURE

Andreski, Stanislav. Military Organization and Society. *Foreword by Professor A. R. Radcliffe-Brown. 226 pp. 1 folder.*

● **Cole, G. D. H.** Studies in Class Structure. *220 p.*

Coontz, Sydney H. Population Theories and the Economic Interpretation. *202 pp.*

Coser, Lewis. The Functions of Social Conflict. *204 pp.*

Dickie-Clark, H. F. Marginal Situation: *A Sociological Study of a Coloured Group. 240 pp. 11 tables.*

Glass, D. V. (Ed.). Social Mobility in Britain. *Contributions by J. Berent, T. Bottomore, R. C. Chambers, J. Floud, D. V. Glass, J. R. Hall, H. T. Himmelweit, R. K. Kelsall, F. M. Martin, C. A. Moser, R. Mukherjee, and W. Ziegel. 420 pp.*

Glaser, Barney, and **Strauss, Anselm L.** Status Passage. *A Formal Theory. 208 pp.*

Jones, Garth N. Planned Organizational Change: *An Exploratory Study Using an Empirical Approach. 268 pp.*

Kelsall, R. K. Higher Civil Servants in Britain: *From 1870 to the Present Day. 268 pp. 31 tables.*

König, René. The Community. *232 pp. Illustrated.*

● **Lawton, Denis.** Social Class, Language and Education. *192 pp.*

McLeish, John. The Theory of Social Change: *Four Views Considered. 128 pp.*

Marsh, David C. The Changing Social Structure in England and Wales, 1871-1961. *272 pp.*

Mouzelis, Nicos. Organization and Bureaucracy. *An Analysis of Modern Theories. 240 pp.*

Mulkay, M. J. Functionalism, Exchange and Theoretical Strategy. *272 pp.*

Ossowski, Stanislaw. Class Structure in the Social Consciousness. *210 pp.*

SOCIOLOGY AND POLITICS

Crick, Bernard. The American Science of Politics: *Its Origins and Conditions. 284 pp.*

Hertz, Frederick. Nationality in History and Politics: *A Psychology and Sociology of National Sentiment and Nationalism. 432 pp.*

Kornhauser, William. The Politics of Mass Society. *272 pp. 20 tables.*

Laidler, Harry W. History of Socialism. *Social-Economic Movements: An Historical and Comparative Survey of Socialism, Communism, Co-operation, Utopianism; and other Systems of Reform and Reconstruction. 992 pp.*

Mannheim, Karl. Freedom, Power and Democratic Planning. *Edited by Hans Gerth and Ernest K. Bramstedt. 424 pp.*

Mansur, Fatma. Process of Independence. *Foreword by A. H. Hanson. 208 pp.*

Martin, David A. Pacificism: *an Historical and Sociological Study. 262 pp.*

Myrdal, Gunnar. The Political Element in the Development of Economic Theory. *Translated from the German by Paul Streeten. 282 pp.*

Verney, Douglas V. The Analysis of Political Systems. *264 pp.*

Wootton, Graham. Workers, Unions and the State. *188 pp.*

FOREIGN AFFAIRS: THEIR SOCIAL, POLITICAL AND ECONOMIC FOUNDATIONS

Bonné, Alfred. State and Economics in the Middle East: *A Society in Transition. 482 pp.*
Studies in Economic Development: *with special reference to Conditions in the Under-developed Areas of Western Asia and India. 322 pp. 84 tables.*
Mayer, J. P. Political Thought in France from the Revolution to the Fifth Republic. *164 pp.*

CRIMINOLOGY

Ancel, Marc. Social Defence: *A Modern Approach to Criminal Problems. Foreword by Leon Radzinowicz. 240 pp.*
Cloward, Richard A., and **Ohlin, Lloyd E.** Delinquency and Opportunity: *A Theory of Delinquent Gangs. 248 pp.*
Downes, David M. The Delinquent Solution. *A Study in Subcultural Theory. 296 pp.*
Dunlop, A. B., and **McCabe, S.** Young Men in Detention Centres. *192 pp.*
Friedlander, Kate. The Psycho-Analytical Approach to Juvenile Delinquency: *Theory, Case Studies, Treatment. 320 pp.*
Glueck, Sheldon, and **Eleanor.** Family Environment and Delinquency. *With the statistical assistance of Rose W. Kneznek. 340 pp.*
Lopez-Rey, Manuel. Crime. *An Analytical Appraisal. 288 pp.*
Mannheim, Hermann. Comparative Criminology: *a Text Book. Two volumes. 442 pp. and 380 pp.*
Morris, Terence. The Criminal Area: *A Study in Social Ecology. Foreword by Hermann Mannheim. 232 pp. 25 tables. 4 maps.*
Trasler, Gordon. The Explanation of Criminality. *144 pp.*

SOCIAL PSYCHOLOGY

Bagley, Christopher. The Social Psychology of the Child with Epilepsy. *320 pp.*
Barbu, Zevedei. Problems of Historical Psychology. *248 pp.*
Blackburn, Julian. Psychology and the Social Pattern. *184 pp.*
● **Fleming, C. M.** Adolescence: *Its Social Psychology: With an Introduction to recent findings from the fields of Anthropology, Physiology, Medicine, Psychometrics and Sociometry. 288 pp.*
● The Social Psychology of Education: *An Introduction and Guide to Its Study. 136 pp.*
Homans, George C. The Human Group. *Foreword by Bernard DeVoto. Introduction by Robert K. Merton. 526 pp.*
Social Behaviour: *its Elementary Forms. 416 pp.*

Klein, Josephine. The Study of Groups. *226 pp. 31 figures. 5 tables.*
Linton, Ralph. The Cultural Background of Personality. *132 pp.*
Mayo, Elton. The Social Problems of an Industrial Civilization. *With an appendix on the Political Problem. 180 pp.*
Ottaway, A. K. C. Learning Through Group Experience. *176 pp.*
Ridder, J. C. de. The Personality of the Urban African in South Africa. *A Thematic Apperception Test Study. 196 pp. 12 plates.*
● **Rose, Arnold M.** (Ed.). Human Behaviour and Social Processes: *an Interactionist Approach. Contributions by Arnold M. Rose, Ralph H. Turner, Anselm Strauss, Everett C. Hughes, E. Franklin Frazier, Howard S. Becker, et al. 696 pp.*
Smelser, Neil J. Theory of Collective Behaviour. *448 pp.*
Stephenson, Geoffrey M. The Development of Conscience. *128 pp.*
Young, Kimball. Handbook of Social Psychology. *658 pp. 16 figures. 10 tables.*

SOCIOLOGY OF THE FAMILY

Banks, J. A. Prosperity and Parenthood: *A Study of Family Planning among The Victorian Middle Classes. 262 pp.*
Bell, Colin R. Middle Class Families: *Social and Geographical Mobility. 224 pp.*
Burton, Lindy. Vulnerable Children. *272 pp.*
Gavron, Hannah. The Captive Wife: *Conflicts of Household Mothers. 190 pp.*
George, Victor, and **Wilding, Paul.** Motherless Families. *220 pp.*
Klein, Josephine. Samples from English Cultures.
  1. Three Preliminary Studies and Aspects of Adult Life in England. *447 pp.*
  2. Child-Rearing Practices and Index. *247 pp.*
Klein, Viola. Britain's Married Women Workers. *180 pp.*
  The Feminine Character. *History of an Ideology. 244 pp.*
McWhinnie, Alexina M. Adopted Children. *How They Grow Up. 304 pp.*
Myrdal, Alva, and **Klein, Viola.** Women's Two Roles: *Home and Work. 238 pp. 27 tables.*
Parsons, Talcott, and **Bales, Robert F.** Family: *Socialization and Interaction Process. In collaboration with James Olds, Morris Zelditch and Philip E. Slater. 456 pp. 50 figures and tables.*

SOCIAL SERVICES

Bastide, Roger. The Sociology of Mental Disorder. *Translated from the French by Jean McNeil. 264 pp.*
Carlebach, Julius. Caring For Children in Trouble. *266 pp.*
Forder, R. A. (Ed.). Penelope Hall's Social Services of Modern England. *352 pp.*
George, Victor. Foster Care. *Theory and Practice. 234 pp.*
  Social Security: *Beveridge and After. 258 pp.*

● **Goetschius, George W.** Working with Community Groups. *256 pp.*

Goetschius, George W., and **Tash, Joan.** Working with Unattached Youth. *416 pp.*

Hall, M. P., and **Howes, I. V.** The Church in Social Work. *A Study of Moral Welfare Work undertaken by the Church of England. 320 pp.*

Heywood, Jean S. Children in Care: *the Development of the Service for the Deprived Child. 264 pp.*

Hoenig, J., and **Hamilton, Marian W.** The De-Segration of the Mentally Ill. *284 pp.*

Jones, Kathleen. Lunacy, Law and Conscience, *1744-1845: the Social History of the Care of the Insane. 268 pp.*

Mental Health and Social Policy, 1845-1959. *264 pp.*

King, Roy D., Raynes, Norma V., and **Tizard, Jack.** Patterns of Residential Care. *356 pp.*

Leigh, John. Young People and Leisure. *256 pp.*

Morris, Pauline. Put Away: *A Sociological Study of Institutions for the Mentally Retarded. 364 pp.*

Nokes, P. L. The Professional Task in Welfare Practice. *152 pp.*

Timms, Noel. Psychiatric Social Work in Great Britain (1939-1962). *280 pp.*

● Social Casework: *Principles and Practice. 256 pp.*

Trasler, Gordon. In Place of Parents: *A Study in Foster Care. 272 pp.*

Young, A. F., and **Ashton, E. T.** British Social Work in the Nineteenth Century. *288 pp.*

Young, A. F. Social Services in British Industry. *272 pp.*

SOCIOLOGY OF EDUCATION

Banks, Olive. Parity and Prestige in English Secondary Education: a Study in Educational Sociology. *272 pp.*

Bentwich, Joseph. Education in Israel. *224 pp. 8 pp. plates.*

● **Blyth, W. A. L.** English Primary Education. *A Sociological Description.*
  1. Schools. *232 pp.*
  2. Background. *168 pp.*

Collier, K. G. The Social Purposes of Education: *Personal and Social Values in Education. 268 pp.*

Dale, R. R., and **Griffith, S.** Down Stream: *Failure in the Grammar School. 108 pp.*

Dore, R. P. Education in Tokugawa Japan. *356 pp. 9 pp. plates*

Evans, K. M. Sociometry and Education. *158 pp.*

Foster, P. J. Education and Social Change in Ghana. *336 pp. 3 maps.*

Fraser, W. R. Education and Society in Modern France. *150 pp.*

Grace, Gerald R. Role Conflict and the Teacher. *About 200 pp.*

Hans, Nicholas. New Trends in Education in the Eighteenth Century. *278 pp. 19 tables.*

● Comparative Education: *A Study of Educational Factors and Traditions. 360 pp.*

Hargreaves, David. Interpersonal Relations and Education. *432 pp.*
● Social Relations in a Secondary School. *240 pp.*
Holmes, Brian. Problems in Education. *A Comparative Approach. 336 pp.*
King, Ronald. Values and Involvement in a Grammar School. *164 pp.*
● **Mannheim, Karl,** and **Stewart, W. A. C.** An Introduction to the Sociology of Education. *206 pp.*
Morris, Raymond N. The Sixth Form and College Entrance. *231 pp.*
● **Musgrove, F.** Youth and the Social Order. *176 pp.*
● **Ottaway, A. K. C.** Education and Society: *An Introduction to the Sociology of Education. With an Introduction by W. O. Lester Smith. 212 pp.*
Peers, Robert. Adult Education: *A Comparative Study. 398 pp.*
Pritchard, D. G. Education and the Handicapped: *1760 to 1960. 258 pp.*
Richardson, Helen. Adolescent Girls in Approved Schools. *308 pp.*
Simon, Brian, and **Joan** (Eds.). Educational Psychology in the U.S.S.R. *Introduction by Brian and Joan Simon. Translation by Joan Simon. Papers by D. N. Bogoiavlenski and N. A. Menchinskaia, D. B. Elkonin, E. A. Fleshner, Z. I. Kalmykova, G. S. Kostiuk, V. A. Krutetski, A. N. Leontiev, A. R. Luria, E. A. Milerian, R. G. Natadze, B. M. Teplov, L. S. Vygotski, L. V. Zankov. 296 pp.*
Stratta, Erica. The Education of Borstal Boys. *A Study of their Educational Experiences prior to, and during Borstal Training. 256 pp.*

SOCIOLOGY OF CULTURE

Eppel, E. M., and **M.** Adolescents and Morality: *A Study of some Moral Values and Dilemmas of Working Adolescents in the Context of a changing Climate of Opinion. Foreword by W. J. H. Sprott. 268 pp. 39 tables.*
● **Fromm, Erich.** The Fear of Freedom. *286 pp.*
The Sane Society. *400 pp.*
● **Mannheim, Karl.** Diagnosis of Our Time: *Wartime Essays of a Sociologist. 208 pp.*
Essays on the Sociology of Culture. *Edited by Ernst Mannheim in co-operation with Paul Kecskemeti. Editorial Note by Adolph Lowe. 280 pp.*
Weber, Alfred. Farewell to European History: *or The Conquest of Nihilism. Translated from the German by R. F. C. Hull. 224 pp.*

SOCIOLOGY OF RELIGION

Argyle, Michael. Religious Behaviour. *224 pp. 8 figures. 41 tables.*
Nelson, G. K. Spiritualism and Society. *313 pp.*

Stark, Werner. The Sociology of Religion. *A Study of Christendom.*
  Volume I. *Established Religion. 248 pp.*
  Volume II. *Sectarian Religion. 368 pp.*
  Volume III. *The Universal Church. 464 pp.*
  Volume IV. *Types of Religious Man. 352 pp.*
  Volume V. *Types of Religious Culture. 464 pp.*
Watt, W. Montgomery. Islam and the Integration of Society. *320 pp.*

SOCIOLOGY OF ART AND LITERATURE

Beljame, Alexandre. Men of Letters and the English Public in the Eighteenth
  Century: *1660-1744, Dryden, Addison, Pope. Edited with an Introduction
  and Notes by Bonamy Dobrée. Translated by E. O. Lorimer. 532 pp.*
Jarvie, Ian C. Towards a Sociology of the Cinema. *A Comparative Essay
  on the Structure and Functioning of a Major Entertainment Industry.
  405 pp.*
Rust, Frances S. Dance in Society. *An Analysis of the Relationships between
  the Social Dance and Society in England from the Middle Ages to the
  Present Day. 256 pp. 8 pp. of plates.*
Schücking, L. L. The Sociology of Literary Taste. *112 pp.*
Silbermann, Alphons. The Sociology of Music. *Translated from the German
  by Corbet Stewart. 222 pp.*

SOCIOLOGY OF KNOWLEDGE

Mannheim, Karl. Essays on the Sociology of Knowledge. *Edited by Paul
  Kecskemeti. Editorial note by Adolph Lowe. 353 pp.*
Stark, Werner. The Sociology of Knowledge: *An Essay in Aid of a Deeper
  Understanding of the History of Ideas. 384 pp.*

URBAN SOCIOLOGY

Ashworth, William. The Genesis of Modern British Town Planning: *A Study
  in Economic and Social History of the Nineteenth and Twentieth Centuries.
  288 pp.*
Cullingworth, J. B. Housing Needs and Planning Policy: *A Restatement of
  the Problems of Housing Need and 'Overspill' in England and Wales.
  232 pp. 44 tables. 8 maps.*
Dickinson, Robert E. City and Region: *A Geographical Interpretation.
  608 pp. 125 figures.*
  The West European City: *A Geographical Interpretation. 600 pp. 129 maps.
  29 plates.*
● The City Region in Western Europe. *320 pp. Maps.*

Humphreys, Alexander J. New Dubliners: *Urbanization and the Irish Family. Foreword by George C. Homans. 304 pp.*

Jackson, Brian. Working Class Community: *Some General Notions raised by a Series of Studies in Northern England. 192 pp.*

Jennings, Hilda. Societies in the Making: *a Study of Development and Re-development within a County Borough. Foreword by D. A. Clark. 286 pp.*

Kerr, Madeline. The People of Ship Street. *240 pp.*

● **Mann, P. H.** An Approach to Urban Sociology. *240 pp.*

Morris, R. N., and **Mogey, J.** The Sociology of Housing. *Studies at Berinsfield. 232 pp. 4 pp. plates.*

Rosser, C., and **Harris, C.** The Family and Social Change. *A Study of Family and Kinship in a South Wales Town. 352 pp. 8 maps.*

RURAL SOCIOLOGY

Chambers, R. J. H. Settlement Schemes in Africa: *A Selective Study. 268 pp.*

Haswell, M. R. The Economics of Development in Village India. *120 pp.*

Littlejohn, James. Westrigg: *the Sociology of a Cheviot Parish. 172 pp. 5 figures.*

Williams, W. M. The Country Craftsman: *A Study of Some Rural Crafts and the Rural Industries Organization in England. 248 pp. 9 figures. (Dartington Hall Studies in Rural Sociology.)*

The Sociology of an English Village: *Gosforth. 272 pp. 12 figures. 13 tables.*

SOCIOLOGY OF INDUSTRY AND DISTRIBUTION

Anderson, Nels. Work and Leisure. *280 pp.*

● **Blau, Peter M.,** and **Scott, W. Richard.** Formal Organizations: *a Comparative approach. Introduction and Additional Bibliography by J. H. Smith. 326 pp.*

Eldridge, J. E. T. Industrial Disputes. *Essays in the Sociology of Industrial Relations. 288 pp.*

Hetzler, Stanley. Technological Growth and Social Change. *Achieving Modernization. 269 pp.*

Hollowell, Peter G. The Lorry Driver. *272 pp.*

Jefferys, Margot, *with the assistance of Winifred Moss.* Mobility in the Labour Market: *Employment Changes in Battersea and Dagenham. Preface by Barbara Wootton. 186 pp. 51 tables.*

Millerson, Geoffrey. The Qualifying Associations: *a Study in Professionalization. 320 pp.*

Smelser, Neil J. Social Change in the Industrial Revolution: *An Application of Theory to the Lancashire Cotton Industry, 1770-1840. 468 pp. 12 figures. 14 tables.*

Williams, Gertrude. Recruitment to Skilled Trades. *240 pp.*

Young, A. F. Industrial Injuries Insurance: *an Examination of British Policy.* *192 pp.*

ANTHROPOLOGY

Ammar, Hamed. Growing up in an Egyptian Village: *Silwa, Province of Aswan. 336 pp.*

Brandel-Syrier, Mia. Reeftown Elite. *A Study of Social Mobility in a Modern African Community on the Reef. 376 pp.*

Crook, David, and **Isabel.** Revolution in a Chinese Village: *Ten Mile Inn. 230 pp. 8 plates. 1 map.*

The First Years of Yangyi Commune. *302 pp. 12 plates.*

Dickie-Clark, H. F. The Marginal Situation. *A Sociological Study of a Coloured Group. 236 pp.*

Dube, S. C. Indian Village. *Foreword by Morris Edward Opler. 276 pp. 4 plates.*

India's Changing Villages: *Human Factors in Community Development. 260 pp. 8 plates. 1 map.*

Firth, Raymond. Malay Fishermen. *Their Peasant Economy. 420 pp. 17 pp. plates.*

Gulliver, P. H. Social Control in an African Society: a Study of the Arusha, Agricultural Masai of Northern Tanganyika. *320 pp. 8 plates. 10 figures.*

Ishwaran, K. Shivapur. *A South Indian Village. 216 pp.*

Tradition and Economy in Village India: *An Interactionist Approach. Foreword by Conrad Arensburg. 176 pp.*

Jarvie, Ian C. The Revolution in Anthropology. *268 pp.*

Jarvie, Ian C., and **Agassi, Joseph.** Hong Kong. *A Society in Transition. 396 pp. Illustrated with plates and maps.*

Little, Kenneth L. Mende of Sierra Leone. *308 pp. and folder.*

Negroes in Britain. *With a New Introduction and Contemporary Study by Leonard Bloom. 320 pp.*

Lowie, Robert H. Social Organization. *494 pp.*

Mayer, Adrian C. Caste and Kinship in Central India: *A Village and its Region. 328 pp. 16 plates. 15 figures. 16 tables.*

Smith, Raymond T. The Negro Family in British Guiana: *Family Structure and Social Status in the Villages. With a Foreword by Meyer Fortes. 314 pp. 8 plates. 1 figure. 4 maps.*

DOCUMENTARY

Meek, Dorothea L. (Ed.). Soviet Youth: *Some Achievements and Problems. Excerpts from the Soviet Press, translated by the editor. 280 pp.*

Schlesinger, Rudolf (Ed.). Changing Attitudes in Soviet Russia.

2. *The Nationalities Problem and Soviet Administration. Selected Readings on the Development of Soviet Nationalities Policies. Introduced by the editor. Translated by W. W. Gottlieb. 324 pp.*

SOCIOLOGY AND PHILOSOPHY

Barnsley, John H. The Social Reality of Ethics. *A Comparative Analysis of Moral Codes. 448 pp.*

Douglas, Jack D. (Ed.). Understanding Everyday Life. *Toward the Reconstruction of Sociological Knowledge. Contributions by Alan F. Blum. Aaron W. Cicourel, Norman K. Denzin, Jack D. Douglas, John Heeren, Peter McHugh, Peter K. Manning, Melvin Power, Matthew Speier, Roy Turner, D. Lawrence Wieder, Thomas P. Wilson and Don H. Zimmerman. 358 pp.*

Jarvie, Ian C. Concepts and Society. *216 pp.*

Roche, Maurice. Phenomenology, Language and the Social Sciences. *About 400 pp.*

Sklair, Leslie. The Sociology of Progress. *320 pp.*

International Library of Social Policy

General Editor Kathleen Janes

Jones, Kathleen. Mental Health Services. *A history, 1744-1971. About 500 pp.*

Thomas, J. E. The English Prison Officer since 1850: *A Study in Conflict. 258 pp.*

Primary Socialization, Language and Education

General Editor Basil Bernstein

Bernstein, Basil. Class, Codes and Control. *2 volumes.*
  1. *Theoretical Studies Towards a Sociology of Language. 254 pp.*
  2. *Applied Studies Towards a Sociology of Language. About 400 pp.*

Brandis, Walter, and **Henderson, Dorothy.** Social Class, Language and Communication. *288 pp.*

Cook, Jenny. Socialization and Social Control. *About 300 pp.*

Gahagan, D. M., and **G. A.** Talk Reform. *Exploration in Language for Infant School Children. 160 pp.*

Robinson, W. P., and **Rackstraw, Susan, D. A.** A Question of Answers. *2 volumes. 192 pp. and 180 pp.*

Turner, Geoffrey, J., and **Mohan, Bernard, A.** A Linguistic Description and Computer Programme for Children's Speech. *208 pp.*

Reports of the Institute of Community Studies and the Institute of Social Studies in Medical Care

Cartwright, Ann. Human Relations and Hospital Care. *272 pp.*
Parents and Family Planning Services. *306 pp.*
Patients and their Doctors. *A Study of General Practice. 304 pp.*
Dunnell, Karen, and **Cartwright, Ann.** Medicine Takers, Prescribers and Hoarders. *About 140 pp.*
● **Jackson, Brian.** Streaming: *an Education System in Miniature. 168 pp.*
Jackson, Brian, and **Marsden, Dennis.** Education and the Working Class: *Some General Themes raised by a Study of 88 Working-class Children in a Northern Industrial City. 268 pp. 2 folders.*
Marris, Peter. Widows and their Families. *Foreword by Dr. John Bowlby. 184 pp. 18 tables. Statistical Summary.*
Family and Social Change in an African City. *A Study of Rehousing in Lagos. 196 pp. 1 map. 4 plates. 53 tables.*
The Experience of Higher Education. *232 pp. 27 tables.*
Marris, Peter, and **Rein, Martin.** Dilemmas of Social Reform. *Poverty and Community Action in the United States. 256 pp.*
Marris, Peter, and **Somerset, Anthony.** African Businessmen. *A Study of Entrepreneurship and Development in Kenya. 256 pp.*
Runciman, W. G. Relative Deprivation and Social Justice. *A Study of Attitudes to Social Inequality in Twentieth Century England. 352 pp.*
Townsend, Peter. The Family Life of Old People: *An Inquiry in East London. Foreword by J. H. Sheldon. 300 pp. 3 figures. 63 tables.*
Willmott, Peter. Adolescent Boys in East London. *230 pp.*
The Evolution of a Community: *a study of Dagenham after forty years. 168 pp. 2 maps.*
Willmott, Peter, and **Young, Michael.** Family and Class in a London Suburb. *202 pp. 47 tables.*
Young, Michael. Innovation and Research in Education. *192 pp.*
● **Young, Michael,** and **McGeeney, Patrick.** Learning Begins at Home. *A Study of a Junior School and its Parents. 128 pp.*
Young, Michael, and **Willmott, Peter.** Family and Kinship in East London. *Foreword by Richard M. Titmuss. 252 pp. 39 tables.*

Medicine, Illness and Society
General Editor W. M. Williams

Robinson, David. The Process of Becoming Ill.
Stacey, Margaret. *et al.* Hospitals, Children and Their Families. *The Report of a Pilot Study. 202 pp.*

Routledge Social Science Journals

The British Journal of Sociology. *Edited by Terence P. Morris. Vol. 1, No. 1, March 1950 and Quarterly. Roy. 8vo. Back numbers available. An international journal with articles on all aspects of sociology.*

Economy and Society. *Vol. 1, No. 1. February 1972 and Quarterly. Metric Roy. 8vo. A journal for all social scientists covering sociology, philosophy, anthropology, economics and history.*

Printed in Great Britain by Lewis Reprints Limited
Brown Knight & Truscott Group, London and Tonbridge   21972

14